Powerful Partnerships in Student Success: Schools, Families and Communities

Edited by

Nicholas D. Young, Ph.D., Ed.D.
and
Christine N. Michael, Ph.D.

Learning Disabilities Worldwide (LDW) continues its mission to serve as a global advocate for individuals with learning disabilities, their families, and the professionals who work with them; and would like to thank all dedicated people who share this commitment. LDW has also broadened its focus to promote high quality education for all children and adults, which explain why it currently offer programs, and publishes material, on a range of contemporary educational topics.

We wish to offer special recognition to Mary Laity for her timely and professional copy layout services that made the final publication of this book possible, as well as to the co-editors, Drs. Nicholas D. Young and Christine N. Michael, and every contributing author of *Powerful Partners in Student Success: Schools, Families and Communities*. This book seeks to build enduring bridges between the important educational stakeholders. We also wish to thank the members of the governing and advisor board of Learning Disabilities Worldwide, under the capable leadership of its Executive Director, for their support of this book project designed to help students achieve greater levels of academic success through uniting the efforts of the important adults in their lives.

Last, but not least, the co-editors would like to personally thank Amelia Carlson, Didi Firman and Elizabeth Jean for offering superb editorial assistance throughout the various phases of this project.

©2012 LDW (Learning Disabilities Worldwide)

Published by Learning Disabilities Worldwide, Inc.
PO Box 142
Weston, Massachusetts, 02493
978-897-5399

www.ldworldwide.org

All rights reserved LDW® 2012.

ISBN 978-1-930877-03-0 - $49.95

No part of this publication may be reproduced in whole or in part, or stored in a retrieval system or transmitted in any form or by any means, electronic, mechanical, photocopying, recording, or otherwise, without the written permission of the publisher.

Printed in the United States.

Other LDW Publications

Books edited by Teresa Allissa Citro
Parenting the Child with Learning Disabilities: The Experts Speak
Successful Lifetime Management: Adults with Learning Disabilities
Transitional Skills for Post Secondary Success: Reflections for Students with Learning Disabilities
Many Shades of Success: Other Views of Post-Secondary Options

Books edited by Georgios D. Sideridis and Teresa Allissa Citro
Research to Practice: Effective Interventions in Learning Disabilities
Classroom Strategies for Struggling Learners
Strategies in Reading for Struggling Learners

Books edited by Nathalis G. Wamba and Teresa Allissa Citro
Learning Differences: Research, Practice and Advocacy

Books edited by Nicholas D. Young and Christine N. Michael
Creative Solutions to Contemporary Challenges in Small and Rural Schools Across America

Children's Book Co-Authored by John Golden and Teresa Allissa Citro
I am Full of Possibilities: Oliver Gets Tested

To order please visit
www.ldworldwide.org

About the Book Cover

Front Cover

This photograph was taken at Westminster Center School (Westminster, VT) of student, Chelsea Wilder, reading to community volunteer, Alma Beals and her lab, "Maddie."

Photograph taken by Missy Maloney Wilkins, Ph.D.

Back Cover

This photograph was taken at Landmark College (Putney, VT) where students and professors join teachers from Westminster Center School for a team building activity.

Photograph taken by Missy Maloney Wilkins, Ph.D.

About the Editors

Dr. Nicholas D. Young has worked in diverse roles in education for more than twenty years, serving as a director of student services, principal, graduate professor, higher education administrator, and superintendent of schools. He holds numerous degrees from Austin Peay State University, Westfield State University, Western New England University, Union Institute & University and American International College, including a Ph.D. in Educational Administration and an Ed.D. in Psychology. Dr. Young previously served as the President of the Massachusetts Association of School Superintendents, completed a distinguished Fulbright Program focused on Japanese educational systems, and was recognized as the Massachusetts Superintendent of the Year in 2010. He has also served for more than twenty-seven years to date in the U.S. Army and U.S. Army Reserves; and he is currently the Commanding Officer for the 405th Combat Support Hospital, USAR, located in West Hartford, CT. Dr. Young is a frequent presenter at state, national and international conferences and has published widely on a number of topics in education, leadership and psychology.

Dr. Christine N. Michael is a more than thirty-year educational veteran with a variety of professional experiences. She holds degrees from Brown University, Rhode Island College, Union Institute & University, and the University of Connecticut, where she earned a Ph.D. in Education and Human Development and Family Relations. Previous work has included middle and high school teaching, higher education administration, college teaching, educational consulting, literacy development, Head Start, Upward Bound, GED preparation, and the federal Trio programs. She is a licensed principal and superintendent in the State of New York. Her interest in small and rural schools is currently expressed through work in rural Kentucky, the Western Slope of Colorado, Standing Rock Indian Reservation schools, and the Adirondack Mountains of New York.

The two editors have previously published several articles and chapters in addition to co-editing and co-authoring the following books together: *Counseling in a Complex Society: Contemporary Challenges to Professional Practice* (2007), *Counseling with Confidence: From Pre-service to Professional Practice* (2009) and *Creative Solutions to Contemporary Challenges in Small and Rural Schools Across America* (2010).

Introduction

Edited By:

Nicholas D. Young, Ph.D., Ed.D.

and

Christine N. Michael, Ph.D.

If the phrase "it takes a village to raise a child" has become too trite or overused, it is incumbent upon our society to invent another one that stresses the absolute necessity of viewing families and communities as integral partners in the process of promoting student development in K-12 institutions. Studies of high performing schools—whether public, private, religious, technical, alternative, or charter— show consistently that positive parental and community engagement in the daily life of the school is one of the primary elements in achieving that high performance.

The gifts engaged families and communities can give to our schools are numerous. These span the spectrum from philosophical support, such as affirming the school's mission and values, to a willingness to invest valuable resources –fiscal, human, experiential, or geographic. In a period of extreme economic uncertainty, compounded by a recent array of natural disasters, schools are stressed and family security frayed. As this book is being completed, Hurricane Irene, for example, has postponed the opening of schools up and down the East Coast. In hard-hit areas such as Vermont and upstate New York, schools that survived the flooding and mud slides are serving as emergency shelters for the homeless instead of opening their doors to students. In those unlucky communities in which schools, homes, and businesses were damaged or destroyed, students are out in the community performing service to those who are suffering losses. Additionally, community members are working within the ravaged school buildings to make them operational again. It is precisely in times like these that schools, families and communities need to seek newfound synergy.

Historically, the notion that the school should be in the community and the community in the school was not assumed. Parents were expected to leave the education of their children in the capable hands of teachers and educators' authority was rarely challenged. The nature of our earlier economy left precious time for parents and community members to take part in school-day activities; outside of school hours, students joined their families in the work of the fields, factories, and homes.

It is also impossible to ignore the fact that the very definition of "family" has been radically altered in the last decades. Throughout the history of American education, "family" has been synonymous with the nuclear unit of heterosexual parents and their biological children. Today, "family" is as diversely defined as the country is pluralistic. Real relationships must be created and those relationships must acknowledge the variables of divorce, immigration, homelessness, language, culture, sexual orientation, adoptive or foster parenting, socio-economic status, and disability—to name just a few. In some cases, grandparents are raising their grandchildren, while in others; children and adolescents essentially are their own parents. Each family configuration has its unique assets to share with the larger school community even as it presents individual challenges.

Likewise, the notion of "community" has grown in complexity. What once was defined by geography, with the presumption of a high degree of cultural homogeneity and communally-held values and beliefs, has now in so many locations become a mélange of different backgrounds, languages, cultures, values and traditions, not to mention diverse experiences of and expectations for the institution called "school." If you throw in membership that may or may not see itself as a component part of the school- community dyad—the childless/childfree, second home owners, those learning in a distance format, "snow birds," or businesses that are not locally owned or associated—and the quest to convince all constituents they must champion the local school becomes all the more daunting. While the historical notion of "common ground" among community members may be obsolete, we must find a contemporary corollary in at least "shareable ground," on which everyone in the community sees him or herself as a "booster."

This book was conceived as a partnership with current educators who know the need for vital school-family-community collaborations first hand. Organized around three salient themes, the book illustrates strategies that work rather than dwelling on the challenges confronting us. It is hoped that readers will be inspired to adopt or adapt these ideas to use in their own practice. In "Families as the Foundation," authors share their strategies for developing and nurturing powerful relationships with their students' families. The chapter topics range from a discussion of the crucial nature of respectful conversation to effective communications in a high-tech era. Chapters included in "Community Connections" illustrate how such entities as public agencies and private foundations can join with schools to increase their assets and reap mutual benefits. The final section, "Case Study Successes, is comprised of case studies of individual schools and initiatives that have been found to be effective in strengthening the relationships between the critical constituencies. The editors close the book with a reflection on best practices in community building from educators around the country. All chapters are intended to offer models of success that can be "stolen" or serve as springboards for future strategizing in readers' own settings.

Editors' Note

The editors wish to express their deepest gratitude to the educators who shared with them the challenges and successes they have experienced in forging stronger bonds among school constituents, families, and local communities. Their creative approaches to building the powerful partnerships that support positive student development are to be celebrated. The editors freely acknowledge that the contributors to this book are professional educators and the voices heard here are theirs while underscoring that there is much fertile ground left for research that relies on the perceptions of parents, community members, and students themselves. And while this book cannot possibly capture all of the nuances and complexities of daily life in the diverse schools in our society, it is hoped that it will engender discussions among all of the key stakeholders as they continue to strive for collaborations that ensure the best futures possible for each and every student.

NOTES

NOTES

Contents

Section One
Families as the Foundation

Chapter One 3
How Parent Teacher Organizations Work
to Build Collaborative Relationships
Lynne M. Celli

Chapter Two 13
When Parents Lose Their Kids to the Journey
Called "Growing Up": How Schools Can Respond with Empathy
Marianne R. Young

Chapter Three 27
Social Justice Starts at Home
Dorothy Firman

Chapter Four 41
Using Technology to Strengthen the School
and Family Relationship
Sharon Goulet & Marisa A. McCarthy

Chapter Five 53
Promoting School, Home and Community Communication
Sharon MacDonald

CONTENTS

Chapter Six.. 65
The Power of School/Family Partnerships
Linda E. Denault

Chapter Seven... 77
It Takes a Community to Create Student Success for Foster Youth
Robert D. Mack

Section Two: Community Connections

Chapter Eight 93
**Building True Ties between Technical
Schools and their Regional Communities**
Judith L. Klimkiewicz

Chapter Nine 101
**How Community Agencies and Civic Groups
Can Contribute to Student Success**
Julie M. DeRoche

Chapter Ten 113
**Securing Student Success: The Increasing Role
of Local Private Foundations**
Nadine B. Binkley

Chapter Eleven 123
**Community Involvement and School Safety:
Thoughts on Streamlining the Process**
Warren Corson III

Chapter Twelve 143
Building Real Relationships in a Rural Setting
Neil Gile

Chapter Thirteen 155
**Using Technology to Foster Purpose and
Community in the School Setting**
Meryl L. French

Section Three: Case Study Successes

Chapter Fourteen.. 169
Promoting Collaboration Across Constituency Groups:
Lincoln Middle School
Timothy Allen

Chapter Fifteen.. 181
A Case Study in Collaboration: The Orange Elementary School
Paul Burnam

Chapter Sixteen 196
Free Union Country School: A Portrait of Community Caring
Sarah Goodbar

Chapter Seventeen 211
Did the KIPP Schools Get It Right?
Shanda Lazare

Chapter Eighteen 223
New Leadership Charter School
Michael D. Moriarty & Jennifer S. Alexander

Closing

Chapter Nineteen... 235
"The Welcome Mat Is Out": Reflections on What Works in Building Strong School, Family and Community Partnerships
Christine N. Michael & Nicholas D. Young

Section One
FAMILIES AS THE FOUNDATION

CHAPTER ONE

How Parent Teacher Organizations Work to Build Collaborative Relationships

By: Lynne M. Celli

Building Collaboration with PTAs/PTOs

There are many ways Parent/Teacher Associations (PTAs) and Parent/Teacher Organizations (PTOs) can work with schools and school districts to build collaborations across many constituencies. Examples of necessary components for collaborative relationships in school districts and within individual schools to build this collaboration for all families and community organizations include welcoming environments, well-developed and implemented communication systems, advocacy for all students, and a shared decision-making process. These factors are four of many variables that are instrumental in creating collaborative environments. However, research supports they represent the most critical in working toward a collaborative environment for all constituencies.

Creating a Welcoming Environment

The first component important to the process of building collaboration within schools is a focus on designing and implementing a welcoming environment. Creating a welcoming environment in schools may seem to be a simple task. Contrary to perception, creating this type of environment is really very complex. It is complex because it is more than just technical work and a process. It more importantly involves adaptive work and processes. The technical work of creating a welcoming environment in a school is merely developing the procedures and processes that are superficially necessary to be in place for the desired outcome – a friendly, warm, and welcoming environment. This technical work includes what the school district and the individual schools do to build this type of environment. This work may include planning Open Houses and providing weekly or monthly newsletters to both the parents and community members. It may also include the steps parents, visitors, and community members being required to take part in procedures when they enter a school or when they wish to visit a school for a specific purpose. Technical work for building a welcoming environment in a school also includes articulating in writing through all school publications the clear expectations for involvement in a school. Additionally, the procedures and processes for participation in the school environment include posting information that is able to be clearly seen and understood by all constituencies who may enter the building and wish to be involved with the culture and life of the building.

Further, there is the adaptive work necessary for building a welcoming environment in a school setting that leads to overall collaboration. This adaptive work is much more difficult to develop and achieve. The adaptive work involves putting into practice on a regular basis, with sincerity, what it articulates and communicates to the school community at-large. An example of putting into practice the adaptive work is creating a culture and mindset of all personnel approaching their work on a daily basis from a "customer service" perspective. The question needing to be answered is "What is the feeling that our partners and our guests in a building sense when they enter?" Is the feeling that they only see and read the technical words about creating a welcoming environment? Or, does it transcend to the adaptive processes, to everyone typically having a smile on their face and are eager to welcome visitors and assist in any way possible to make them fee part of the community of the school? A practical example of this includes always offering a warm greeting to whoever might enter the building – from the most difficult parent, to the most difficult School Committee member, to the most difficult community member who does not have children in the school or in the school district, and is still a taxpayer in the community. In many ways, this example points to the development and implementation of an ongoing positive attitude and looking at the school as a part of the larger community and the need to be a viable component of the community at-large. The struggle for some schools comes from the fact that implementing this positive attitude on a regular basis contradicts the way some schools have historically operated – as individual organizations working toward individual and independent goals. Therefore, this welcoming environment needs to play a critical role in the organization of a school.

Fostering Strong Communication

The next component for building collaborative relationships is communication. In thinking about how important regarding the enormous concept of communication, one must acknowledge without it, relationships will most assuredly breakdown. In terms of the importance of building relationships between organizations such as PTAs, PTOs, and schools; communication, some would argue, is the foundation for all the work. The most current census data of 2000 state the percentage of families who do NOT have students in the school system in 75% or greater (United States Census 2000, 2000). This means that in any given city or town, only approximately 25% of the taxpayers has students in the school system. It, therefore, becomes critical that schools develop and implement an inclusive and comprehensive communication system. This inclusive and comprehensive communication system must thoughtfully address the need for ongoing, open, and transparent dialogue between all constituencies of a community. Most importantly, this communication is critical for that 75% of residents who would not naturally receive or be able to participate in dialogue with a school by virtue of not having students present in the school. As Mary Ann Stewart, President of Massachusetts State PTA, (2010 – 2012) quoted in an interview, "schools need to encourage back and forth dialogue by 'inviting' communication with everyone in the community." It cannot be expected to happen by default. It becomes the responsibility of the personnel in the school and the school district to develop a process that makes practical this "invitation" to communicate and to dialogue. Ms. Stewart further encourages schools to keep current and accurate databases with contact information for not only their school personnel but expanded databases that are inclusive of different groups within the community such as the Senior Citizens and the League of Women Voters. There needs to be outreach on a regular basis whereby school personnel provide outreach to all in an effort to encourage the consistent updating of contact information. This will assure the schools always have the most recent contact information for all and will allow the efficient dissemination of many different types of information pertinent to the individual school or the district as a whole. Disseminating the "good news" and current events not only help parents of students within a school to be regularly updated on the progress a school is making, but allows people within a community to feel confident about the work being done at schools and how funding is positively being used in within the system. Furthermore, Westmoreland, Rosenburg, Lopez, and Weiss (2009) state that in order for collaborative relationships to be developed and fostered, these communication systems must be robust in nature. Everyone involved in a community must reach out to all constituencies to share information in thoughtful and relevant ways. In addition, making collaboration and family engagement a formalized process in the district and in individual schools by setting measurable goals for this work, communicates the importance of this relationship.

Advocating for the Needs of Students

In addition to providing a welcoming environment and promoting open, honest, transparent communication, advocacy must be present for the students. This component of the process to promote ongoing collaboration is critical in order to successfully build relationships with schools, parents, and communities. Advocating for students is multifaceted and must be done in a tiered approach. This approach includes beginning with advocating at the national and state level to assure adequate funding for schools whether these schools are urban, suburban, or rural. Adequate funding promotes healthy morale, not only within a school system, but also within communities at-large. Most states have state-level advocacy groups with local representation that have formal processes and procedures for communicating and reaching to the federal level and these processes communicate unique and specific needs of individual states and local school districts. These state-level groups become the voice of the school districts, the parent community, and local municipalities. They bring current data, information, and funding needs to the table, in order to ensure the dialogue will take place at the federal level. This step in the advocacy process is very important as school districts and communities use this communication vehicle to assure they have a "federal" voice in all debates and discussions that may impact policy decisions both short-term and long-term and have direct effects on district-level work.

The next step in the advocacy process is the state-level groups who work on the state level to provide advocacy in individual state legislatures (National Standards for Family-School Partnerships, 2007). Advocacy for students in an ongoing and timely way is, in many ways, the key to successfully obtaining resources necessary to maintain a quality school system. As Westmoreland, Rosenburg, Lopez, and Weiss (2009) have discussed, it is critical for families to be engaged at many levels. They emphasize that family engagement not only promotes advocacy for school districts on many levels, but additionally opens the lines of communication that are important as stated above, as well as builds capacity in the community, the district, and the individual schools. This increased capacity allows a school district to continually set high standards for students and teachers as well as continue to set goals for continued improvement in all aspects of the school and the school district.

Shared Decision-Making

The final focus for building collaboration with schools, families, and community organizations is shared decision-making. Jeynes (2003 and 2007) has found through research increased family involvement in the educational process within a school district and at the individual school level increases student achievement. It is with this end in mind we highlight shared decision-making. Examining carefully how everyone interacts with the students will paint a clear picture if shared decision making is truly happening or just written on a site council plan or a strategic plan. Asking questions such as, How do the site council recommendations change practice on a day-to-day basis? How much does the site council plan impact students? Are parents involved in the school regularly and are the parents involved in meaningful ways? When the data from questions such as these are analyzed and tracked and the results of involvement are coupled with the trends, it becomes clear as to the extent of the inclusionary nature of a school. It becomes "....creating a buzz within the community..." Stewart (2010). If there is a positive "buzz" within the community from people involved in the shared decision making, it is clear people feel welcomed, their suggestions and involvement have been taken seriously and incorporated into the "life" of the school. As Karen Mapp (2007) states, schools are considered a community. This is especially true when the community members involved see the results of their work, whether it be as members of a site council or as a volunteer in some capacity within the school.

Additionally, shared decision making has to be taken to the district level. Pragmatic and practical examples of this include a superintendent's advisory council, evident responsiveness to reasonable expectations stated at school committee meetings, or in other public forums. It is important to emphasize here the expectations mentioned here must be reasonable and within the best interests of the school district as a whole, without personal agendas involved. Further, school boards or school committees have a responsibility to plan and implement this process. In collaboration and cooperation with school district leadership, school boards or school committees should develop comprehensive trainings to encourage quality and substantive community participation in the school system. However, often this is difficult since first school boards and school committees must understand their role in the organization. In order for the concept of shared decision making not to just be ongoing jargon for all members of a school district, all parties need to learn and acknowledge their appropriate roles and responsibilities within a school district. This is easier stated, than applied, as the education piece for school board members and school committee members is essential. At this critical juncture, the comprehensive training for board and committee members is not currently taking place. Instead board and committee members are typically given one day training and left to their own devices to interpret their appropriate roles and responsibilities with minimal experience and training often make decisions significant to a school district.

As emphasized, if shared decision making is to be taken seriously by all constituencies, it must be encouraged and embraced by all parties up to and including the school board or the school committee. A way to emphasize the importance of shared decision-making is committing to transparency and integrity. Specific steps for involvement with the process of transparency and integrity must be clearly communicated. These steps include when the school staff develops and implements specific steps to welcome ALL parents in the many facets of the school. As stated in *The Missing Piece,* school staff should offer learning opportunities for parents and communities members so the participants in the shared decision making feel informed and vital (Kentucky Department of Education, Commissioner's Parent Advisory Council, Final Report, 2007). School staff must encourage, support, and expect parents, and community to be involved in the school, as well as with school improvement decisions on an ongoing basis. It is important the school staff take seriously their role in providing professional opportunities and workshops that are easily accessible to the whole parent community around their shared role in the school and in the school district. It is always through education that the community becomes a true partner and is fully invested. "When people see that you are listening and that they are indeed decision makers with you, their motivation changes dramatically" (Vella, 2002, p. 137).

Closing Thoughts

In essence, there are several ways that PTAs and PTOs can work to build collaboration with schools, families, and community organizations. Creating a welcoming environment, encouraging consistent communication which is open, honest, and transparent, in addition to advocating for students, and applying the theory of shared decision making are four of the critical components to this process. When all constituencies feel welcomed, they will be motivated to become involved in the school district, as well as involved with individual schools in ways they feel will make the most positive contributions. When there is effective communication within the community and all constituencies, the collective community feels they are a vital part of the school district, regardless if they have children in the schools or do not have children in the schools. This component is vital, especially when school districts look to communities for additional funding to improve and expand programs and/or improve the physical buildings. Many times this comes in the form of an override. Without the support of the community as a whole, overrides fail. Open, honest, transparent communication encourages all community members to be "invested" members of the school district and "take ownership" of the initiatives. Reciprocal advocacy for students with a school system by all members of a community, parents, and other community members is also critical to create the collaborative environment. When reciprocal advocacy for children is common practice, members of the community and parents feel a compelled responsibility for the success for the district as a whole and achievement of ALL children. Lastly, when shared decision-making is not only encouraged but practiced, the parents and community come together and work together to make all important decisions affecting children. There are mechanisms such as advisory committees that are valued, in place, and their work is often implemented. It is important to note the four components of building collaboration with schools, families, and community organizations mentioned here are not exclusive on the process. However, work on implementing them in a comprehensive and substantive way will prove to build a thriving school district within a community, where no one can tell where one begins and the other ends.

References

Education Alliance. (2008). *How can state education agencies support district improvement? A conversation amongst educational leaders, researchers, and policy actors*. Providence, RI: Brown University.

Elmore, R. (1995). Getting to scale with good educational practice. *Harvard Educational Review*, 66(1), 1-26.

Jeynes, W. H. (2007). The relationship between parent involvement and urban secondary school achievement: A meta-analysis. *Urban Education*, 42(1), 82-110.

Jeynes, W. H. (2003). A meta-analysis: The effects of parental involvement on minority children's academic achievement. *Education and Urban S ociety*, 35(2), 202-218.

Kentucky Department of Education, Commissioner's Parent Advisory Council, Final Report. (2007).*The missing piece of the proficiency puzzle – Recommendations for involving families and community in improving student achievement*.

Mapp, K., Johnson, V. R., and Davies D. (2007) *Beyond the bake sale: The essential guide to family-school partnerships*.

Marzano, R. J., Waters, T., and McNulty, B. A. (2005). *School leadership that works: Fromresearch to results*. Alexandria, VA: Association for Supervision and Curriculum Development (ASCD).

Popham, W. J. (2008). *Transformative assessment*. Alexandria, VA: Association for Supervision and Curriculum Development (ASCD).

PTAs National standards for family-school partnerships. (2007). http://www.pta.org/national standards.asp

Public Education Network. Using NCLB to improve student achievement: An action guide for community and parent leaders. www.publiceducation.org/pdf/nclb/nclbbook/pdf

Reeves, D. B. (2006). *The learning leader: How to focus school improvement for results*. Alexandria, VA: Association for Supervision and Curriculum Development (ASCD).

Stewart, M. *Best practices for schools, family, and community engagement Subcommittee Report: Recommendations for the Lexington School Committee*. June 2010.

Stewart, M. (2010, August 26). Massachusetts State PTA President 2010 – 2012.

United States Census 2000. (2000). Retrieved from http://www.census/gov/main/www/cen2000.html

Vella, J. (2002). *Learning to listen, learning to teach: The power of dialogue in adult education.* San Francisco, CA: John Wiley & Sons.

Wallace Foundation Report Chapter 2.1 *How districts harness family and community energy for school improvement.* pgs. 107 – 125.

Westmoreland, H., Rosenburg, H. M., Lopez, M.E., and Weiss, H. (July 2007). *Seeing is believing: Promising practices for how school districts promote family engagement.* http:www.hftp.org/publications-resources/browse-our-publications/seeing-is-believing-promising-practices-for-how-school-districts-promote-family-engagement.

Author Note
Lynne M. Celli, Ph.D.

Lynne M. Celli has been the Superintendent of Schools for the Swampscott Public Schools since 2010. Prior to assuming this position, he served in a variety of other positions during this twenty-nine career in education to date including elementary teacher, K-12 principal, college professor, and educational consultant. She holds a BA in Sociology and Education from Clark University, a M.Ed. Curriculum, Instruction, and Administration from Boston College, and a Ph.D. in Curriculum, Instruction, and Administration from Boston College. She was named to the International Who's Who of Professional Educators in 2000.

NOTES

CHAPTER TWO
When Parents Lose Their Kids to the Journey Called "Growing Up": How Schools Can Respond with Empathy

By: Marianne R. Young

The Parent Perspective

For parents, the real question is: do we like their children? In her 2003 book, *The Essential Conversation: What Parents and Teachers Can Learn from Each Other,* Sarah Lawrence Lightfoot explores the relationship between the parent and teacher. In her reflections on the parent-teacher conference she notes,

> "Parents come to the meeting, sit facing the teacher in the chairs that their children inhabit each day, and begin to feel the same way they felt when they were students – small and powerless. And when the teachers offer observations and evaluations of their students, they are often using values and frameworks carved out of their own early childhood experiences."

If we are going to create schools that support what years of research tell us, that students who are in the company of invested and interested adults do better in school than students without this presence, we have to change some of our behaviors. If we are going to create schools that support what Epstein and colleagues point out in their handbook, *School, Family and Community Partnerships,* that "the way schools care about children is reflected in the way schools care about the children's families," (2002), then we have some changing to do.

The Transformative Moment

Kevin was enrolling in seventh grade, and he and his mother were enthusiastic. A special education student with a history of behavioral issues, Kevin and his mother attended the summer IEP meeting and shared with us their anticipation of a new beginning. They were so glad to be joining our middle school, and were certain that Kevin could and would be successful. After all, the elementary school teachers did not know how to reach Kevin.

We reviewed the IEP and put plans in place to assure Kevin's success. Kevin's schedule would include both required classes and electives of interest, time for academic support, Kevin's mother would be notified immediately should anything go awry.

The first day of school was a success. On the second day of school, Kevin skipped a class. Within two weeks, Kevin's mother had been contacted numerous times. Kevin was cutting classes, stealing, and disrespectful behavior was becoming the norm. Each conversation concluded with "thank you," and hope for a better day tomorrow. Then, I arrived at school one morning to find Kevin's mother waiting for me. I discovered that she had changed the dynamic.

Kevin's mother ranted about the school, about the teachers and about me. She informed me that we were failing her son, that we did not know what we were doing, and that she was tired of receiving phone calls from me. She chastised me, implied my incompetence, and was clear that she was no longer participating. We had better figure out what we were doing and were going to do for her son.

I was taken aback. I wasn't expecting this reaction, was not prepared for it, and at the close of our meeting found myself devastated. What happened? What had I missed? I spent the day and evening questioning myself. Where had I gone wrong? Maybe I was incompetent. Maybe I was in the wrong profession, had been wrong all along about my ability to lead a school.

It was not until the next morning that I was able to see clearly that her reaction was not about me, nor about the school. Kevin's mother's reaction was about her son, her hopes and her dreams, her disappointments and her life. Certainly our work at school was not without its shortcomings, neither did it warrant such anger. Kevin's mother needed us to be both the cause and the salvation of her son's failures at school.

The Theory

The parenting process is a loss process arguably beginning at the child's birth. However, when the child reaches school age, reaches adolescence and fully engages in the journey called "growing up," the process of letting go and the sense of loss for parents is considerable. While we in schools are championing and inviting their involvement, parents are turning their children over to the care and influence of strangers called teachers. Our society requires this; our humanness has reservations. While parents are attending school meetings and conferences, concerts and science fairs in an effort to remain involved, their children spend their days in an environment that does not include their parents. Whatever our attempts to include parents, we still ask that they leave their children with us.

"Part of letting our children go is also letting them be, and that means letting go of our expectations for them. For consciously or unconsciously, even before they were born, we dream many dreams about what kind of children we want." (Viorst, 1986, p. 209) Letting our children go. Saying goodbye to long-held dreams and hello to new realities. This is what the parents of our students are engaged in; this is what they bring to our schools.

If we accept and support the research, then we must include and support parents as well as other adults significant in the lives of our students. We have to welcome parents not simply for their baking and fundraising skills, but as individuals who are on a very personal, very challenging journey and essential to our students' academic lives. If we espouse partnership and collaboration, then we must work to create relationships with parents dedicated to the success of our students. We do that by treating parents well, with empathy, honesty and mindfulness. As Willy Loman said in *Death of a Salesman*, "Attention must be paid." Attention to the humanness of each adult – parent and teacher alike – who works on behalf of our children.

I propose that the school-parent relationship travels through stages and that being mindful of these stages as we work with parents improves relationships, results in holistic support for students, and thus student development.

Stages in the Parent-School Relationship

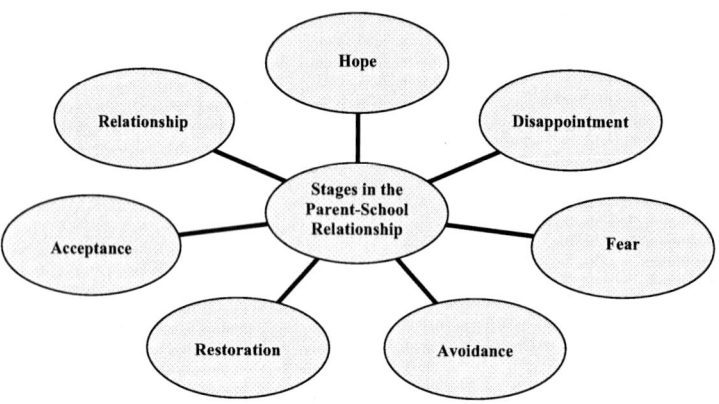

Stage I: Hope

Characterized by anticipation, cooperation, a new beginning ... "Anything we can do."

Sally has arrived with her mother for the first day of kindergarten, and they are both nervous and excited. What will this experience bring? Sally is looking forward to the adventure of school, while her mother looks forward to Sally's academic and social success. Sally's mother hopes that her daughter will be a flourishing student. Either she longs for others to recognize all the wonderful qualities she sees in her daughter, or she longs for the school to save her daughter from her struggles. The anticipation is palpable.

The school, too, is hopeful. The first day of school is the best day of the year. Students are well behaved, teachers well rested. Educators throughout the building are announcing that this is a new day, and we all have a clean slate. Teachers review guidelines and expectations, new books are distributed, pages in the new notebook pages are untouched. We are wearing our new clothes and everything is possible.

This stage is exacerbated when the new school year includes a new school. It is heightened when students are moving from elementary school to middle school, or from middle to high school. It is magnified for students entering kindergarten. It is especially intensified if the move to this new school has been deliberate and intended to solve past difficulties.

The first day of school is one of the most hopeful of days of the year and most certainly one that evokes powerful memories. Parents remember the smells of new lunch boxes and pencil boxes, their favorite or least favorite teacher, and see this day as the close of summer and the opening of the future. We are filled with hope.

Stage II: Disappointment

Characterized by disbelief, a sense of being let down, … "I can't believe it. What happened?"

The state of hopefulness, as with the remaining stages, can last for any length of time. For some students and their parents, it is short lived. For others, it can last through elementary school and wane at the start of middle school. For others still, the hope may not dissipate until the college search and application process begins. While some students deal with academic or social struggles beginning in the primary years, others do not suffer disappointment until much later. For all parents there will come a time of disappointment.

Let us consider Sally. She has acclimated to school and is enjoying herself. She gets along well with others, is appropriate and works hard. But she is struggling with reading. Assessing this as the case, the teacher calls home to notify Sally's parents. Certainly, the teacher thinks they will be grateful for the call so that Sally will not fall through the cracks. Still, they react with disappointment. The teacher views the call as proactive, timely and responsible. The parents hear that Sally is struggling with reading, hence she is imperfect. What seems to the teacher to be news parents will want to know, the parents view this as news they need to know, but certainly do not desire.

Sally's parents may have suspected that their daughter would struggle with reading. Max's parent may have suspected that he would have difficulty making friends. Alicia's parents may have assumed that she would sail through her first year in middle school as she sailed through elementary school. Gabe, in his junior year of high school, receives his first "C."

This first disappointment, however minor, is a disappointment nonetheless. This is when the work begins. We are engaged in the process of loss.

"Mourning the loss of a child, or the hope of the child-who-was-to-be, may begin at any stage of the parenting process and may need to be acknowledged and understood by the outside world as well as those who experience the loss." (Viorst, 1986, p. 205)

While Viorst is discussing the death of a child, or the termination of a pregnancy, the stage of disappointment is a loss for the parent. Parents are in a state of disbelief, because either nothing similar has ever occurred before, or because they were certain that the behavior would not happen again. During the stage of hope, the parent welcomed communication from the school, and while now they understand the need for the communication, it is not a conversation they relish. Simply put, they are disappointed, but they will move forward.

At this stage parents are generally still cooperative and willing to work with the school. They will attend required meetings, support any disciplinary action, and offer to support the school's initiatives at home. The parent is not happy, nor is he/she willing to abandon hope.

Stage III: Fear

Characterized by questioning, a change of attitude ... "What about the other kids?"

This is the stage that often takes teachers and administrators by surprise, the stage that significantly changes the dynamic. This is often the time school leaders become defensive because the parent begins to change the conversation from cooperation to indignation.

For the sake of discussion, let us return to Kevin's story. Up until this point, Kevin's mother had been cooperative. Although disappointed by such early-in-the-year problems, she remained willing to support the school's decisions. Then came the proverbial straw and Kevin's mother moved from disappointment to fear. Kevin's mother experienced a change of attitude and began to question the school.

Here, parents will frequently look to others as a barometer and compare their children to other children. Questions will arise around fairness and equity. A parent will start to look more closely at the teacher and point out shortcomings. Often the conversation will include queries about the details of the situation, the intricacies in the interaction, or the quality of the efforts made on the part of the school. Driven by the fear that nothing is changing or the fear that things are falling apart, parents will search for an explanation, for a cause. The reaction is defensive in nature, and often will include accusations and hostility.

Sally is not reading because the teacher does not know how to teach her to read. "I know other students are having the same trouble." "Kevin would not steal. I've heard that there are other kids who steal." I know other kids who have had trouble with that teacher." "My son does not do drugs. I know. He tells me everything."

Stage IV: Avoidance

Characterized by denial, blame, evasion ... "The school...the teacher...is not doing its job."

During Stage III (Fear), parents begin questioning the integrity of the school's work. While they may still acknowledge a redeeming quality or two, and the parent has not completely shut down communication, this next stage brings blame and eventually silence.

As with all the stages, the degree to which we are involved in this exchange varies according to the situation, the family and the school, but all parties are intricately connected. The parent is feeling a sense of futility, a tendency to give up, and strong desire to stop the conversation. The parent may announce, "You're on your own!" to either the school or the student. The parent may simply request a change of placement. Often the parent will threaten to take the student "out of *this* school." Possibly the procuring of a lawyer is threatened, but always is the intimation that they have done all they can do, and they will no longer participate. Requests to parents to come to school and retrieve their child are met with disdain, frustration. Canceling meetings, personal attacks and accusations are not uncommon. Parents who are divorced begin to ask that the school contact the other parent. Should parents need to attend meetings, there will be no banter, no social niceties. The time educators and parents spend together, if any, will be strained and marked by what is *not* said.

Stage V: Restoration

Characterized by willingness, listening, initiation ... "Can I come in?"

Regardless of the reaction the school has had to the previous stages, but most certainly influenced by the reaction, parents will return to support their children, however faultily. They may be limited in their capacity or hindered by forces beyond their control, but they almost always return. They must. They need for their children to be in school or find an alternative. Alternatives are hard to find.

The parent is beginning to know his/her child in new ways, recognizing patterns, understanding limitations, and dealing with difficulties. Although the parent remains disappointed, he/she is taking the first steps toward acceptance. "Sally is a good kid, really. I hate to watch her struggle. Homework is such a chore. What should we do?" "Kevin is Kevin. He drives me crazy. I don't know what to do, but he has to be in school. Could we meet?"

Stage VI: Acceptance

Characterized by yielding, openness ... "What do you suggest?"

Restoration and acceptance are closely linked and yet quite distinctive. While restoration allows the parent to renew conversation with the school, acceptance restores the parent-student relationship as well. Throughout this process, while tension is ebbing and flowing between the parent and the school, so too is the dynamic between the parents and student. Initially, the parent and student bring home the news from school and work in a spirit of cooperation and an eye on resolution. As the discord at school heightens, the atmosphere at home is strained. Such is the nature of conflict.

There is a climactic moment. Whether wrought by another incident at school, an occurrence in the home, or a seemingly non-related event, the parents reach a turning point. What may begin as resulting resignation will often culminate in acceptance.

Stage VII: Relationship

Characterized by appreciation, gratitude ... "It's okay. Thank you."

Given that the school, through the work of its leaders, has maintained throughout this cycle a calm respect for the individuals and a willingness to work for the benefit of the student, the parties will undoubtedly return to a state of relationship. The parent will once again, or maybe for the first time, see the school as an ally rather than as an enemy and return to a place of cooperation. Should efforts have been particularly successful, there will be gratitude. Should efforts have resulted in a peaceful coexistence, there will be evidence of concurrence.

Although the parent may not be witnessing in the life of their child that for which they had once hoped, they will have arrived at a place where they can once again glimpse the uniqueness of their child.

Considerations

As is the case with criticism of Kübler-Ross' work, classifying or attributing stages to any process has its limitations. "What was described ... become[s] prescribed." (Fulton, Metress, p. 315) Nonetheless, if school leaders use this cycle as a way of approaching discourse with parents, the results are irrefutable. In addition, educators would do well to consider these other factors contributing to the parenting process, the stages of grief and mourning, and the parent-school relationship.

Guilt

Parents bring to the table disappointments and shortcomings. Their own. Maybe they did not finish school themselves. They are not available enough or think they aren't earning enough. Often they are divorced or going through a divorce, a traumatic time for all. Are they struggling with alcoholism or drug addiction?

Each time the school contacts a parent with news that is less than impressive, a parent is forced to consider their role and their influence in their child's life. None of us is without some disappointment. When we look at our children, as cliché as it sounds, we hope for better. If a parent is unable to facilitate the better, he/she is left questioning his/her ability to parent.

Loneliness

When school leaders work with parents and see the fear set in, we are also watching the characteristics of loneliness. Loss is lonely. Grief can be isolating. Although we *know* we are not the only ones ever to suffer a loss, the journey through grief and mourning is a most personal affair. It is easy to feel alone.

We call from our schools to inform the parent of a problematic situation. The parent enters the requisite meeting alone. Later in the evening, parents are home with their child dealing with the situation alone. The family is confronting the situation alone and tends to believe they are the only family in this state of affairs. When the student cries, "I'm not the only one who did it!" the parent has no evidence. The parent wants to believe it is so, may even know it is the case, but this is a solitary affair. "I don't care what anyone else did. You are my child. You are the one I'm concerned about." Singular pronouns. Singular journey.

Time

When Sally was in kindergarten and was struggling with reading, her parents were disappointed. When Sally reaches middle school and is still reading below grade level, being offered Title I services and earning average or below average grades in class, the parents are anxious. Not only is she having difficulty reading, she is becoming reluctant. When Sally enrolls in high school and gives up the hope of college, her parents are angry. What will become of her?

The stages of the parent-school relationship are evident at any grade level. They are amplified in high school. Time is running out. Research tells us that many children do not learn to read until third grade. This is a benchmark, but fourth grade is still only fourth grade. The non-reading is certainly a concern, but the student will probably, eventually come into her own, a parent thinks. One day it will just click. But high school. That is another story. Sally's not on the college track because she cannot pass the advanced courses. Too much reading. Sally failed the statewide test the first time she took it. She has to give up after school activities or her part-time job to attend tutoring sessions. If she does not graduate, what will she do?

Morality

Cutting class. Difficulty making friends. Cheating. Aggressive behavior. Drug involvement. So often, the nature of the troubling behavior in which the student is engaged is laden with moral nuances. These are the "bad" behaviors.

The principal calls the parent and informs the parent that his/her son or daughter has been engaged in a situation that is not acceptable at school. While the parent may consider the behavior incidental, it nonetheless warranted a call from the principal who is the arbiter, the person they themselves avoided when they were in school. Similarly, should the call come from the teacher, the parent once again is contacted by the one who once held power over them, the one who knows everything, who is smart and educated. The parent is once again a child, a student. Inherent in this interaction is the undertone of judgment. While the range of behaviors may vary in degrees of morality, the call from the school does not. Calls from school are bad.

The Diagnosis

When terminally ill patients enter the second stage of Kübler-Ross' stages of death and dying, they are angry with the doctors, maybe with God, and with the diagnosis. (Kübler-Ross, 1969, p. 222)

So, too, are parents angry with the diagnosis, and educators provide the diagnosis: -ADD, ADHD, dyslexia, IQ tests, achievement tests, standardized tests. We continually give parents information that smacks of diagnosis. We do so in definitive terms followed by a recommendation for treatment. In a brief conversation or a short meeting, the parents have been issued the conclusion and solution. Their reaction tells us the story.

The School in the Parent-School Relationship

In our quest to provide excellent educational opportunities to all students, it is easy for educators to lose sight of the most powerful influence: the humanness of our constituents. How quickly we move through parent conferences, doling out information about our students from one parent to the next. How seldom we make phone calls home, so that when one is made it is monumental in the life of the family. How ritually and singularly we recognize successes.

We know that partnership with parents is essential to student success. Let us then pay attention to how we invite them into relationship with us.

Language

The written and spoken word is our tool for success in creating partnership with parents. The words we choose, our tone of voice and the frequency of our verbal interactions are key to creating and maintaining relationship with parents. We cannot stop the process parents go through as they deal with disappointments and struggles, but we can control how we discuss our students and our reaction to parental behavior. We can set the tone.

Our vocabulary and our behavior should demonstrate our willingness to listen, to consider and to collaborate. However, our words should be strong. Whether the issue is owned by the student or the school, we need to speak clearly about the situation, take responsibility when the cause is with us, and hold both the students and ourselves accountable.

The language we use when communicating with parents should be compassionate. Yes, the situation warrants clarity and strength, but the parent deserves compassion. Have we, teachers and administrators, suffered similar losses? Can we remember times when we, too faced disappointment? Parents will look to the school for leadership and for resolve hoping it will do for their child what they cannot. We should provide this, certainly, and with compassion.

The school should remain eternally hopeful. We are working with young people, works in progress. The choices students make during their school years will most definitely influence their futures, but will not finish them. As we reflect on our own growth and development, we will see that many of our successes, moments when we were most proud of ourselves were experienced in adulthood. As learners, we were far more open in college and in our post-graduate work than we were as adolescents. We must recognize this in our students and provide the hope parents need when they have lost it for themselves.

We must be ever affirming. The culture of the school must be one where students are recognized regularly for their daily successes and in authentic ways. Parents need to know that even while a particular situation is problematic, their child does in fact contribute to the school community. If the culture of the school is one where each and every individual is valued, then the misbehavior or the struggle experienced by the student must be addressed in light of its impact on the community, not as a personal judgment. The words we choose to address the student, regardless of who the student is, must demonstrate respect. The words we choose to address the parent must be equally respectful.

Again, *if* we are true to that which we espouse – that the role of the parent in the life of our students is significant and needed – then there are a few simple but ever important steps we can take to ensure its presence.

- Listen. Listen to what is being said and not said. Hear what the parent is saying about his/her child, him/herself, his/her struggles.
- Make the extra phone call. Call when there is good news to share. Just call.
- Create a support group. Following the "if we build it, they will come" philosophy, hold coffee hours at several different times and invite parents in to talk with us and with each other.
- Know the services and programs in the community and use them. Specialists who reside in our communities are often very willing to help us help our parent community. Ask.

- Maintain your focus on and vision for the student.
- Do not blame.

Our goal is partnership. Our goal is excellence. We cannot achieve our goals without the support of our students' parents. They are our community.

Following recent parent conferences a teacher commented to me, "You know, I think parents just want to know that their child has been noticed."

References

Blank, M. and Kershaw, C. "Designing Collaborative Educator-Parent Partnerships." *Practitioner.* Virginia: NASSP. Vol. 25.

Fulton, G. B., and Metress, E. K. (1995). *Perspectives on Death and Dying.* Boston: Jones and Bartlett Publishers, Inc.

Kübler-Ross, E. (1997). *On Death and Dying.* New York: Collier Books.

Lawrence-Lightfoot, S. (2003). *The Essential Conversation: What Parents and Teachers CanLearn from Each Other.* New York: Random House.

McEwan, E.K. (1998). *Angry Parents, Failing Schools: What's Wrong with Public Schoolsand What You Can Do About It.* Harold Shaw Publishers.

O'Connor, N. (1994). *Letting Go With Love: The Grieving Process.* Mariposa.

Author Note
Marianne R. Young, MA

Marianne Young has been the principal at Monument Mountain Regional High School in Great Barrington, Massachusetts since 1999, save two years when she served as the Superintendent of the Lenox Public Schools. Ms. Young began her tenure in educational leadership in a small Vermont middle/high school following years of teaching English. She holds a BA in Secondary Education and English from the University of Rhode Island, and a MA in Education Leadership from Vermont College of Norwich University. Ms. Young has presented her work on the parent-school partnership and other educational topics at conferences sponsored by organizations such as ASCD and MSSAA. She is an instructor for Massachusetts College of Liberal Arts and a member of the School Leaders Network.

Correspondence concerning this chapter should be directed to the author at marianne.young@bhrsd.org.

CHAPTER THREE

Social Justice Starts at Home

By: Dorothy Firman

Defining Social Justice

The consideration of social justice is one that has slowly but surely moved through many fields in the United States, from politics to education to religion to psychology and social services. Issues of social justice in education are particularly poignant as schools across the country face issues of bullying in unprecedented numbers. Adams, Bell and Griffin (2007) refer to social justice as both a process and a goal.

> "Social justice includes a vision of society in which the distribution of resources is equitable and all members are physically and psychologically safe. We envision a society in which individuals are both self-determining (able to develop to their full capacitates) and interdependent (capable of interacting democratically with others). Social justice involves social actors who have a sense of their own agency as well as a sense of social responsibility toward and with others and the society as a whole. These are conditions we wish not only for our own society but also for every society in our interdependent global community" (p. 2).

Carlisle, Jackson and George (2006) define social justice *education* as "the conscious and reflexive blend of content and process intended to enhance equity across multiple social identity groups (e.g., race, class, gender, sexual orientation, ability)…" (p. 57). Moving beyond the role of schools in the quest for social justice, the Center for Family, Community, and Social Justice (2011) refers to the "persistent struggle" for, among other things: equal human and civil rights; fair economic, educational and social opportunities; dignity and respect for all; elimination of societal prejudices; and equal access. Issues of social justice are clearly relevant to all school systems and inevitably to all families with school children and ultimately, of course, to all global citizens. Oxfam (2006) includes a commitment to social justice and equity, as well as a value and respect for diversity in their goal of developing responsible global citizens. From the classroom to the globe, social justice stands at the forefront of our need and our mandate—as individuals, families, communities and countries.

Social justice then, as a theme that addresses broad stroke issues of injustice, power abuse, oppression, diversity, and equality, in the end, comes down to the smallest acts of violence, of disrespect, of aggression, or of fairness, justice and goodness. These qualities or behaviors, the good and the bad, are hard to teach and the call to justice needs to be answered at all levels. Schools need social justice curricula; communities need awareness of and active engagement with issues of social justice; political systems need to squarely face their complicity in social injustice while correcting and creating laws and norms to support justice. And families, each and every one, need to embed socially just values in their daily lives. For long before children enter pre-school or connect with their larger community in any way, the earliest lessons will have been learned.

Social Justice and Academics

While schools seek to address social justice, for all of the right reasons (equity, fairness, true democracy, inclusion, among others), they are burdened with an embedded split between the "social" welfare of students and the "academic" welfare. "Increasingly, educational leaders are faced with tremendous pressure to demonstrate that every child for whom they have responsibility is achieving success— often defined as performance to a designated standard on a single standardized test" (Shields, 2004, p. 109). Research is growing that maintains there can be no separation of one of these goals from the other: that, in fact, social justice in the schools is a key factor in creating academic success for *all* students (Dover, 2009; Carlisle, Jackson & George, 2006). The National Association of Educational Progress notes a racially correlated achievement gap (1999). The Gay, Lesbian, Straight Education Network (2003) points to social oppression as an explanation for increased drop out and suicide rates among LGBT students. The economic reality of public school funding based on the local tax base assures better educational opportunities for children in wealthier communities (Dover, 2009). The list goes on.

Schools and Families

As schools continue to gear up towards greater academic success for students, as well as greater social justice, the question remains what else needs to be done to promote positive student development in the arena of social justice. It is clear that students who live in a socially just environment do develop more positively and are better prepared for life as adults in a diverse and global environment. Likewise, students who have strong and healthy family connections are better equipped for both academics and life outside of school. The issue of family/school relationships is one that is being given more attention, attention that is much needed, because it is true that it take a village to raise a child. It has been noted that better school/family communication (Dover, 2009) creates more social justice and we know that more social justice creates better academic outcomes. Thus the circle widens and the family and school, working together will improve both the lived experience of social justice and the positive outcome of success in academics.

While beyond the scope of this chapter, it is clear that the communities, from the local town to the global "village" in which families and school are housed have an equally important role to play in promoting social justice, well being and positive development for children and the adults in their world.

The Role of Families in Social Justice Education

Given the key importance of family in the lives of children, as it pertains to any and every aspect of a child's life, it is crucial to include, and in fact, live, the values, theories and strategies of social justice education in the home life of the child. While schools hold a major key to social justice, for it is in schools that children most actively engage in social situations, the family offers children the first template for relationship. And social justice, at is core, is about relationships. Barr (2005) notes that interpersonal skills, "the intimacy and autonomy strategies needed to make and maintain good relationships" (p.149) are a key to creating a social justice orientation in young people.

And families are the first role models. The effects of this early "imprinting" are long lasting and form the basis for the deepest level of conditioning. Families teach the first set of ethical and social guidelines. These teachings are overt and covert. They are often the most powerful and almost always the first set of rules to live by.

What guides healthy relationship behavior? What creates an ethical, socially just stance in life? What are the guiding principles that help children become good and conscious members of their society? These questions move us into larger worlds of psychology, philosophy, ethics and even theology, but for our purposes here, it is safe to say that early family life sets the stage for children to develop attitudes, beliefs and corresponding behaviors that are socially just. The earliest psychosocial development is in the family. And supporting children in becoming, themselves, socially conscious and just starts at home.

Good Things Families Do

How do families and family life help support children in being socially aware and socially just? Looking at some key themes in social justice education will allow us to look, through the lens of families, at strategies and practices that promote social justice and in doing so promote positive development for children. As parents themselves become more conscious and as schools create a social justice curriculum and actively promote social justice as the bedrock of education, more and more families will be positively influenced in this direction. And, as always, if we look around, we will see families, consciously and unconsciously, working towards social justice with their children, not because they have been trained to do so, but because, to them it makes sense and it reflects their own deeply held values.

Socially just parenting has always existed, though it has not often been addressed. Parenting books and classes have historically focused on what we have come to think of as the parents' domain: sleeping; eating; discipline; awareness of development; homework; chores; when to call the doctor, etc. Implicit in many of these themes are issues of social justice, but rarely named as such. Thankfully, this is changing and even the term *socially just parenting,* is showing up in the literature, in communities and in conversations. The Socially Just Parenting Project (sociallyjustparenting.org), among others, invites a deeper and ongoing exploration of the responsibility of parents in educating for social justice.

Looking at some of the "best practices" in socially just parenting reminds us just how easy it is to take that next step from "good enough" parenting to "good enough and socially just" parenting. What are best practices? *Children of Character: A Parent's Guide* (Reuben, 1997) offers some guidelines. They include the key issue of being a "moral" role model, as well as teaching values and responsibility. More basically, the author points to the core aspects of good parenting as the building blocks for good socially just parenting: unconditional love and building self-esteem. Beyond those "good enough" parenting realities, Reuben focuses on "teachable moments", those moments that appear, unplanned, when a lesson can be learned, a value instilled, a moment of justice noted or created. They exist so often that any parent will have access to them.

Each case vignette, presented below, comes from real people's stories, some public, some private and each points to possibilities for families in choosing to create a better world for their children *and* a better world for other people's children.

First Comes Love, Then Comes.....

When Andrea Ayvazian and Michael Klare got together as a couple they were already deeply committed to social justice. Says Andrea: "When we connected as a couple, it seemed clear to us that we should take the next step—by not taking the next step" (Ohlson, 2001, p. 3). Even before considering the questions of social justice and children, which they would do later when their son was born, they could not move into the culturally sanctioned institution of marriage, because to them, those rights were being denied to many of their fellow citizens. Long before even one state in the US passed legislation to allow gay marriage, Andrea and Michael were taking a stand. Ayvazian notes that choices like these are not simple or easy. This is a stand that comes at a cost. Beyond whatever social pressures or familial issues might be raised in such circumstances, the pure financial reality of this choice has had an influence on their lives from the moment they did not got married, long past the time they had a child. Two health insurance policies are carried, since there is no family plan, and even vacations that offer "family" discounts are rejected, unless those discounts are also given to gay and lesbian families.

When families live what they want to teach their children, the message is brought home in the most authentic and meaningful way possible. What children see their parents doing tells them as much or more than what they hear their parents tell them. Much later, Andrea, in her ongoing work as a social activist, noted the importance of role models as an essential aspect of being an ally. "Not only does allied behavior contribute to an increase in equity and a decrease in violence, but allies provide positive role models that are sorely needed by today's young people" (Ayvazian, 2007, p. 227).

Read to me

For academic success, it has long been clear that reading to children is a big jump-start on education. At the same time, the content or the quality of what children are taking in, through reading or television, or living in their families, are sowing deep seeds that will support—or sabotage—the building of a social justice consciousness in children. It may well have been the publication of *Heather has Two Mommies* (1989) by Leslea Newman that planted the seed for a movement to create books that embraced diversity, and focused on social justice. At the time, however, it created a stir and a strong negative reaction that went so far as public, negative, comment on the floor of the Senate and the banning of the book in many environments (www.articleworld.org). But the people whose lives were positively impacted, both lesbian and gay parents and parents with a social justice orientation, welcomed the book with open arms. It has become the trailblazer and today, while still in the minority, there are books to be had for children of all ages that tell good stories with good and just themes. By 2002, *King and King* (de Haan & Nijland) was published. The classic stories of love and family, the fantastically appealing "happily ever after" stories, now included a much wider, much more accurate picture of who it is that gets to fall in love and be happy. Today stories for children holding a social justice perspective, in many arenas of life, continue to become available, offering parents a powerful way to share deep values with their children. (See, among others: Jane Adams Peace Association Children's book awards; Cooperative Children's Book Center; Social Justice Picture Books)

Barbie

Many a parent, coming of age in a socially conscious culture, have contended with the issue of toys for their children. Parents rightfully ask questions from "Do we give our child a toy gun?" to "What about Barbie?" There are, of course, no easy answers, perhaps not even "right" answers, but questions like these invite social awareness and offer yet another moment to move towards socially just parenting. Barbie is iconographic of one important piece of a societal oppression: the sexualization of girls and women. Families make all sorts of decisions to deal with this issue, often creating polarization with their daughters (and sometimes sons) or giving up their own strong values.

One family worked hard to balance their only child's desire for that particular doll, with their own social values. Barbie showed up, as she often does, on a birthday, given by well meaning family and friends. Ellen, then 6, was thrilled. Mom and dad were not. "At 6? Really? She needs a big busted, high heels wearing doll?" Their solution, one they worked with over the next 3 or 4 years until Barbie was no longer of interest to Ellen, was to create a different Barbie world. Instead of Barbie pools and Barbie Corvettes, the parents looked long and hard for dolls of similar size in a variety of racial and cultural diversities. At a next holiday the parents bought Ellen a globe and spent time playing with it and organizing the dolls around their countries of origin. When the family went on vacation, mom proposed to Ellen that Barbie join the Peace Corps. The conversation that was elicited added a dimension to Barbie's world (and more importantly, Ellen's). Barbie was gone when the family returned from vacation, but the conversation and visits to books about various countries that Barbie might be, in the Peace Corps, continued. Honoring a commitment to their honesty with Ellen, Barbie returned. And along with the diversity of friends she had before she left, she now had more, and new clothes, new friends, even new accessories, all representing a diverse world.

Recently Ellen (now 25) packed up and gave away her Barbie doll collection. In it, one tall white blond Barbie, one American Indian woman, one white young girl, one Arabian man, one African woman, one dog, one cat. And lots of shoes.

Barbie Redux

Galia Slayen took the Barbie doll issue one step further. Having struggled with an eating disorder when she was in high school, Galia conquered that issue and got conscious about some of its roots. One of them was Barbie. "I'm not blaming Barbie (for my illness)- she's one small factor…" But a factor worth thinking about and talking about. Slayen, while still a high school student made a life size Barbie doll. "I'm blond and blue eyed and I figured that was what I was supposed to look like" (Marsh, 2011).

What does an adult sized Barbie look like? She's 6 feet tall, has a bust of 39 inches and a waist that is 18 inches. And, say researchers in Finland, she would not have the 17-22% body fat required for a woman to menstruate (Winterman, 2009).

Boys Will be Boys

Cheryl Kilodavis, herself the child of African American and Caucasian heritage, struggled as child to understand the big questions. One of them had to do with judgment and why people felt it was okay to judge others. Years later, as a mother to two boys, she wrote a book, *My Princess Boy* (2010). All she set out to do was to explain to her son's teachers why he was "unique", why he wore sparkly dresses and loved the color pink. The book had, not surprisingly, a strong anti bullying message and somehow it went viral. Like *Heather has Two Mommies,* it collected its share of hostility as well, but out of it also grew deeper parent awareness and the growth of "Princess Boy/Strength Girl Acceptance Groups" now running nation wide. Their mission? "To accept and celebrate the unique person within all of us" (myprincessboy.com).

Correction

When Joe, now a school guidance counselor was a little boy, his father took him, for the first time, from the suburbs of New Jersey into NYC for a sports event at Madison Square Garden. He no longer remembers what sports event or what teams were involved, but he remembers (and still close to tears as he tells it) seeing a homeless man lying on the street. He tried to go over to see the man, to figure out why he was lying down, maybe to help him, but dad pulled him away by the hand and could offer no explanation. The man was still there when they came out and again Joe wanted to do something, though he knew not what. He could not even understand why there was a man lying on the sidewalk. And dad didn't know how to explain and didn't know what to do but to hurry on and focus on the game.

Somewhere along his way to adulthood Joe determined that he would not recreate that scene. His own life involved work with social service organizations, social justice causes and finally work with school children. When he first ventured into the streets of Boston with his young sons, he was surprised to find himself in the same situation. There, on a cold winter's day, was homeless person, lying on the streets. Whatever their task at hand was that day, Joe doesn't remember. What he does remember is taking his kids aside and talking to them about the man on the street and asking them what they wanted to do. Their decision was to buy a blanket to give the man. Stepping away from the plans at hand, they found a store, bought a blanket and returned to give it to the person who was in need.

Father Knows Best

Jabari Natur started his quest for social justice when he was listening to the radio with his young daughters and heard a rap song (much of it "bleeped out") that offended him and made his young daughters mad. His strategy, instead of pulling away from the material, was to take his daughters on-line to see the lyrics (in all their vividness) and to begin talking to them about what these songs said and what they meant. Over time, he encouraged his daughters to write a letter to the particular rap artist that they had been hurt by, telling him that his lyrics were disrespectful to women. These 9 and 10 year-old girls did that and went further (with dad's help) by turning their letter into a song and their song into a music video. Uploaded onto U-tube, the song had more than 750,000 hits within a week. The newly created musical group, *Watoto on the Nile,* composed of two girls from Baltimore, began to speak back to the adults in their world. Their father noted that "silence gives consent" and he worked hard not to allow that silence in his family (Charnas, 2011).

Giving and Getting

Parents, in this culture, are caught in an orientation of materialism. Advertising reminds us of what we "need to have" to be happy. Children, particularly vulnerable as they are, are bombarded with messages about having and getting and owning and needing everything they see. What does it mean for a culture when a popular bumper sticker states that the one who dies with the most toys wins? Short of turning away from the culture at large, living a deeply alternative lifestyle, even living off the grid, there are few situations that protect children and parents from the culture's demands to consume. What's a parent to do? There are no easy answers, but parents far and wide are making decisions that offer their children a larger view of the world, a fairer view of the world and view in which a child's desires for this or that toy are important and valuable... and not the only issue at hand.

One family (and likely many more) gives their children an early Christmas present. They are middle class and have enough money to really give the kids what they want. And this first present is generous. They give each child, starting at age 3 a gift of $100.00. But with the gift comes a responsibility. For weeks before the end of the year, appeals come for all the charities, all the non-profits, all the local and national and international appeals to support good works. In this family, each child chooses how (after much discussion) to gift their money. Each represented cause is talked about. The children engage with the literature, with each other, with the parents. They can give any amount to any organization that has sent an appeal. The resulting donations may appear odd to those who receive them. $26.00 to Unicef? $14.00 to Doctors without Borders? $7.00 to the local theater group? And $55.00 to Save the Hummingbird? While the parents encourage the conversation, answer the questions and help the children think (and feel) their way through the decisions, the children, in the end, are making choices. They are becoming global citizens and social activists.

And countering the trend of holiday "madness" in this country, there are many families who don't make that giant thanksgiving meal, but instead take their children to help at the local soup kitchen. And there are those who turn Valentine's day into a love-for-the-larger world holiday. And others who remember the origin of the many holidays and celebrate their original meaning, not the materialized version that comes across our airwaves. Even birthdays, that oh-so-special time of "me" can be turned into an opportunity for a larger justice: a school in which children "give" a book to the library on their birthday; a family who uses birthdays as an opportunity to let go of toys that a child has in order to consciously share those benefits with others; a family who asks their child to appreciate what they have and to give back.

And There Is More

Across the board, if we look, we can find families making decisions every day that encourage social justice in their children; families that live in a socially just way. Whatever the particular issue of justice is, there are people taking a stand in families, in schools and in communities to change our world.

Linda Carney-Goodrich (2011) moved from being poor to being middle class and now worries about instilling social justice values in her middle class kids. Issues of classism are at the forefront of her parenting (*Middle Class Brats?*).

Brad Roth, a dancer, noticed that the brother of a child in his ballet class was in a wheelchair. Jordy snuck off to another ballet room, while Ashley had her lesson, and he began to "teach" ballet barre exercises to some kids who were also waiting. Brad promptly facilitated the creation of a dance performance for Ashley and Jordy at the Special Olympics World Games. His three daughters now dance with him in his mixed ability dancing company (Roth, 1997).

Susan and Tereza (no last names listed) started a blog called *White Anti-Racist Parent*. It's stated goal is to be a "place for open dialogue around raising anti-racist consciousness and racial justice in the white community." Susan and Tereza are not experts, nor are any of the people whose stories we've heard. Tereza comments: "Do I really know what it takes to be an anti-racist parent, and what's more, do I dare call myself one? At this stage, perhaps I'm more of a wannabe. My desire to get out of my head and start taking action led me to starting this blog." (http://www.whiteantiracistparent.blogspot.com/)

Conclusion

All of us should heed the call to be wannabes, to be beginners, to take a first step, and to keep consciously moving on this most important journey. Owen (2011) in his chapter "Fathering for Social Justice" notes three characteristics of what he calls "anti-oppressive parenting." These are: knowledge, practice and character. Knowledge includes the education that parents need to understand oppression, its history and its reality in culture. For more on that learning curve, visit The Socially Just Parenting Project (sociallyjustparenting.org) where there is a comprehensive list of books for just this process of gaining knowledge. Practice, Owen's second task, gives us permission to be imperfect and to learn as we go. It also reminds us that this work is not theoretical. As parents and families we must change our lives in little and big ways to create the arena in which social justice can grow. This is where we find our "teachable" moments. Look to your schools and your community to see opportunities to engage in these important issues, as adults, as parents and as families.

Finally Owen's vision of building virtuous character in our children, takes us back to the key realization that it is in parenting our children, from the day they are born, that character is built. The earliest messages for children about relationship come before they have language or cognition to understand. The good enough parent is the first teacher of social justice and this teaching begins at birth. By the time the child is old enough to internalize verbal messages, guidance, rules and practices of social conduct and morality, the parent, siblings, extended family and social environment—whatever it is— are the teachers. In the same way that we teach our children to brush their teeth and look both ways before crossing the road, we must teach them to be fair and kind and thoughtful. And as we are role models, the first and most profound of the many that they will see, we must practice what we preach. Each parent who teaches, practices and lives through the call of social justice helps create a healthier child and a better world.

References

Adams, M., Bell, L. & Griffin, P. (eds). (2007). *Teaching for diversity and social justice*. New York: Routledge.

Ayvazian, A. "Interrupting the cycle of oppression: The role of allies as agents of change" in Young, N. & Michael, C. (2007) (Eds). *Counseling in a complex society: Contemporary challenges to professional practice*. Amherst, MA: Synthesis Center Press.

Barr, D. (2005). Early adolescents' reflections on social justice: Facing history and ourselves in practice and assessment. *Intercultural Education,* 16(2), 145-160.

Carlisle, L., Jackson, B. & George, A. (2006). Principles of social justice education: The social justice education in schools project. *Equity & Excellence in Education,* 39, 55-64.

Carney-Goodrich, L. (2011). *Middle Class Brats?* [Web Log Message] Retrieved from: http://www.classism.org/middle-class-brats.

Center for Family, Community, and Social Justice. (2011). http://www.cfcsj.org/.

Charnas, D. (2011). Girls who denounced Lil Wayne: "We were mad". *Newsone for Black America.* Retrieved from: http://newsone.com/nation/dcharnas/watoto-from-the-nile-interview-open-letter-lil-wayne-girls/.

De Haan, L. & Nijland, S. (2003). *King and King.* New York, NY: Tricycle Press.

Dover, A. (2009). Teaching for social justice and k-12 student outcomes: A conceptual framework and research review. *Equity & Excellence in Education,* 42 (4), 506-524.

Heather Has Two Mommies (nd). Articleworld.org. Retrieved from http://www.articleworld.org/index.php/Heather_Has_Two_Mommies.

Kilodavis, C. (2010). *My Princess Boy.* New York, NY: Aladdin.

Kilodavis, C. (2011). Cheryl's Bio. Retrieved from: http://www.myprincessboy.com/bio.asp.

Marsh, L. (2011). Life size Barbie gets real women talking. *Today.com.* Retrieved from http://today.msnbc.msn.com/id/42595605/ns/today-today_people.

National Association of Educational Progress. http://nces.ed.gov/nationsreportcard/ltt/.

Newmann, L. (1989). *Heather has Two Mommies.* Northampton, MA: In Other Words Publishing.

Ohlson, K. (2001). Marriage: For better? For worse? *Oberlin Alumni Magazine.* 97(2). Retrieved from: http://www.oberlin.edu/alummag/oamcurrent/oam-fall2001/marriage.html

Owen, D. (2011). Fathering for Social Justice. In Nease, L. & Autsin, M. (Eds.), *Fatherhood-philosophy for everyone: The Dao of daddy.* New York: Wiley Blackwell.

Oxfam (2006). Key elements of global citizenship. *Oxfam Education.* Retrieved from: http://www.oxfam.org.uk/education/gc/curriculum/key_elements.

Roth, B. (1997). Dancing with disabilities. *Association for the Advancement of Psychosynthesis.* Retrieved from: http://www.aap-psychosynthesis.org/resources/articles2/roth.htm.

Shields, C. (2004). Dialogic leadership for social justice: Overcoming pathologies of silence. *Educational Administration Quarterly.* 40 (1). 109-132.

The Gay, Lesbian, Straight Education Network. (2003). http://www.glsen.org/cgi-bin/iowa/all/home/index.html

The Socially Just Parenting Project (sociallyjustparenting.org).

Winterman, D. (2009). What would a real life Barbie look like? *BBC News/Magazine* Retrieved from: http://news.bbc.co.uk/2/hi/uk_news/magazine/7920962.stm. *White Anti-Racist Parent.* (http://www.whiteantiracistparent.blogspot.com/).

Author Note
Dorothy Firman, Ed.D.

Dorothy Firman is a professor of psychology and a licensed mental health counselor in Massachusetts. She did her doctoral studies at the University of Massachusetts-Amherst. Dr. Firman is the president of a local not-for-profit educational organization, The Synthesis Center, in Amherst. She is the author of a number of books, including a series of books on the mother/daughter relationship.

Corespondence concerning this chapter should be directed to the author at: dfirman@comcast.net.

NOTES

CHAPTER FOUR

Using Technology to Strengthen the School and Family Relationship

By: Sharon Goulet & Marisa A. McCarthy

Introduction

It is critical for schools to support the learning that goes on at home in order to build and sustain strong relationships between school and families. Educators and the school communities have a responsibility to the children to understand the communities they live in and integrate the current trends that will assist in this process. Technology can be used to broaden opportunities for whole learning communities and their families. Technology is being taught in school and creates a perception that only the children of today's society need to learn these skills in K-12 programming and for higher education. The key to increasing student performance and strengthening family relationships is to combine the two components. The learning process involved with integrating technology into the schools and the homes of our students open opportunities to obtain valuable job skills, enhance education, and it helps the families have more control over their financial situations.

It is without question that our children are worth developing and sustaining positive relationships between school and families. Why do parent become defensive when attempting to collaborate with their child's teacher? Why do educators become defensive when criticized by parents? How do we as a society mend this relationship to support our children's emotional and educational needs? Tech Goes Home (TGH) has been a successful pilot program in a Boston area middle school. Lilla G. Frederick Middle School has found a prescription to increasing student learning while also increasing parental involvement. Building trust and effective community programming were critical components in educating the families in the Frederick Pilot Middle School through the leadership of Deb Socia, founding principal.

Increasing parental involvement in the students' education allows for all participants to gain valuable job skills, enhance education, and take control of finances. Hayes (2007) reports that two-thirds of American children live in homes with two parents and of these homes 35% are black non-Hispanic children. One out of every five children live in poverty, including 33% of black and 29% are Hispanic children. Furthermore, one third of American high school students' drop out of school and within the last twenty-five years suicides have tripled with students between the ages of fifteen and twenty-four. The need for a stronger partnership between schools and families is critical in supporting academic and emotional security to solidify a positive experience for the future of our children.

Technology Goes Home

TGH began eleven years ago through the collaboration of Mayor Menino and the Boston Public Schools. TGH is a school-based, family broadband education program that is recognized by the Federal Communications Commission (FCC) National Broadband Plan for excellence in broadband adoption programming in addition to being Verizon's National Tech Savvy Award recipient. TGH has influenced over five thousand Boston families in forty-three Boston public schools according to DeGennaro (2010) as of November 2010. The program requires twenty-five hours of technology training sessions which are provided by the TGH initiative at the Frederick. Upon completion of the training the students and parents are skilled in how to use the computers to meet important educational life goals. After being trained the families may choose to purchase a computer for the discounted price of $50.00. Although families at Fredrick Pilot Middle School are welcome to participate in the TGH program, due to the high interest in the program sign-ups are limited and seats are filled on a first-come, first-serve basis. As outlined on the TGH website, the program has two sets of goals: School-Based TGH and Community-Based TGH.

Goals of the School-Based TGH Program:

To encourage parents and children to work together toward a common goal

To enhance the relationship between parents and teachers

To help children improve their academic performance

To help adults acquire 21st Century technology skills

To empowers children and adults to advocate for themselves and their community

Goals of the Community-Based TGH Program

To help provide technology access, training, and hardware to members of the Boston community

To enhance the relationship between members of the community and community institutions such as Community Centers, Housing Associations, and Public Libraries

To help adults acquire 21st Century technology skills

To expose citizens to the many online resources offered by the City of Boston and our many partners

To empower adults to advocate for themselves and their community

According to the Frederick Pilot Middle School data recorded the first year, the population for TGH was 86% people of color. 41% had a primary language other than English. 82% did not have a college diploma. 34% did not have high school diplomas, and 60% had an income of lower than 20,000 dollars per year. When the Deb Socia, Principal of the Fredrick Pilot Middle School, considered these statistics it was inevitable that the goal of increasing student performance could only improve with positive collaboration between the school and the students' home lives. Technology needed to be in the homes as well as in the schools to bridge together school and home.

At Frederick Pilot Middle School in Boston, Massachusetts a pre-survey was given to all of the parents interested in the initiative. According to the TGH pre-survey 67% of parents reported that TGH was the first time parents had participated in any event in their child's school. Considering that the youngest students in the program are 5th graders, this percentage illustrates a significant need for family and school connections to be made. According to the post survey, 99% of parents reported they would be more involved now. 96% of parents reported the program improved their relationship with their child's teachers, and 96% of parents reported they would use technology to communicate with their child's teachers. 80% of the parents reported they were more likely to use online financial resources, 88% of parents were more likely to use job related online-resources, and 98% of the parents reported they were likely to recommend TGH to other community families. Additionally, in the pre-survey, parents reported that the reasons they chose to participate in TGH were: for the computer 24%, for the training 38%, to spend time with their child 28%, to know their child's teachers 2%, and for any other reasons 7%.

Community Programming through Technology Goes Home

Applying 21st century skills in the classroom requires a collaborative effort between schools, family and the community in order to help our students achieve success. It is the educator's responsibility to establish and sustain connections with parent. "Parents want to be involved and we need to find ways to invite them that lead to real connections. Bake sales just do not cut it" says Deb Socia, Director of Tech Goes Home (TGH) serving Boston Public Schools. Advantages of effective partnerships with parents include better attendance, effective homework production, increased motivation to learn, better behavior, higher graduation rates, and increased enrollment in higher education (Price, 2001). It is critical the school recognizes that effective partnerships with families are characterized by establishing clear and defined responsibilities, effective and open communication, mutual respect, and a common vision of the goals for the students to achieve success (NAIS, 2004).

Parental involvement their child's education is critical for student success. How can educators move away from the "bake sale" era to strengthen school and family relationships and move forward using 21st century skill in technology? Lilla G. Frederick Middle School in Boston, Massachusetts has been successful in "opening the digital doors" to support learning and create opportunities to improve the lives of children. The Frederick Middle School community has experienced demographic inconveniences, socioeconomic challenges and underperforming academic scores have contributed to their history of being at risk for academic failure (DeGennaro, 2010). TGH works to educate children and their families who lack financial resources, non-English speakers, and community members that lack access to the hardware, Internet connections. TGH provides the skills and knowledge of boradband's life-relevance to maximize the use of technology and strives to establish and sustain relationships with the community members. The use of this technology has supported growth and learning for the students at the Frederick while bridging the gap between schools and family relationships. This digitally ambitious community has positively redefined the relationships between Parents and Schools.

The Leader behind Technology Goes Home

Deb Socia is the Executive Director of TGH and founding principal of the Lilla G. Frederick Pilot Middle School in Dorchester, Massachusetts and has been committed to the Frederick community for the last 7 years. As an educator since the early 1980's, Socia has supported the growth and learning of thousands of parents and students. Throughout her tenure in education, Socia has worked as a Dean of Curriculum and Instruction, a central office Curriculum Coordinator, an administrator in a residential treatment center and the Program Director for Coalition of Essential Schools, as well as a 7th and 8th grade math teacher.

Socia believes parents are essential to ensuring successful student achievement. Deb's personal philosophy on effective improvement in the home to school connection is:

"Parents want to be involved and we need to find ways to invite them that lead to real connections. Bake sales just don't cut it. If you have an event and parents do not come, it is your fault. Either the event was not engaging or meaningful to your families, or the timing was not convenient, or the invitation did not make the right connection. Parents want their children to be successful and we need to be more open to partnering with them. "

-Deb Socia

Through the development and implementation of TGH, Socia hoped to develop a heightened level of student and parent engagement to the Frederick Pilot Middle School. Her passion and success with TGH at Frederick Middle School has inspired Socia to share the process behind this highle effective, quality program with other districts in order to increase family-school engagement, and ultimately increase student success. The Frederick Had over 200 families one year go through the program. The outcome is encouraging because in retrospect there were only 670 families per year across the whole city of Boston. At open house in 2010, 800 family members were in attendance and 1200 people were in attendance at graduations and other outside events

In Socia's experience TGH has provided the best parent engagement strategy thus far in education. TGH brings families into the building and into the classroom and then transcends that connection to the home, which is where learning begins. Through TGH, parents become acquainted with the teacher and the school experience in a very unique way. The parent and teacher make a connection that goes beyond the classroom and the results have illustrated that graduates now have a person they know well, trust, and can feel comfortable that their best interests are being considered from the start. In addition, TGH allows for the parent and child to swap roles. Often the child is more knowledgeable than the parent when it comes to technology, therefore, TGH provides the students an opportunity to act as the teacher to their parents and truly own the learning process. This role change strengthens the relationship between the parent and child and creates an opportunity to open the door to stronger communication between families. According to Socia, "There is just no downside!"

The staff at Frederick Pilot Middle School has worked extremely diligent with fidelity to earn the trust of families and the community that benefit greatly from TGH over the last eleven years. Especially because this Lower Boston community has suffered damage due to poverty and lack of knowledge or access to the internet. TGH has worked to undo damage that has occurred in order for families to heal and for lifelong learning to take place. The lack of trust or unsupportive attitudes toward schools have manifested from negative experiences that families have encountered within their school communities. TGH is successfully proving that in today's society families can trust schools and it is important the schools provide that foundation to foster a positive relationship between the home and school.

Using Technology to Improve Your School and Community Relationships

Planning and development, implementation and management, and monitoring and evaluation are three steps to improving your school to community relationships through the use of technology. By strengthening the relationship between families and educators, students will become empowered and their motivation for learning increases. Behavior issues decrease and it allows the teachers to use the art of instruction more effectively and confidently. Student learning also increases when families are given a voice. Bringing the internet and laptops into the home increases teacher-parent communication and creates a common and level ground that can often be an intimidation factor between educators and parents. In order for this process to be executed effectively, educators must begin to increase their knowledge base in technology so that learning can optimally infuse the relationship between homes of students and their schools.

In 2004, the National Association of Independent Schools (NAIS, 2004) reported suggestions for schools to work effectively with parents. Some of these suggestions include, but are not limited to:

- Contact parents early on to report positive behavior
- Write a monthly newsletter that updates parents on classroom learning and activities
- Invite parents into the classroom and assign them tasks
- Inform parents on how they can support classroom behavior in their home via contract requiring them to make children complete homework and other home learning activities
- Address parent concerns head on
- Consider having a parent meeting in the first month of school to give expectations on student achievement and behavior, leave time for questions

Although these suggestions are meant to encourage a stronger relationship with parents they can also be perceived as dominating and professionally omniscience. Families that lack the education or resources to support their child's academic growth as expected by the school may be perceived as an intimidating expectation and task. TGH has used the specific concept of technology to support the relationships between parent-teacher, parent-child, and sometimes between immigrant and home country to increase motivation for learning through school-family values. Socia states that her philosophy in training her staff, students, and parents is based on "three legs of a stool." The three critical components are: training, hardware (netbook), access (Internet). The teachers at the Frederick Pilot Middle School are intensely trained to achieve high rates of participation and success. Using Google Gmail students are required to help their parents set up their own email accounts. All teachers have their own email accounts and by having the students work through this process both parents and students understand that the line of communication between parent and teacher is open and welcomed. This process establishes a bond between teacher and parent and has resulted in improved student behavior, increased performance, and parental support (DeGennaro, 2010).

Conclusion

More research needs to continue about technology being used to support school-family relationships to bridge the gap between the school and community partnerships to increase student performance. The research analyses the implementation of technology within the schools. Educators are primarily focusing on how to make the connections between technology and the students. Current research inevitably must focus on how to create the connections between schools and the family by using technology. Technology is being introduced into all aspects of life and TGH has ignited motivation and effective communication that has increased the value of using technology as a community building tool. Steven Jones, an expert in cyber communication states, "Information, Internet and Community" (*Cybersociety*), the nature and power of computer-mediated community are not created by the communication medium, they are attained through it. That is, human desire to communicate is the motivating force that determines both the level and kind of communication achieved" (AEL, p. 6, 2003).

Building and sustaining connections between schools and their families through using technology is a process that requires consistency and fidelity in development, implementation, and an effective evaluation process. TGH is a model community project that has transformed the lives of the students' and their families to grow and learn together. Healthy relationships between learning communities and schools require both groups of people to communicate respectfully, honestly, and listen objectively to support and increase learning. Socia has led her team at Frederick Pilot Middle School to build an admirable and model learning community while creating opportunities for the future of their students. Children are the primary focus of schools and their families in addition children are the future of our existence. It is the children that provide hope and direction for educators and families to co-exist in a nurturing and fulfilling relationship. Together schools and families can make a positive difference in our children's lives to make the world a better place.

References

DeGennaro, D. (2010). Opening the digital doors. *Educational Leadership,* 68(3), 73-76.

NAIS. (2009, March). *Parents working with schools/schools working with parents.* Retrieved February 1, 2011, from www.nais.org/about/seriesdoc

AEL. (2003). Interactions: A summary of research on school-community relationships. *The Regional Educational Laboratory At Ael,* 2-12.

Hayes, W. (2007). The need for parental involvement gaining parental support. In *All new real-life case studies for school administrators* (pp. 54-61). Lanham, United Kingdom: Rowman and Littlefield Educatiion.

Hayes, W. (2007). *All new real-life case studies for school adminstrators.* Lanham, United Kingdom: Rowman and Littlefield Education.

Socia, D. (n.d.). *Technology goes home.* Retrieved from www.techgoeshome.org/home

D. Socia, personal communication, January 6, 2011.

D. Socia, personal communication, February 17, 2011.

unknown. (2011, February). *Creating strong relationships between schools and families.* Retrieved from www.educatorsforsocialchange.org/resources

Authors' Note
Sharon Goulet, M.Ed

Sharon Goulet has been the Supervisor of Special Education for Chicopee High School since 2010. Prior to assuming this position, she served in a variety of other positions during this thirteen-year career in education to date including elementary and secondary special education teacher in physical education, health, math, ELA, science, and social studies. She holds a BA in Movement and Sport Studies with a minor in Health Studies from Springfield College, and a M.Ed. in Special Education for American International College. She is a doctoral candidate in Educational Leadership and Supervision at American International College.

Marisa A. McCarthy, CAGS

Marisa A. McCarthy's extensive experience working in both educational and clinical settings includes work as a director of pupil services, special education administrator, school adjustment counselor, and mental health clinician. She is a Ed.D. candidate in Educational Leadership and

Supervision at American International College. Ms. McCarthy received her BA in Psychology from Western New England College and her MA and CAGS in Educational Psychology from American International College.

NOTES

NOTES

CHAPTER FIVE

Promoting School, Home and Community Communication

By: Sharon MacDonald

Introduction

In order to establish better family and school communication, school systems need to be creative, encouraging and initiate powerful programs in an effort to improve school and home communication. Traditional PTA's and/or PTO's thrive at the elementary levels yet fail more often than succeed at the middle and high school levels. Education has undergone "struggles" in both middle school and high school communication efforts between school and home. A strong sense of communication between staff, students and families promotes the most productive schools. Professor John Seyfarth from Virginia Commonwealth University reminds us of research done by Thompson in 2003 that showed high performing school systems provide "nurturing, supportive and respectful relationships with parents, students and staff therefore creating a strong positive school climate and also maintain high performance communication with both internal and external stakeholders including inviting their input" (*Seyfarth, p. 5*).

We are facing a national dropout crisis with the most recent statistics stating that "30 percent of all students dropout before twelfth grade and nearly 50 percent of Black and Latino students do not complete high school (*Bridgeland, Dilulio & Morison 2006; Thornburgh 2006*). In 2010, approximately 7,000 students nationally dropped out of school each day or approximately one student dropped out somewhere across the nation every twenty-six seconds (*Superintendent's Report, April 6, 2011*).

The Annenberg Institute for School Reform has released, as of April 4, 2011, some alternatives to traditional approaches to public school reform. Their studies suggest that the voices of students and families are too often ignored and that it is time that we stop the debating and begin to realize that we need to focus on "how best to reform the nation's public schools— particularly those in low-income and working-class neighborhoods and communities of color--" (*Press Release April 4, 2011, Annenberg Institute for School Reform*). The study states three very important points in their VUE, Summer 2007edition:

- At its' most effective, a learning community is one whose members have a shared purpose; supportive relationships among people of varying levels of expertise; and a repertoire of routines and activities. (*p. 20*)
- A personalized school culture at every level of education is a critical component and that those components include all staff that is truly committed to living every moment where "individual uniqueness is honored, engaged, and respected. Staff are responsive to students' cognitive, emotional, and physical needs. (*p.41*)

- As a community we all have to strive to work network together "to ensure that all students' basic needs, such as housing, healthcare, and childcare, are being met; this allows students to focus their attention on their studies." (p. 41).

Elementary School Initiatives

One national initiative for promoting more effective family and school communication is the Parent-Teacher Home Visiting Project (PTHVP) that was studied in 2004 within the Harvard Graduate School of Education and the Annenberg Institute for School Reform. The project was initiated in four states in 2007, and grew to ten states by 2010. All of this has been made possible with funding through a combination of state, federal and foundation support. The core design of the program is based on the "fundamental respect of family assets and the building of capacity of both the educators and the families to support the academic and social success of every child". The program is also "grounded in community organizing theory and practice" (*Parent-Teacher Home Visiting Project- An Approach to Evaluation*, p. 5).

The Home Visitation Project also presents other noted core values: 1. Families and teachers are equally important co-educators where the family is the expert on the child and the teacher is the expert on the curriculum to be mastered, and 2. Before information about academic status can be effectively shared, positive communication must be established and barriers addressed (*Parent-Teacher Home Visiting Project*, p. 7). The national project model suggests that an outside community agency provides the training as well as the funds to pay the staff for their time beyond the normal school day. It further suggests that the school initiative begins with a team of teachers volunteering to undergo training and then having those teams go out in pairs to visit homes in hopes of establishing a rapport and connection with those specific families. The goal is to visit with these families in their homes at least three times during the school year. Initial studies found that visiting ALL homes rather than selected families made the most sense for a genuine feeling of trust however that may be impractical for all schools to be able to implement.

The Parent-Teacher Home Visiting Project has proven to be successful at several schools in Massachusetts, one of the original four states to participate in the project. For the 2010-2011 school year, the Springfield school district, one of the largest inner city school districts in Massachusetts, formed a partnership with their teachers union and four of their elementary schools where each school received $25,000 to pay their teachers to make these home visits. The program was funded through the National

Education Association Foundation as part of its Closing the Achievement Gap Initiative. Many teachers agreed to go the extra step for their students and their parents are appreciative. One mother said that the visits "helped her daughter avoid failing first grade" and went on to state "the visits made her feel respected" (*Springfield Republican,* December 12, 2010, C2).

The tone of the home visit is to be information sharing, establishing a caring connection to one another and promoting the critical need for the continuation of ongoing communication. An important first step in communication is having the teachers ask these parents what dreams they have for their children. Initial studies have found that most inner city parents have the modest dream of wanting their students to graduate high school and become productive members of society. The dream of a college education for many inner city parents is still not the norm. Three years ago five males at an alternative middle school in Springfield were asked what their dream was and they all agreed that it was "to make it to the age of twenty-one". Educators have a responsibility to work with all of these families to help them believe that college is a real possibility for every child. We need to show parents that we all need to work together to help raise our children in the inner city together by believing and supporting them in every way that we can.

Duggan Middle School is one of the four main middle schools in the inner city of Springfield, MA with a current student enrollment of 440 middle school students. Duggan was one of the first schools in the city of Springfield to volunteer to pilot the Home Visitation Program in 2006. There were report forms to be completed to document the visits, a compact agreement to be signed by the student, parents and the teachers as well as regularly scheduled staff reporting at meetings to share the success/failures and to compare strategies and outcomes. A "real story" from that school was when one of the teachers reported out on her experience with one of her students that was selected for a home visit. That student had made quite an impression on the staff very early on in the new school year. Almost everyone in the entire school knew who he was because he was a very mature, well dressed, vocal, sixth grade boy who appeared to be misplaced in the sixth grade for several reasons. Larger in size than the average sixth grader, he was always getting the attention of the girls. He thrived on getting their attention each and every day and as a result of all of that notoriety, his focus was definitely not on academics. Teachers had him on their concern list. The image that he portrayed at school was that of a young man who had an extensive up to date wardrobe and that pleasing his peers was his number one priority. Because of the way he was groomed and dressed every day it was "assumed" that he probably came from a stable middle class family situation. Much to the surprise of the teachers that did the home visit, as well as to the staff that heard the report sharing afterwards, the situation was very different!

The teacher continued to report that the teachers were invited in to a rather sparsely furnished apartment where mom was lying on the living room floor on a mattress with a very young baby beside her. There was a small table containing a television and lamp in the room and that was all. During the conversation that took place in that visit it was shared that the family had no other furniture. The visitation team learned that the middle school student was the oldest of three children and mom was the sole support of the family. They also learned that this student actually borrowed his clothes on a daily basis from his cousin because he did not have any appropriate school clothes of his own. Lastly, the student also shared with the teachers that he had some insurance money coming to him because he was injured in a car accident and that when he got the insurance settlement money he was going to use it to buy a bedroom set for his mom. The visitation committee members gained an entirely different perspective on that student after the report was given that they will never forget!

Another important focus of the Parent-Teacher Home Visiting Project is the reduction of barriers perceived and/or real that impact our work with inner city children in particular. Statistics reveal over and over that there are not enough minority teachers and administrators in proportion to the inner city school student populations. One minority middle school student stated it very clearly when he said to his very white guidance counselor who wanted to set up a home visit that she "didn't understand his world." She reassured him that was exactly why she wanted to come to his home so that she could begin to understand things from his perspective. She did go. His family was honored and he was shocked at the same time. It was a memorable exchange for all parties involved.

The Parent Facilitators Initiative

A second successful initiative has been the establishment of Parent Facilitators in many of the elementary and middle schools in Springfield, MA. In the Springfield model the facilitator position is a paid position. The key to the success of the program is an active, caring parent facilitator who also works well with staff within the school. That can be a rare match so when it does happen a school should treat it as a very precious gem! The expectations for success within the school may be greater than when the president of the PTO/A is a volunteer.

Duggan Middle School stands out once again because they have another successful model program where their Parent Facilitator who was coerced into returning to the school setting last year after retiring from her position as a longtime paraprofessional within the same building. She has the ability to create her individualized work schedule, the freedom for flexible hours, and works "part-time" yet gives almost full-time to the position due to the nature of her enthusiasm for what she does. She works closely with her building principal and staff to provide parents with networking opportunities through numerous informational outreach programs. She coordinates a community tag sale for the school complete with carnival rides and a food festival that promotes fellowship as well as a fundraising opportunity for the school. Participants wait every year to reserve their space "rain or shine". She has also coordinated a community spaghetti supper where community members started lining up an hour before the event was even scheduled to begin for two years in a row! Her third successful program has been an annual Grandparents Luncheon in recognition of the many grandparents that are raising their children today as the primary "parent". These have been successful initiatives in one specific middle school. Her genuine caring nature for working with families of the students at her school is evident in everything that she does! This Parent Facilitator truly represents reaching out into the community on a daily basis helping the families in her school feel welcomed, encouraged and reassured on a daily basis. This same Parent Facilitator also promotes diversity programs during Black History Month where students perform dances, recite poetry and share cultural foods with each other in another enriching way. The school hosts a number of Somalian refugee students who have been especially honored to participate in these programs every year. She goes above and beyond to make sure that these students are included, feel valued and are respected. As a committed educator, she exemplifies in every way the need for the personalization of every student's education and getting the students engaged in any way possible.

Inner City School Initiatives

Families living in poverty and surrounded by the influences of street gangs are very difficult challenges for families to overcome. It takes a lot of hard work; encouragement and understanding of what many parents are dealing with today. Schools are finding it necessary to become more proactive in assisting these families with both resources and moral support. The city of Springfield, in Massachusetts with a student body population of over 26,000, had seventeen murders in 2010. In the first four months of 2011 there were seven more murders. In both 2010 and 2011, most of those victims were under the age of twenty-one and gang related incidents.

In 2008, a middle school 14-year old girl in the same city was murdered on the front porch of a main street at 10:30 p.m. on a school night just two blocks from a well-respected four year college campus. Four days later her best friend's family came to the school to inform her that her brother was arrested and charged with that murder. How does one live with the fact that her brother murdered her best friend? That incident was also gang related- a young adult male person pulled the fourteen-year old girl in front of him and she was shot instead. All of these young adults had parents with dreams for their children. Several of these young men were avid basketball players, one a soccer star; those parents dreamed of watching their sons play sports in college. Those dreams did not include the real life situations of hearing that their child had been stabbed across the street from that same college and died after crossing the street in an attempt to get to the college for assistance. Nor did any parent deserve to receive news nine days later that their child at the age of seventeen was gunned down in retaliation inside a favorite city park where children are supposed to feel free to be able to come and play. Yet, these are all incidents that did occur in Springfield, MA in the first half of 2011.

Those dreams also did not include visualizing the murder of a young mother in April 2010, inside her mother's apartment in front of her younger sister while her fourteen month old son hid in another room. She became the sixteenth victim in the city in 2010. In August 2011 her mother, sister, her father gave testimony in court about how it has left them devastated and changed their lives forever. She was shot by four bullets with one hitting her brain all in front of her then twelve year old sister. Her sister had difficult times getting through some days in seventh grade because as she describes it "ever since that day, I really can't sleep and I wake up crying and wishing my sister was still here" (*Springfield Republican, p. 17*). The shooter convicted of her murder in August lived just down the same street from them. Two weeks later in the upstairs apartment of the same building the seventeenth victim was a 16-year-old male.

Instead of happy dreams about college and careers for that young mother and her upstairs neighbor, the survivors had to bury them, one family has relocated due to the trauma of the situation, and the survivors still struggle with the ongoing nightmares associated with that event as the first family also now helps to raise their two year old grandson and nephew. As much as they love him, he reminds them of his mother every time they look at him. She was described as an innocent victim who was working hard to pursue her dream of becoming a nurse to help others. How do we as a school system and a community assist these families to cope with that pain and still go to work and/or come to school prepared to focus on academic learning with enthusiasm on a daily basis? These are just a sampling of the actual realities of the youth murdered in Springfield over the past four years and their family's broken dreams. How can we as a nation better address this violence?

Believing in the Dream of Graduating High School

The reality of graduating high school does need to be addressed in the inner cities because many urban schools still have a high school dropout rate of well over 50%. Last year in 2010 in Massachusetts, the city of Springfield had a dropout rate that was three times the state average with 144 seniors that were "almost there" yet could not find it in themselves to be able to continue on to actual graduation. In 2010 Springfield's graduation rate was ranked the second worst in the state of Massachusetts; second only to Holyoke, Massachusetts. (*Superintendent's report*, August, 2010). College has still not become the realistic dream for many of these families. Educators in our profession need to be committed to helping these families realize that with hard work on the part of the student, the determination of the family, continual encouragement and support from educators along with financial and continuous community support; *college can continue to be a realistic dream* for their children.

The Gateway to College Initiative

Gateway to College is one of these national initiatives available to high school students who are sixteen to twenty years old, at risk of dropping out of high school due to previous retentions or other negative situations, have earned at least 6.5 high school credits and want to take advantage of an additional opportunity to realize the potential to graduate. The program started ten years ago at Portland Community College to assist high school dropouts to be able to continue their education. The Bill & Melinda Gates Foundation has funded the Gateway to College program through its Early College High School initiative since 2003. The Gateway to College Program is currently available on at least twenty-six college campuses in sixteen states across the country. Massachusetts is fortunate to have three college campuses, ranking right up there with California and Texas, while the other thirteen states have only one or two locations available.

Selected students from the Holyoke and Springfield school systems who have earned at least 6.5 credits in either school district may attend Holyoke Community College's Gateway to College Program in Holyoke, Massachusetts for free once they are interviewed and accepted. The Bill and Melinda Gates Foundation has reached out to support these families from the inner cities of Holyoke and Springfield by making the cost of this program free to those students while students from surrounding suburbs desiring to attend have to pay approximately $8,000 for the same opportunity.

These students receive a college id., tokens for bus transportation and lunch along with free rental of textbooks etc. The students spend the first semester in high level study skill strategies classes and then go on to complete the graduation course requirements necessary for their respective school district. They are assigned "Resource Specialists" who act as their coaches, mentors and advisors. This wrap-around support helps to keep the students on the right track to be successful. Once high school graduation requirements are met, each student, at his/her own pace, rolls right over into the college program the following semester. Families are thrilled to see their children be afforded an additional opportunity of hope. They see their child receiving a second chance to get back on track and see the dream of graduation become a reality for their child.

The "Last Scholarship Dollars" Initiative

For the past two years, Springfield Promise "Last Scholarship Dollars" has been an additional incentive program available for Springfield, Massachusetts public and charter school students who find that their financial award does not entirely cover their need at the colleges they have been accepted to. These additional scholarships are need-based and help to bridge the remaining financial gap for the college expenses for these students. After colleges have seen what financial aid is returned to them from other students that were accepted yet chose to attend another institution, they make those additional dollars available to students from the inner city that have not had all of their financial aid needs met through grant opportunities. Boston has a similar program where they have documented that "over the last two years, 40% of Boston Public School Valedictorians have an average unmet need of nearly $5,000" (accessboston website). This is a wonderful opportunity to assist those students with the most financial need make college dreams become reality!

The Community Networking Initiative

Community networking with area businesses also makes it possible for high schools to fund additional opportunities for all students. Massachusetts Mutual Insurance Company, headquartered in the city of Springfield, Massachusetts, provides the entire cost for all of the city of Springfield's tenth grade students to take the PSAT as preparation for the eleventh grade testing opportunity. Studies have shown that students do better if they have the opportunity to experience taking the test for the first time in the tenth grade.

Mass Mutual also provides very generous scholarship opportunities for nine metropolitan areas throughout the country for students of African-American/Black, Asian/Pacific Islander of Hispanic descent by providing 27 $5,000 scholarship opportunities to qualifying students with concentrations in the fields of business, economics, financial planning, management, marketing and/or sales. Springfield school students are one of the nine cities where this additional opportunity is available to them. The beauty of these scholarship opportunities is that they are renewable each year students are in college! Mass Mutual is also a financial contributor to the Big Brothers/Big Sisters Mentoring Program within the Springfield city schools as well.

Closing Thoughts

Interest and enthusiasm in program offerings makes many things possible! A passion for programs you believe in can become a reality with a little creativity and a lot of perseverance! Continuing to collaborate with administration and staff and making community connections are several recent initiatives that will benefit our students as we prepare them for the 21st Century. School administration and staff need to continue to reach out in the community and assist families to make their educational dreams come true for all of our youth! Once again we are reminded that a strong sense of communication between staff, students, families and community members is needed in order to promote the most productive schools and to help our families to reach for the dream of a college education for all of the youth of today. All of the stakeholders need to continue to communicate in productive and creative ways together.

A free and appropriate education is a basic human right here in the United States and we need to continue to reach out to families so that they can understand the special gift provided for all of their children and encourage them to help their children take advantage of this amazing opportunity! As educators, we also need to be there within the community to support our families through the difficult times and assist in getting them all of the resources that they may need as they move forward together to make pleasant dreams become a reality for more of our children.

References

Ingram, Alan, Superintendent's Report given to School Counselors, August 6, 2011.

Lemmel, D. and Steinberg Seidel, S.; *"Alternative High Schools: Pioneering Promising Practices for Blending Academic and Extended Learning Opportunities"*, Voices in Urban Education, Annenberg Institute for School Reform, Summer 2007.

Gateway to College National Network, 2009-2010, Portland, Oregon.

Life sentence given for killing. (2011, August 17, 2011). *The Republican*, pp. A1, A17.

Mapp, K. L., Harvard Graduation School of Education; *Parent-Teacher Home Visiting Project-An Approach to Evaluation Report*; October 23, 2010 Annual Meeting.

Press Release April 4, 2011) Annenberg Institute for School Reform Launches Center for Education Organizing.

Seyfarth, J. (2007). *Human resource Leadership for Effective Schools* (5th ed.). Allyn & Bacon (pub).

Author Note
Sharon MacDonald, M.Ed.

Sharon MacDonald is currently the Guidance Department Chair at Forest Park Middle School in Springfield, Massachusetts. She has also served as the Guidance Department Chairs at Duggan Middle School where she was also an active participant in the first year of the Parent-Home Visitation Project as well as at one of the high schools in the city as well where her students participated in the Mass Mutual Incentive Program. Previous to her guidance experience she was a classroom teacher of Health and Physical Education in a suburban community outside of Springfield, Massachusetts where she also resides.

Sharon was given the Margaret Addis Award in 2009 by the NEASC for her work with minority students in urban schools. She completed her degrees at Springfield College with a B.S. majoring in Health and Physical Education and a M. Ed. in Counseling and Psychology. She is currently pursuing her doctorate degree at A.I.C. in Educational Leadership and Supervision.

Correspondence concerning this chapter should be directed to the author at zontagram13@gmail.com.

NOTES

CHAPTER SIX

The Power of School/Family Partnerships

By: Linda E. Denault

The Challenge

In the 21st century, a key word in every field and endeavor is collaboration. In order to succeed in the new global economy, young people must be able to think critically and solve problems, particularly in a collaborative manner. Thus, the challenge for educators is to help all students to be successful academically, but not in only a traditional paper-pencil way. As students are expected to work cooperatively and collaboratively, the brokering of many partners to accomplish tasks in the real-world settings for which we are preparing them is essential; these settings and partnerships must be modeled for students throughout their public school education. As Epstein's, 1995 research points out:

> "There are many reasons for developing school, family, and community partnerships. ... However, the main reason to create such partnerships is to help all youngsters succeed in school and in later life. When parents, teachers, students, and others view on another as partners in education, a caring community forms around students and begins its work. ...The external model of overlapping spheres of influence recognizes that the three major contexts in which students learn and grow – the family, the school and the community ... The model of school, family, and community partnerships cannot simply produce successful students. Rather, partnership activities may be designed to engage, guide, energize, and motivate students to produce their own successes" (p. 701-702).

Therefore, word "community" must take on a broad meaning. How can this be accomplished, especially during times of fiscal uncertainty for our public schools? One answer may rest in the growing number of educational foundations that have arisen in communities across the nation. Here is one example from a two-town regional school district in central Massachusetts that is using its educational foundation as a vehicle for positive change within the community.

Background

As we focus on the paradigm shift from teaching to learning, a key element that cannot be ignored in order to promote student development is the sense of community that must be built. But what exactly is community? According to Sergiovanni, community can be defined as follows... "communities are collections of individuals who are bonded together by natural will and who are together binded into a set of shared ideas and ideals. This bonding and binding is tight enough to transform them from a collection of 'I's' into a collective 'we' " (1994, p. xvi).

Community is not a new idea, but one that doesn't always receive the attention or credit that it deserves as a powerful agent of change and forward progress. In describing his idea of the Basic School, Ernest Boyer said it well:

After completing our research, we concluded that the most essential ingredient of a successful school – the one idea that holds it all together – is best described by the

simple word 'connections.' An effective school connects people, to create *community*.

An effective school connects the curriculum to achieve *coherence*. An effective school

connects classrooms and resources, to enrich the learning *climate*. And an effective

school connects learning to life, to build *character* (1995, p. 6-7.).

The sense of community that both Sergiovanni and Boyer describe speaks to the development of the whole child in a learning environment that connects community in rigorous, relevant, and authentic ways. Linda Darling-Hammond defines environments that support meaningful learning in successful schools of today as those that feature the following attributes:

- Active in-depth learning
- Emphasis on authentic performance
- Attention to development
- Appreciation for diversity
- Opportunities for collaborative learning
- Collective perspective across the school
- Structures for caring
- Support for democratic learning
- Connections to family and community

No one of these features alone can ensure that students will be both challenged and supported in their learning. Schools must weave these strands into a tightly interknit tapestry if they are to support both competence and community (Darling-Hammond, 1997, p. 107).Therefore, what better way to build community than to expand the sense of community beyond the walls of the school, not only in the learning activities that take place, but in the funding that makes those activities possible? "When mutually supportive, the relationship between school and communities can lead to shared programs for the benefit of all ... Only by building and strengthening their links with other institutions in the community can schools achieve their full mission" (Danielson, 2002, pp. 67, 73). In the

21st century, schools cannot be expected to operate in isolation with limited resources to keep their offerings current. "Schools cannot do it alone. The people of the community must join together to create a supportive learning environment dedicated to removing obstacles to student success" (Zimmerman-Orozco, 2011, p. 70).

One Community's Response

As communities across the nation struggle to finance education adequately, the idea of non-profit support through educational foundations has become increasingly popular. Although such foundations may vary in their purpose and the nature of their support, the Dudley-Charlton Education Foundation, Inc., has been true to its goal of enriching students' K-12 educational experiences, as it distributes funds through grants that are teacher initiated and that provide innovative opportunities for enriching students' learning experiences and promoting instructional excellence. Grant awards that also partner with community businesses or organizations or extend the learning experiences into the local community are given funding priority. This standard is appropriate in that "extended learning opportunities provide authentic learning experiences for all types of students. ...Students who are engaged are capable of far greater rigor" (Freeley & Hanzelka, 2009, p. 65, 67).

Now successfully operating, the foundation became a reality just two short years ago, with the encouragement of the district's superintendent. That is when a group of adults, representing a fairly broad cross-section of the local population, came together to form an education foundation for this two-town regional school district, located in suburban/rural southern Worcester County. At one time, these two towns, Dudley and Charlton, had as many cows as people, but, during the boom of the late 1980's, they witnessed tremendous growth, resulting in vanishing farms and in the doubling then tripling of the population. With the influx of many young families, the schools changed, too, with each community now boasting a new middle school and, in Charlton, a new elementary school as well. Although this tremendous increase in population included a relatively heavy influx of professionals that boosted the per capita income as well as property valuations, the accompanying increase in taxes has kept the fiscally conservative district from supporting its schools any greater than the minimum level of funding that is required by state statute. Thus, in spite of relative affluence among several segments of the population, there are no "extras" in the annual school budget to meet the increasing demands of education in the 21st century. Thus, the need for a non-profit organization to step forward to provide additional support for the schools was clear. After all, "schools cannot meet society's demands and unfold the full potential of every child without the help of the entire community. From an initial focus on civic values and cultivating basic skills in reading, writing, and math, public schools have broadened their curriculum over the past century to include a dizzying array of programs. Schools need community support to successfully prepare children for their multifaceted lives beyond school" (Vollmer, 2011, p. 71).

The group that came together around this common goal of supporting the local public schools formed the Board of Directors of the Dudley-Charlton Education Foundation. The board consisted of a cross section of residents of the towns in terms of professions, gender, ages, longevity within the district – a lawyer, an accountant, two businessmen, two bankers, a former superintendent of schools, a college professor, a stay-at-home mom, a secretary, a local journalist, and a stay-at-home dad, with the superintendent of schools serving as an ex-officio member. Convinced that the district needed additional funds to help its students remain competitive for college and/or the work force of the 21st century, the Board of Directors drew up an organizational plan, adopted by-laws, filed for legal recognition as a non-profit organization, and started to plan for the future. Their intent was to raise funds to enhance, extend and enrich the education of Dudley-Charlton students at all grade levels, pre-K -12, not to supplant funds that are the regular fiscal responsibility of the district, but to raise funds that would provide the means to go above and beyond the typical programs in promoting student achievement. Funds have been raised in two major ways: an annual appeal that culminates in a gala dinner dance and silent auction and a nine-and-dine golf tournament. Both occur locally in conjunction with area businesses and are generously supported by the local banks as well as parents and the community at large.

In order to ensure that the funds raised achieved the stated goals, the board determined that the money would be distributed through a grant process, with applications open to all teachers and staff in the district. Criteria for the grants stressed innovation and creativity, helping students stretch beyond the basic curriculum with new techniques, projects, and/or technologies, with particularly emphasis on authentic community connections. The larger the number of students impacted, the amount of collaboration evident, and the greater the possibility that the grant could be replicated, then the more favorably the grant was looked upon as the board made its funding decisions.

This special grant program, developed and funded by the DCEF, has had a variety of positive results in terms of school-community relationships and, most importantly, in terms of student achievement. In general, through outreach by the DCEF Board, the wider school community has become more aware of the needs and the accomplishments of the regional school district. Beyond fund-raising through an annual appeal, a gala dinner-dance, and a golf tournament, this outreach has included visits to the Board of Selectmen, televised in the respective towns, School Committee meetings, also televised, and other school/local affairs, sharing the message of the DCEF and its mission and goals, and especially sharing the successes of its grant programs within the district.

How is this non-profit organization an example of school, family, and community working together to promote student achievement? The following examples of the wide range of successful grant programs sponsored to date by the DCEF should provide the answer as to how this organization is fulfilling that important role.

Grant Funds at Work

At the high school level, "Broadway Connect" enhanced the arts program by offering choral students and student in the show choir (singers and dancers) a unique opportunity to learn directly from Broadway artists to create a mini-Broadway show at the high school. Through the grant, the music department was able to bring members of the cast of "Wicked" from Boston to work directly with the students, providing classes in vocal techniques, ensemble performance techniques, acting, choreography, make-up, and special effects. The culmination of these master classes was a public performance/concert featuring both students and guest artists that was based on scenes from "Wicked." It was a tremendous success and enjoyed by a full house that represented a wide cross-section of the community. It was also taped for local able access, allowing all residents of both towns to enjoy the show from home. In addition, students later took a field trip to Boston to see a live performance of "Wicked" and to reconnect with the artists under whose direction they had worked so closely.

Highlighting the benefit to another discipline, "Engineering Projects in Community Service" (EPICS) opened the door to students' participation in a program originating from Purdue University. With grant funding, one of the science teachers and a group of interested students formed an after-school club that partnered with a local wildlife sanctuary, Capen Hill, to build an interactive display to highlight the difference between modern weather instruments and vintage or traditional weather equipment. Beyond the problem solving, engineering, and team-building skills acquired through this project, students learned civic responsibility and program management. As a permanent meteorological display at Capen Hill, this learning opportunity was a true example of community service learning and will have a lasting benefit to the entire community. This project is an excellent example of new skills for the 21st century in action.

"These new skills include the capacity to:
- Design, evaluate, and manage one's own work so that it continually improves
- Frame, investigate, and solve problems using a wide range of tools and resources
- Collaborate strategically with others
- Communicate effectively in many forms
- Find, analyze, and use information for many purposes
- Develop new products and ideas"

(Darling-Hammond, 2010, p. 2).

With a less than strictly an academic focus, "Rachel's Legacy" provided a timely and powerful opportunity for students and parents to confront the issue of bullying prevention in a meaningful way and to foster a more positive and peaceful school environment. Through this special assembly, provided through grant funds, Craig Scott, brother of Rachel Scott, the first victim of the 1999 Columbine School shootings, visited Shepherd Hill Regional High School and presented a heartfelt and memorable message to the entire school community. This was an appropriate expenditure of academic grant funds in that "the responsibility is on all educators to take an ethical stance against the intolerance, the hatred, and the violence that is common in society and that can spill over into schools. If the schools mirror society, then it is up to educators to transform the culture in schools to reflect upon and critically analyze morn than the core of their knowledge, but also their ways of knowing within a social learning environment where they form relationships and develop moral judgments" (Hollingshead et. al, 2009, p.115).

At the middle school level, the grant awards allowed for a reaching out to a large number of at-risk students while making a significant K-16 connection. Middle schoolers identified as being at risk of school failure were paired with mentors within the school. Research supports a focus on such "connectedness" in schools as a way to increase student success. "School connectedness refers to an academic environment in which students believe that adults in the school care about their learning and about them as individuals. … Although connecting students to school is important at all grade levels, it's especially crucial during the adolescent years" (Blum, 2005, p.16). These adult mentors checked with these students on a daily basis to offer support regarding homework and any other school and/or home issue they were experiencing that was problematic to them. As a result of this ongoing effort, identified students showed both improved attendance and increased achievement as reflected in their course averages and report card grades. However, one of the best components of the program, and probably the least able to be measured in a quantifiable way, was the K-16 connection that enabled these students to spend time at Worcester Politechnical Institute (WPI), touring the campus, attending/ participating in a robotics class, and talking with college students. For these at-risk teenagers, the world of college was opened up as a real possibility for their own future. Introducing middle school students to the college environment is in line with current innovative initiatives that have begun across the nation to integrate high school with college by focusing on accelerating rather than remediating to support students at-risk of dropping out of high school (Steinberg & Allen, 2009). Thus, the potential here for a long-term impact is enormous.

Also at the middle school level was an interdisciplinary project that created much excitement in the community as well as at the school was the E-2 Club. The "Emerging Entrepreneurs (E-2) Club" provided for an innovative application of academic skills to an authentic business endeavor. Guided by their teachers, approximately 40 students in grades 6-8 organized and operated their own restaurant (the "Recipe for Success Kitchen"), learning from local businesses all the essential aspects of food service including how to plan a menu, purchase the correct quantities of food, food preparation, how to advertise, design aesthetics, establish seating capacity, food service, and clean-up. On one evening each week, for three consecutive weeks, the E-2 Club transformed the school's cafeteria into a dining room that would rival any popular restaurant. Open to the public, with special invitations to local senior citizens, the restaurant welcomed diners literally on a red carpet and offered them either of two menu choices that were prepared and served by the students while pleasant background music played. Not only did this make for a fine dining experience for the community, but students put their math, problem-solving, health/ nutrition, language arts, and visual arts skills to work in a collaborative school-community setting. As a bonus benefit, any proceeds above and beyond expenses were donated to the local food bank in support of needy families in the area. It is easy to see why this project was an extraordinary learning experience that was a favorite for students, teachers, parents and the community ... a perfect model of how education foundation funds were used to enhance student learning in meaningful real-world settings.

At the elementary level, social studies was the academic focus of the "Hands-on Geography" grant that afforded fourth graders the opportunity to reach beyond their textbooks and take part in an interactive program designed to teach geographic skills and to familiarize students with U.S. landforms and the states themselves as well as many important places around the globe. Inspired by their participation in this grant-funded program, teachers and student have been working on other models of their own creation to make the learning of social studies more hands-on and engaging. Presenting content in innovative ways that are more visual and kinesthetic than language-based can be a valuable tool for differentiating instruction and requiring students to think about content in new ways. (Marzano, 2010)

Even at the kindergarten level, education foundation funds have had a positive impact, helping these young learners use 21st century skills to build phonology and other basic reading skills. "Technology is all about engagement ...The iGeneration is immersed in technology. Their tech world is open 24/7. Now, we need to take advantage of their love of technology to refocus education. In doing so, we'll not only get students more involved in learning, but also free up classroom time to help them make meaning of the wealth of information that surrounds them" (Rosen, 2011, p.15). District kindergarten teachers did just that. Through grant funds, they were able to purchase a small set of iPads to be shared in centers among the kindergarten classes. Using a variety of applications designed for the primary grades, instruction can be differentiated to meet a wide range of learner needs in beginning reading. Given this individualized nature of the program's design, each kindergarten student has been able to progress at his/her own rate. Use of this technology has been highly motivating and engaging for these young children.

Conclusion

It is evident that an education foundation can make a significant contribution toward building a community of learners and providing an incentive to teachers to tap their own creativity as they stretch themselves and their students in innovative ways, maximizing student interest in learning and, hence, promoting greater student achievement. As community-based organizations, education foundations help extend the outreach of schools beyond their walls, enlisting the support and cooperation of the entire community and then giving and/or sharing the rewards of their endeavors back to the community.

Often times, learning today can be considered non-traditional in its focus and format. Education foundations can support this shift in learning and help communicate the worthiness of such changes. "What is needed are schools that make it possible for the vast majority of students to do what a generation ago it was assumed that perhaps only 15 to 30 percent of the students could do: think creatively; master intellectually demanding concepts; analyze propositions in their cultural, historical, and economic contexts; reason well; and argue persuasively – in sum, evidence of the traits of well-educated citizens who are prepared to participate fully in the life of a modern democratic state and in an economy where the ability to think, reason, and use one's mind well is the key to access and to success. And these things must be done in an environment where most of the assumptions upon which the traditional structure of schools is based are no longer valid" (Schlechty, 1997, p. 235-236).

Given the challenging fiscal times in which we live, an education foundation can also be a way to fund enriching activities that would otherwise be eliminated or go unfunded in a "bare bones" school budget. In so many ways, education foundations are "win-win" propositions for school communities (students, teachers, administrators, parents, and the general public) that are serious about supporting local public education, as such endeavors enrich the school experience for students, increasing the students' motivation and enthusiasm for learning that ultimately increases their achievement. Isn't that good for the community and for the nation as well?

References

Blum, R. W. (2005). A case for school connectedness. *Educational Leadership,* 62 (7), 16-20.

Boyer, E. L. (1995). *The basic school: A community for learning.* Princeton, NJ: The Carnegie Foundation for the Advancement of Teaching.

Danielson, C. (2002). *Enhancing student achievement: A framework for school improvement.* Alexandria, VA: ASCD.

Darling-Hammond, L. (2010). *The flat world and education: How America's commitment to equity will determine our future.* San Francisco: Jossey-Bass.

_____. (1997). *The right to learn: A blueprint for creating schools that work.* San Francisco: Jossey-Bass.

Epstein, J. L. (1995). School/family/community partnerships: Caring for the children we share. *Phi Delta Kappan,* 76 (9), 701-713.

Freeley, M.E. & Hanzelka, R. (2003). Getting away from seat time. *Educational Leadership,* 67 (3), 63-67.

Hollingshead, B., Crump, C., Eddy, R. & Rowe D. (2009). Rachel's challenge: A moral compass for character education. *Kappa Delta Pi Record,* 45 (3), 111-115.

Marzano, R.J. (2010). Representing knowledge nonlinguistically. *Educational Leadership,* 67 (8), 84-86.

Rosen, L.D. (2011). Teaching the igeneration. *Educational Leadership,* 68 (5), 10-15.

Schlechty, P.C. (1997). *Inventing better schools: An action plan for educational reform.* San Francisco: Jossey-Bass.

Sergiovanni, T. J. (1994). **Building community in schools**. San Francisco: Jossey- Bass.

Steinberg, A. & Allen, L. (2011). Challenging assumptions: Helping struggling students succeed. *Phi Delta Kappan*, 92 (5), 21-26.

Vollmer, J. (2011). Welcome to the great conversation. *Educational Leadership*, 68 (8), 69-73.

Author Note
Linda E. Denault, Ed.D.

Currently, Dr. Denault is a professor in the education department at Becker College, Worcester, MA, and serves on the faculty of the educational doctoral program at American International College in Springfield, MA. Prior to working at the college level, Dr. Denault was the superintendent of schools for Palmer Public Schools and Monson Public Schools, both in Massachusetts. Throughout her forty-plus years in education, she has filled a variety of roles, mainly at the elementary school level, including classroom teacher, reading supervisor, assistant principal, principal, and curriculum coordinator. She holds a B.S. in elementary education from Worcester State, M.Ed. in reading from Worcester State, a C.A.G.S. in leadership and administration, also from Worcester State, and an Ed.D. from the University of Massachusetts-Amherst in educational policy, research and administration.

Dr. Denault can be reached for comments or questions at ledenault@aol.com.

NOTES

CHAPTER SEVEN

It Takes a Community to Create Student Success for Foster Youth

By: Robert D. Mack

Introduction

Children who are removed from their biological parents due to neglect or abuse are placed in the custody of the Department of Children and Families in Massachusetts. Approximately 423,000 school-aged youth are in foster care and live primarily in foster homes, group homes, or residential institutions or they are in kinship care (U.S. Department of Health and Human Services, 2009). About three-fourths of these children are ultimately placed in foster homes (Buehler, Rhodes, Orme, & Cuddeback, 2006) that provide both physical safety and basic needs. The other quarter is placed in kinship care or group homes. Social workers become the legal guardians of youth in care and maintain responsibility, as agents of the State, for them. There is no shortage of data that emphasize that youth in foster care face increased barriers in life (e.g., fetal drug effects, neurobiological problems, attachment disruptions, multiple caretakers, abuse, neglect, inadequate social support, poverty, parenting problems, and prejudice) (Choice et al., 2001; Emerson & Loveitt, 2003; Evans, 2004; Finkelstein, Wamsley, & Miranda, 2002; Snodgrass, 2010; Zetlin, Weinberg, & Shea, 2010). This population also faces specific educational barriers (e.g., poor teaching, ineffective schools, large classes and schools, poor attendance, and difficult transitions to new schools) (Collins, Spencer, & Ward, 2010; Courtney, Irving, Gorgan-Kaylor, & Nesmith, 2001; Courtney, Terao, & Bost, 2004; Mech, 2003). The outcomes overwhelmingly show that high school graduation, college enrollment, and college graduation rates are all lower than national averages. This population shows increases in homelessness, pregnancy, substance abuse, and dropout rates (Altshuler 2003; Emerson & Lovitt, 2003; Lovitt & Emerson, 2008; Merdinger, Hines, Osterling, & Wyatt, 2005; Pecora et al. 2006).

Successful educational attainment is particularly troublesome for those in this population who are unprepared, as described by Snodgrass (2010), due to lack of stability, multiple school placements, and confused self-identity. According to Mech (2003), "educational attainment is the centerpiece of any strategy that is aimed at preparing foster wards for economic self-sufficiency…too little has been done to open educational opportunities to foster wards or make certain that the placement system conveys a strong message as to the value it attaches to educational achievement" (p. 76). Foster youth need the support of social workers, educational professionals, and foster parents to collaborate and develop *academic care* that provides these youth with stability, empathy, and resources to decrease educational neglect and increase education attainment. This process must be encouraged despite the frequent challenges the child welfare system faces regarding limited ability to share pertinent information with other stakeholders due to confidentiality rules (Choice et al., 2001).

Literature Review

Collaboration

Reform and policy changes have forced many child welfare agencies to move from simply providing physical safety to considering the well being of the whole child (Harden, 2004). It does, however, still remain unclear how this can be accomplished and evaluated. The No Child Left Behind initiative has forced educators to consider this vulnerable population's needs and outcomes focused on "placing foster children within their own home school districts in an effort to preserve educational continuity and minimize disruption in the children's lives" (Wulczyn, Smithgall, & Chen, 2009, p. 35). It is apparent that reform is needed and that both child welfare and the school systems must devise and implement new processes that support cross training and collaboration. Documented in a study by Kutash, Duchnowski, Sumi, Rudo, and Harris (2002) one community developed a program that incorporated school staff (e.g., teachers, psychologists, specialists, and administrators), community agencies (e.g., mental health, juvenile justice, and family services), community members (e.g., parent advocates and area organizations), family members, and other supporters. "The purpose of such a comprehensive team was to integrate services between settings and to use the extensive expertise offered by all members, including the child and family, in a collaborative setting" (Kutash et al., 2002, p. 101).

One exploratory study conducted by Zetlin, Weinberg, and Shea (2010) included participants who served as foster parents, educational professionals and child welfare professionals; the purpose of the study was to learn more about the educational challenges foster youth face and to identify strategies to increase achievement. Foster parents identified a critical issue related to the lack of available resources available for assisting foster youth with the multitude of concerns involving mental health and medical, social, and learning issues. Moreover, the foster parents struggled to have the school acknowledge services related to learning or behavioral needs. Foster parents stated that they advocated for these services without support from social workers. The educational professionals found that greatest issues related to foster youth success are also related to school stability. Foster youth experience traumatic changes when entering the system, and for many youth, those changes continue regularly. These changes include new homes, schools, communities, social workers, and so on. Educational professionals from this study also stressed that teamwork with foster parents was crucial in supporting foster youth properly. Finally, the social workers were criticized for not sharing information with the schools that would be helpful in supporting foster youth. Social workers were cited as having poor follow-through and not providing critical information about foster youth starting or leaving the school. Social workers have the most useful source of information related to the decisions that will impact foster youth and also have the greatest understanding of how the system impacts youth in care. Both of these elements are critical components that can be used to enhance communication and collaboration between child welfare workers and educational professionals.

Altshuler (2003) studied the barriers and successful practices that affect the educational outcomes of youth in care and examined what collaboration is needed between schools and the child welfare system to increase academic success of youth in care. This study involved students, educators, and social workers. Findings included barriers to educational success based on student and teacher responses to foster care placements and the negative affiliation and lack of trust between educational professionals and child welfare professionals. Both groups agreed that a lack of communication existed. This researcher found that in the districts where the relationship between educational professionals and welfare professionals was not adversarial, communication barriers decreased and trust was more evident. Both groups of professionals agreed that in the cases where foster parents were involved at home and in the educational process, those youth had greater educational outcomes.

As reported by Choice et al. (2001), "the child welfare and the educational system work separately from each other. Respondents felt that the schools are primarily concerned with education and may be unaware of the special needs of foster children. Similarly, the child welfare system is primarily concerned with safety and the educational needs of children may be considered secondary" (p. 78) and that many participants in their research felt there was little or no known collaboration. Since in most cases it is unknown when and if such action will happen, it is important to consider the perspectives of those on the front line— social workers, foster parents, and teachers—and to encourage immediate action by these key stakeholders.

The commitment to working collaboratively is necessary and should be considered by welfare agencies. Specifically, this should be a factor when identifying potential foster parents. "Successful foster parenting involves communicating and cooperating with workers from the agency with whom the child is affiliated" (Buehler et al., 2006, p. 537). Additionally, foster parents should partner with mental health providers, court officials, birthparents, and teachers. The assumption is that foster homes will provide secure alternative care that supports safety, educational needs, mental health, physical care, and emotional needs.

Finkelstein, Wamsley, and Miranda (2002) found that foster parents did not connect youths' problems at school to their involvement with foster care. Foster parents reported having little discussion about academics and found that youth in their care generally only approached them on issues related to teachers and peers. Foster parents admitted that their own contact with schools only occurred when initiated by a teacher or administrator. When thus contacted, foster parents reported that they tried to be active in the problem-solving process. Foster parents responded that youth in their care "were doing well in all their classes" (p. 37). The grade reports showed that mean grade for students' math and English scores was 69.2 percent.

Unlike teacher reports, social workers showed a high knowledge and understanding of the impact that foster care has on youth and academic achievement. Social workers also identified this as an area of importance; however, little time was spent on issues outside of behavioral problems. Outside of required visits, social workers reported varying ideas regarding their own responsibility to the education of their foster youth. "Nearly all reported that they offered help to foster parents with registration, monitored children's grades through report cards, and evaluated children's problems and ordered testing or located tutoring. But in many cases the amount of time and effort devoted to these areas was minimal and unpredictable, and education seemed less of a priority than other aspects of a child's case" (Finkelstein, 2002, p. 40).

Teachers and other educational professionals are at the center of the teaching process for youth in care and provide the necessary resources to ensure youth in care are supplied with the tools needed to be successful. Finkelstein et al. (2002) examined the school experiences of foster children from the various perspectives of youth, social workers, foster parents, and school staff. They concluded that schools themselves maintain the strongest connection between foster youth and education. The challenge is that teachers showed little understanding of the difficulties and complexities involved with teaching and caring for foster youth. In many cases, this study showed that teachers believed that the experience was no different than that of other students or that it was the teachers' responsibility to see each student equally. The majority of personal interactions were based on behavior or disciplinary actions. Secondly, teachers and other staff members are often not aware of which students are in care.

Education

Most research on foster youth outcomes presents a bleak picture. Evans (2004) notes that foster youth often face educational neglect and that "acquiring academic competence is a major developmental task for all school-age children; it is important to better understand foster care's impact on academic achievement" (p. 527). He also notes that foster youth enter the system at a disadvantage, with a higher incidence of learning and language problems compared to their peers. Barton (1999) found that 40 percent of foster youth age out of that system into welfare or prison. Only 49 percent are employed and only 54 percent finish high school. Sixty percent of females who had been in care were pregnant within three years of leaving. Only 17 percent were found to be self-supporting. Emerson and Lovitt (2003) observe that foster youth in transition are, in large part, without health insurance and are homeless. They note that 61 percent left care with no job experience or work skills. Foster youth score 15 to 20 percentage points below their peers on standardized state tests (Legislative Analyst's Office, 2009). Finally, those leaving care entered post-secondary educational institutions at a rate of only 10 percent compared to their peers who were not in care and who entered at a rate of 60 percent (Lovitt, 2003).

The research conducted by Merdinger et al. (2005) echoed Emerson and Lovitt (2003) and other findings, such as Martin and Jackson (2002), by stating that poor educational outcomes are attributed to maltreatment, multiple and restrictive placements, changes in schools, instability of environments including peer relationships and low educational expectations from foster parents. Harden (2004) stressed that youth from "unstable environments are more likely to experience developmental difficulties. (1) Children exposed to violence within their homes experience the most deleterious outcomes. (2) Erratic, insecure home environments and a lack of continuity, and constancy in care giving are also associated with poor developmental outcomes" (p. 1). These two variables are greatly connected to children in foster care.

The hope is found in the studies by several researchers who have examined the educational aspirations and achievement levels of youth in care. Courtney, Irving, Grogan-Kaylor, and Nesmith (2001) found that the majority of youth had high educational aspirations and that 79 percent wanted to attend college. During a 12- to 18-month follow-up, the actual educational attainment showed that 55 percent had earned a diploma and 9 percent had entered college. Conversely, Courtney, Terao, and Bost (2004) found the most significant contributing factor to educational attainment to be the student's aspiration to achieve. Factors that contribute to developing aspirations are "socioeconomic status, parents' education, and a climate of educational support in the home, as well as school-related factors such as performance and being held back in early grade levels" (p. 38). In this study, youth were asked to identify the planned level of educational attainment, and the results show that just 11.6 percent planned to obtain only a high school diploma. The other respondents indicated that they hoped to earn college degrees (49%) and to study beyond college (22%).

Martin and Jackson (2002) conducted a study using a sample of high achievers from a previous study that had obtained information using a questionnaire on school care, experience, higher education, employment and current life situations, and family. Their own study used 2- to 3-hour, semi-structured interviews with a total of 38 participants who had a mean age of 26 and 25 of whom had earned post-secondary degrees. The research sought recommendations on how to enhance the educational experience of children in care. The findings revealed that 37 percent of interviewees reported concerns regarding the level of care associated with school attendance. The following recommendations were made by participants: 1) youth should be provided with maximum encouragement to attend school; 2) foster parents and workers need to have increased levels of education and qualifications; and 3) better space and resources should be provided to support youth with studying and completing homework assignments.

Martin and Jackson (2002) state, "attending school regularly whatever else is going on is a prerequisite for academic success, but not always given sufficient importance by social workers" (p. 125). Mech (2003) adds that the educational attainment for foster youth is low because the expectations are low; however, the lack of support and encouragement provided by social workers was potentially linked to the lack of education obtained by the workers. Not having additional education themselves might explain why some social workers place less importance on this area, as well as why they sometimes lack an understanding of how to help foster youth achieve increased academic achievement (Martin & Jackson, 2002). Martin and Jackson state that "the low priority given by the majority of social workers to education" also supports the systematic barriers that are in place for foster youth and their achievement levels.

Academic Care Model

Foster youth need the support of social workers, educational professionals, and foster parents to develop *academic care* that provides these youth with stability, empathy, and resources to succeed academically. Based on the current research, the following model should be considered with the intention of decreasing academic neglect and increasing academic attainment. Academic care is achieved by stakeholders setting high expectations, believing in students' ability to learn and succeed, connecting learning to the students' lives, and developing the appropriate team approach to maximizes collaboration. The stakeholders can achieve this by being open to a team approach and by keeping the youths' best interest, rather than systemic agenda and personal bias, as the focus point. Stakeholders should support the individual and consider the holistic needs of each youth. Relationships should be cultivated to provide youth with safe and trustful connections with adults. Finally, classroom learning should be done in a culturally sensitive environment.

The research has identified strengths from each group: social workers are knowledgeable about the process and can be most empathetic to the situation; foster parents can be a major resource for providing stability; and educational professionals are able to identify and provide the appropriate resources to decrease gaps and increase success. Although each group may have its own strength, it is imperative that each group be willing to include other stakeholders who can contribute to the individual needs of each child including empathy, stability, and resources, and that a single stakeholder not be responsible for creating and maintaining a single component. Connections and collaboration are essential to meeting the greater needs of each foster youth. Social workers can play an essential role regarding empathy. As the research indicates, social workers are found to have a high level of understanding the impact of being in foster care. As foster youth feel isolated and misunderstood, developing empathy is a key component to expanding academic care for youth. Additionally, as teachers have been found to have little understanding of how being in foster care impacts youth and foster parents are found not to be actively involved in the academic needs of youth in their care, these groups can learn from social workers how to change their attitudes or perspectives regarding the impact and outcomes related to academics of youth in care.

Recommendations for social workers to develop academic care include:

- Designate a Foster Care Liaison who can be a primary contact who supports school staff with questions and concerns.
- Recruit foster parents with advanced educational achievement and the desire to make this a major part of their role (Martin & Jackson, 2002).
- Develop a systematic approach that could be utilized by both social workers and foster parents to express the value and encouragement of educational accomplishments (Mech, 2003).
- Professionalize the role of foster parents (Erkut, 1991).
- Clarify roles of social workers and foster parents and systematically develop a team approach to educational achievement.
- Develop a communication plan that emphasizes educational achievement and stresses college opportunities from initial entry into state care.
- Cross training with school departments for social workers to learn more about the schools' cultures, expectations, and general limitations

- Advocate for a process that supports permanent placements, or if a foster home placement must be moved, allow that child to stay at the current school placement.
- To participate in professional development opportunities that bring these key stakeholders together as seen with the Education Collaboration Project (ECP) which promotes open communication, to build relationships among youth in care, education workers, and the child welfare system with the goal of improving school success for students in foster care, and to begin to address issues impeding school success for students in foster care.
- Connect with agencies that are able to provide free academic resources.

Foster parents are essential in developing stability for foster youth. Research supports that foster parents can be key figures in the academic process by collaborating with other professionals, assisting with homework, and providing sufficient time and space to do assignments at home. However, it is most essential that youth are able to maintain a sense of stability, and when youth are not being bounced from home -to -home or from school -to -school, they have a greater chance of developing the emotional and academic skills needed to be successful. Social workers can be more involved in the process of supporting foster parent needs to increase the likelihood that those foster parents will support youth for extended time periods. Educators should be more willing to make adjustments to allow foster youth to remain in a current school, even if the home placement has changed, in order to reduce movement and maintain stability. According to Harden (2004), lack of stability is associated with poor developmental outcomes. Additionally, Harden found that youth with stability showed higher task completion on academic assignments and were less likely to repeat a grade or drop out. Recommendations for foster parents to develop academic care include:

- Provide safety and model healthy lifestyle choices and behaviors
- Promote social, emotional, and learning development
- Be an open collaborator and team member
- Attend workshops and trainings to increase knowledge of working with youth in care
- Express academic achievement as an expectation
- Develop a belief that foster youth can be successful
- Pursue additional education (formal or non-formal)
- Invest in out- of- school activities and homework assignments
- Provide adequate space and resources in the home for youth to complete assignments

Teachers and other education professionals have the ability to develop and execute education plans. Resources for youth in care are extremely important to ensure that they are receiving the support to close the gaps created by the systematic process that causes many foster youth to fall behind and give up. Educational professionals will have limits related to resources, but they should work with social workers and foster parents to ensure that each needed resource is identified and a clear expectation of how the youth will receive the support is assigned. Recommendations for educational professionals to develop academic care include:

- Cross training with Department of Children and Families (DCF) errors for teachers to learn more about the impact that foster care has on youth and academic achievement.
- Develop a culture that is sensitive to foster youth including sympathy for their situations and to assumptions, elimination of activities that isolate (e.g., Mother's Day activities).
- Develop a culture that incorporates foster parents in meetings and conversations and that shows appreciation of both youth and parents.
- A forum to help school staff develop high expectations for youth in care and have long- term conversations regarding academics, including college.
- Protocol for identifying youth in care and creating appropriate means to share information.
- Collaborate with DCF to develop appropriate ways to support youth who transition from school-to-school including enrollment, medical records, academic history, etc. Additionally, develop a culture that helps new students to acclimate quickly to the school.
- Identity additional supports that provides tutoring and other academic services.
- Identify local after-school programs and activities.

Conclusion

These youth are most vulnerable and need the support of the full community. For social workers, foster parents, and teachers, remembering the complexity and multiple layers that are involved with these youths' lives is essential. There is no doubt that this population is extremely vulnerable and suffers academically. The greater question is why stakeholders frequently view the responsibility of these youths' academic achievement as someone else's duty. It is essential for all stakeholders to utilize a collaborative model to develop academic care and fro each to support the process as one member of the team working to create a structure or environment that best supports youth in care. These stakeholders need to work closely and those on the front line have an obligation to instigate and maintain such cooperation.

Each of the components in this model--stability, empathy, and resources—requires both openness to collaboration and the willingness to keep the foster youths' best interest first. While research has indicated that each stakeholder has sometimes blamed the others for the troubles that foster youth face or for other academic problems not addressed, time is better spent reducing the sharing gap and working to develop a clearer expectation of who actually is responsible for the academic care process and what each stakeholder can contribute to that process.

References

Altshuler, S. (2003) From barriers to successful collaboration: Public schools and child welfare working together. *Social Work, 48* (1), 52-68.

Barton, S. J. (1999). Promoting family-centered care with foster families. *Pediatric Nursing, 25* (1), 57-67.

Buehler, C., Rhodes, K.W., Orme, J.G., & Cuddeback, G.S. (2006). The potential for successful family foster care: Conceptualizing competency domains for foster parents. *Child Welfare, 85,* 523-558.

Choice, P., D'Andrade, A., Gunther, K., Downes, D., Schaldach, J., Csiszar, C., & Austin, M. (2001). *Education for foster children: Removing barriers to academic success.* Berkeley, CA: Bay Area Social Services Consortium, Center for Social Services Research, School of Social Welfare, University of California, Berkeley.

Collins, M., Spencer, R., & Ward, R. (2010). Supporting youth in the transition from foster care: Formal and informal connections. *Child welfare, 89* (1), 125-143.

Courtney, M. E., Irving, P., Grogan-Kaylor, A., & Nesmith, A. (2001). Foster youth transitions to adulthood: a longitudinal view of youth leaving care. *Child Welfare, 80* (6), 685-695.

Courtney, M. E., Terao, S., & Bost, N. (2004). Midwest evaluation of the adult functioning of former foster youth: Conditions of youth preparing to leave state care. *Chapin Hall Center for Children at the University of Chicago.*

Emerson, J. & Lovitt, T. (2003). The educational plight of foster children in schools and what can be done about it. *Remedial and Special Education, 24* (4), 199-203.

Erkut, S. (1991). Professionalization of foster parenting. *The Wellesley College Center for Research on Women, 226,* 1-26.

Evans, D. (2004). Academic achievement of students in foster care: Impeded or improved? *Psychology in the Schools, 41* (5), 527-535.

Finkelstein, M., Wamsley, M. & Miranda, D. (2002). What keeps children in foster care from succeeding in school? Views of early adolescents and the adults in their lives. New York, NY: *Vera Institute of Justice.* Accessed online, December 11, 2011. http://www.vera.org/content/what-keeps-children-foster-care-succeeding-schools-views

Harden, B. J. (2004). Safety and stability for foster children: A developmental perspective. *The Future of Children, 14,* (1), 30-43.

Kutash, K., Duchnowski, A., Sumi, W., Rudo, Z., & Harris, K. (2002). A school, family, and community collaborative program for children who have emotional disturbances. *Journal of Emotional and Behavioral Disorders, 10,* (2), 99-111.

Legislative Analyst's Office. (2009). Education of Foster Youth in California. Retrieved on February 18, 2011 from http://www.lao.ca.gov/2009/edu/foster_children/foster_ed_052809.pdf

Lovitt, T., & Emerson, J. (2008). Foster youth who have succeeded in higher education: Common themes. *Information Brief, 7* (1), 1-7.

Martin, P. Y. & Jackson, S. (2002). Educational success for children in public care: Advice from a group of high achievers. *Child and Family Social Eork, 7,* 121-130.

Mech, E. (2003). Education, employment, and income. In E. Mech & H. Clark (Eds.), *Uncertain futures: Foster youth in transition to adulthood* (89-107). Washington, DC: CWLA Press

Merdinger, J., Hines, A., Osterling, K., & Wyatt, P. (2005). Pathways to college for former foster youth: Understanding factors that contribute to educational success. *Child Welfare, 84* (6), 867-896.

Pecora, P. J., Williams, J., Kessler, R. C., Hiripi, E., O'Brien, K., Emerson, J., Herrick, M. A., & Torres, D. (2006). Assessing the educational achievements of adults who were formerly placed in foster care. *Child and Family Social Work, 11,* 220-231.

Snodgrass, K. (2010). Foster youth's achievement & Opportunity Gap. *H-204 Report: Difficult, Not Impossible to Mend.* U.S. Department of health and Human Services. The AFCARS Report Preliminary FY 2009 Estimates as of July 2010 (17).

Wulczyn, F., Smithgall, C., & Chen L. (2009). Child well-being: The intersection of schools and child welfare. *Review of Research in Education,* 33 (1), 35-62.

Zetlin, A., Weinberg, L., & Shea, N. (2010). Caregivers, school liaisons, and agency advocates speak out about the educational needs of children and youths in foster care. *Social Work,* 55, (3), 245-260.

Author Note
Robert D. Mack, M.Ed.

Robert Mack currently works and teaches at Curry College, Milton, MA. Previously he worked with foster youth in the Springfield, MA public school system and later worked with foster youth and foster parents as a therapeutic partner. He also served eight years as an independent contractor with The Mentor Network that provides therapeutic foster care services to children with behavioral, developmental, emotional, or medical needs above and beyond those of average children in foster care. Robert holds a B.A. in Psychology and Criminal Justice from Westfield State University, a M.Ed. in Mental Health Counseling from the University of Massachusetts, Boston, and is a doctoral candidate in Educational Leadership and Supervision at American International College.

NOTES

Section Two
COMMUNITY CONNECTIONS

CHAPTER EIGHT

Building True Ties Between Technical Schools and Their Regional Communities

By: Judith L. Klimkiewicz

Introduction

Technical Schools offer a broad scope of instructional and facilitative resources that are valuable to the communities they serve. These schools are often rich in untapped talents and underutilized facilities that could benefit regional community members and their constituencies. It is the challenge of the Technical School administrative staff to build a relationship with regional communities to advertise the educational and facilitative opportunities available to community members and organizations. This relationship must be reciprocal in nature since its continued existence requires each member's fiscal support for a school district that often represents only 10% to 25% of its school age population. During fiscally challenging times this necessary supportive relationship is even more difficult to foster. Thus, it becomes critically important to increase opportunities for community members to become acquainted with the wide range of resources available at the technical school.

Community Service Projects

Importantly, technical schools focus on delivering back to their constituent communities the real-world applications of their students' technically developed skills. Various student efforts such as improving community infrastructure via building projects, or providing an entertainment venue for community members through theater and arts programs will greatly aid the goal of binding the technical school to the regional communities. Where better to demonstrate that critical skill base than in the communities from which they seek support both fiscally and socially? As Shields stated in Bringing Schools and Communities Together in preparation for the 21st Century: "Such steps increase the opportunity for community members to become acquainted with the schools as well as the school staff to know the community better". Because this relationship must be reciprocal, the school becomes a resource for constituents of the communities. "Community meetings, debates, adult education, local theatrical productions, health screenings, candidate nights… all are legitimate uses of school facilities, and contribute to the well being of the communities", notes Henderson (1990). She adds "Schools that provide their communities a variety of services enjoy a deservedly better reputation. They are also much more likely to have a bond issue (or budget) approved."

A partnership approach gives technical schools and their communities' greater opportunities to determine a wide range of options for school involvement. Support for this community involvement begins with school administrators. Their willingness to work with community members and officials to develop school/community- based projects is critical. Having technical students build an addition to a fire house, renovate the town hall, add handicap accessibility to the local reading room, or install geographic information systems provides an opportunity for students to experience the real world application of their technical skill while providing a much needed capital improvement to one of their district towns for the minimal cost of materials. The key responsibilities of the school administrators are to select projects that are manageable, that have a high likelihood of successful completion, and to remain in constant communication with town officials to ensure that projects run smoothly. Projects that do not progress satisfactorily will negatively impact the partnership approach and create a negative relationship that could adversely affect the future support of the school and their initiatives.

Building Connections to Business, Industry, and Post Secondary Institutions

Vocational-technical school regulations (Chapter 74) also require technical schools to develop advisory committees for each individual approved program area that are made up of members associated with that occupation. The advisory committee of each program area must have members from current businesses (potential future employers), post secondary education representatives, disabled or non-traditional members of the field, a parent, current student and union/apprenticeship representation if it so applies. These program advisory members are required to meet twice annually to review curriculum, learning standards, equipment and the facility area to determine if the technical program is meeting or surpassing the standards of current employers, college representatives, or union requirements. This connection to these additional important members of our wider community is critical to technical education for many reasons; it ensures that our students annually are meeting the ever changing criteria for future employment and college entrance, but additionally we have broadened our community member base and expanded the number of constituents that support us in our regional towns. For example, business partners often donate or contribute to the purchase of much needed technical equipment, digital signage or sponsor students/teachers for professional skills testing and/or cooperative work placement positions.

Colleges often provide technical students with articulation (college) credit for their 3-4 year concentration in a specific area, offer scholarships and dual enrollment opportunities while still in high school. While often considered a money savings for students and parents the advisory member relationship also serves to create another "important" community member that supports our educational mission and justification of our budgets.

The Importance of Union Participation

The union/apprenticeship members of our advisory committees serve the broader purpose of informing us on the projected job opportunities for employment in their fields locally, regionally and nationally. When employment is growing they depend on technical schools to provide them with a highly skilled, trained student already having completed 30-50 percent of their required hours. When times are tougher the apprentice positions although limited are often still offered to the technical school that has a prior established relationship.

Many school districts that serve one community are fully focused on the K-12 system they are mandated to deliver. At regional-vocational technical high schools it is critical to expand your services to community members that are not part of your school age population to enjoy the better reputation that garners your support during difficult times (Henderson, 1990).

Schools for All Ages

Schools should not be viewed as institutions that impart certain knowledge and skills to only their students but serve the general public of all ages in a variety of ways. According to a recent study done by Knowledge Works Foundation, 2003 "Eighty-four percent of the population favors community use of the school facilities after hours and 62 percent favor locating services for children and adults at schools." Schools must focus on teaching and learning but they cannot ignore the needs of the broader community. As quality technical schools we have the equipment and expertise to address this need by drawing community members into the schools for many adult services. The schools can frequently provide specialized job training and certifications in such fields as medical (nursing certifications, dental assistance, and radiology programs), electronics/engineering, cosmetology, hotel/restaurant management and construction fields. In addition most technical schools have the highest levels of software and technology available for the worker desiring to improve his professional skills. These programs are often offered to community residents at reduced or minimal costs through grants and job retraining monies.

During the school day the technical school remains open to the public offering its services to the entire community. Most schools have restaurants, malls, banks, cosmetology and automotive repair facilities that are open daily offering gourmet meals, retail items, nail/hair services, and car repair services at minimal material costs, while school is in session.

Recruitment as a Selective Secondary School

As a secondary selective public school district vocational technical high schools have the additional responsibility to recruit (attract) students at an age when many are tied to peers and the school community. This requires communicating to the parents and students the benefits of acquiring a technical education instead of the traditional one they may acquire at the local high school. This requires a marketing effort on behalf of the technical schools that must take place early and often. Building on the previous stated collaborations with the community helps mitigate some of the negatives associated with being the "other" school. A parent who feels the regional technical school is "part of their community" is more willing to consider the benefits of selecting that type of educational delivery system for their own child. Recent information and studies that have been promulgated by such credible organizations as the Pioneer Institute, Mass Inc, and CNBC lauding the benefits both academically and technically of the career and technical education system of the commonwealth, have helped to alter the previous opinions held by parents. According to the Pioneer Institute – White Paper on Vocational-Technical Education in Massachusetts (2008):Their academic results are due to many factors. They reflect a combination of high expectations by educators and the completion of challenging, rigorous coursework by students. The academic skills necessary for career or college entry and success are gained along with the practical knowledge that elevates vocational-technical education students to the ranks of experts in their fields. (p. 1)

Conclusion

Regional technical schools are more than schools as we traditionally think of them; they are composed of deliberate partnerships that support and strengthen opportunities for students, families and members of their surrounding community. Their success has been built on establishing relationships, collaborating with all segments of the community communicating with clarity and remaining open to all possibilities by seeing through the eyes of others. These intentional partnerships are critical to the regional technical schools continued existence and success and must be an integral part of the schools regular work maintained during these times of dwindling budgets and voter anger. When the community is engaged with the school, resources and benefits flow both ways.

References

Fraser, A.L., (2008). *Vocational technical education in Massachusetts; A Pioneer Institute White paper. No. 42 October 2008,* Pioneer Institute Public Policy Research

Henderson, A. (1990). Guest Commentary. *NCREL Policy Brief, Report 9*

Henderson, A.T., & Berla, N. (Eds.).(1994). *A new generation of evidence: The family is cricital to student achievements.* Washington, DC: Center for Law and Education

KnowledgeWorks Foundation.(2003). Ohio's education matters: KnowledgeWorks Foundation poll. Available: http://www.kwfdn.org/2002_poll/index.php

Fraser, A.L., (2008). Vocational technical education in Massachusetts; A Pioneer Institute White paper. No. 42 October 2008, Pioneer Institute Public Policy Research

Shields, P.M. (1994, September) *Bringing schools and communities together in preparation for the 21stcentury: Implications of the current educational reform movement for family and community involvement policies [Online].* Available: http://www.ed.gov/pubs/ArchGoal

Author Note
Judith L. Klimkiewicz, Ed.D.

Judith Klimkiewicz is Superintendent of Schools for the Nashoba Valley Technical School District, a position she has held since 1996. The Nashoba Valley School District serves 7 communities located in north-central Massachusetts. Prior to her current position, she served as the Commonwealth of Massachusetts State Director of Career and Technical Education, a position she held for several years during the time period of implementation of statewide education reforms. She started her career in education as a secondary social studies teacher, and as Director of Curriculum and Staffing at a regional technical school district. She holds a B.A. in Secondary Education and a M.A. in Education Administration from the University of Massachusetts and Ed.D. in Educational Leadership from Nova Southeastern University.

Correspondence concerning this chapter should be directed to the author at jklimkiewicz@nashoba.tec.ma.us.

NOTES

CHAPTER NINE

How Community Agencies and Civic Groups Can Contribute to Student Success

By: Julie M. DeRoche

A Community's Response to Intervention: Haverhill Youth Mentor Program

This case study describes a large city wide collaborative effort to build a volunteer mentor program for the Tilton Elementary School in Haverhill, Massachusetts. Identified as a Level 3 school, Tilton School is a Title 1 school with a high at-risk student population.

The creation of the Haverhill Youth Mentor Program grew from concentrated collaboration among the following groups at various times during a two year span:

Team Haverhill-Julie DeRoche, United Way-Diane Franz, Haverhill Citizen and Mayoral Candidate-John Michitson, Mass Mentors-Marty Martinez, Public School Collaboration-Haverhill Public School administration, Haverhill Youth Service Agencies-Haverhill Boy's and Girl's Club, Northern Essex Community College, Fiscal Agent-Greater Haverhill Chamber of Commerce and community volunteers who supported us in web-based design, through private donations, and as mentors to Haverhill's children.

City of Haverhill

Haverhill, Massachusetts (Nilsson & Nicol, City of Haverhill, 2011), is located in Northeast Massachusetts along the Merrimack River. Established in 1640 as Pentucket, Haverhill was later incorporated as a city in 1870. Haverhill, Massachusetts' historical and business roots are tied to shoe manufacturing companies. Haverhill's historical and business roots as well as its' early economic success, from large business manufacturing and industries, set the foundation for Haverhill's profitable shoe manufacturing companies. For over 180 years, Haverhill, Massachusetts, led the United States' shoe industry. Today, Haverhill's economic and business base grows with advancement in the biotechnical, manufacturing, and small business industry as well as growth through growth in the downtown's restaurant district. A slowed economy, representative of many urban cities, has recently created pockets of slowed growth and renewal within Haverhill and entities such as the public school system have begun to show the challenges that school districts face amid a slowed economic foundation.

According to the Department of Elementary and Secondary Education's "Level 3 Review" (Massachusetts Department of Elementary and Secondary Education, Level 3 Review, 2010), Haverhill is a very diverse community with ethnic populations that are representative of many diverse cities across the United States. With almost 60,000 residents, the City of Haverhill educates approximately 6,800 students in its public school system. Over the past ten years, the City of Haverhill has become even more ethnically diverse and economically needy. The populations of students' needs represented in the following demographics highlight the school district's diversity: 4.1% African American, 1.7% Asian, 22.7% Hispanic or Latino, 71.1% White, 15.6% First Language not English, 6.7% Limited English Proficient, 20.8% Special Education, 42.4% Low Income, 35.3% Free and Reduced Lunch. The systematic review of the Haverhill Public Schools by the Massachusetts' Department of Elementary and Secondary Education's Center for School and District Accountability, reported many concerns and recommendations for remediation related to student achievement, teaching, and learning across the city's 15 public schools.

Team Haverhill

In 2005, Team Haverhill was created as a grassroots volunteer community group in an effort to engage the community in making Haverhill a better place to live. Team Haverhill's (Karlstad, E. & Mann, A., Team Haverhill, 2011) belief system is evidenced in its' mission statement which identifies Team Haverhill as *"an independent, volunteer action group dedicated to making Haverhill a better place to live, learn, work and play. We pursue this purpose by fostering civic dialogue, organizing hands-on projects, creating a more informed public, and advocating for positive change* (http://www.teamhaverhill.org). This signature statement encompasses the belief system that symbolizes the work that is done through the efforts of the volunteers in this organization. According to Eric Karlstad and Alice Mann (2011), Co-Chairs of Team Haverhill, "since 2006, when Team Haverhill became established as an independent entity, the vision work has continued with periodic community conversations (especially at "Possible Dreams" events) and annual goal-setting by Team Haverhill members" (http://www.teamhaverhill.org).

As a result of Team Haverhill's most recent community achievements and successes, Team Haverhill was recently named 2011 Commonwealth Award winner in the category of Creative Community by the Massachusetts Cultural Council; and the 2011 Greater Haverhill Chamber of Commerce's Small Business of the Year, in the non-profit category.

In 2009, Team Haverhill representatives identified a critical need for academic and social support for Haverhill's youth and worked to create a fully supportive mentoring program for Haverhill's at-risk student population with a host of community volunteers and partners including the Haverhill Girls and Boys Club, Haverhill YMCA, Haverhill YWCA, Haverhill's Girls Incorporated, Northern Essex Community College, Haverhill Public Schools, the Greater Haverhill Chamber of Commerce, Team Haverhill representatives and volunteers, the United Way, and Mass Mentors. An additional number of community representatives supported the Haverhill Youth Mentor Network (HYMN) with private donations to host organizational training from Mass Mentors, enlist volunteer mentors from the community, and create opportunities for community outreach and web-based support for the program.

The foundation for the HYMN initiative began through discussions and brain storming sessions at monthly Team Haverhill volunteer meetings. Discussing ways to support Haverhill's youth and the public school system, these conversations sparked intensive research and collaborative sessions around the supportive measures a community should foster for at-risk students. From the research-gathering and discussion phase, the idea of a mentoring initiative was born. Over the course of the first year of planning, volunteer members of Team Haverhill met with Haverhill's Superintendent of Schools to identify a school that would most benefit from a volunteer-based mentoring initiative. In an effort to build community support with the existing Haverhill youth community service agencies and create a program that fully encompassed the input of existing support structures in place for Haverhill's children, Team Haverhill began to series of organized discussion groups bringing together leaders from the community, schools, and Haverhill's four youth service agencies. Looking to build a mentoring system for the fall of 2010 was the identified goal but building the program slowly continued.

In January of 2010, at Team Haverhill's yearly "Possible Dreams" event, future volunteer mentors were solicited at this community-wide event for mentoring in the fall. At this time, the Team Haverhill co-chair introduced me to Diane Franz, a senior project leader at the United Way. Diane was working on building urban support systems and was very interested in this project. Another coordinator involved in the creation of HYMN was a previous organizer of a mentoring program and mayoral candidate, John Michitson. At this time, the three of us worked at building the HYMN program.

Over the course of 2010, the groundwork for HYMN began to develop. We had a location and students in need but we had no money, no volunteers, and no organizational structure. Questions and issues surfaced regarding the organization of the program: before, after school, or in school mentoring, organizing, training, and recruiting mentors, and creating a safe environment for students. Months into the planning phase, a private donor contacted Team Haverhill after hearing about our proposed mentoring program idea and offered $10,000.00 to support our program's development. Soon after we learned of a very talented mentoring trainer who worked for Mass Mentors and we decided to use our donation to hire Marty Martinez, Director of Program Services, to help us build our program and train our community organizers on strategic planning for developing mentoring programs.

Training with Marty was the turning point for HYMN. The stakeholders at the table learning organizational mentoring measures were: Haverhill's Superintendent and Assistant Superintendent, leaders of the four Haverhill youth service agencies, the principal of Tilton school, administrators from Haverhill Public Schools, Diane Franz from the United Way, Team Haverhill representatives, and a student from Haverhill High School. Over the course of four months, we learned how to: develop an operating budget, create a system for training mentors, create material for webdesign, review space and logistics to determine staff needs, raise funds for HYMN program coordinator, screen interview and hire a HYMN program coordinator, recruit fully screen, and train over 20 volunteer mentors from the community, create media outreach for newspapers and Internet sites, implement an evaluative framework for mentoring process, identify 25 students in need of mentoring, and kick-off the mentoring program in October 2011.

Haverhill Youth Mentor Network

HYMN is a fully functioning school-based mentoring program at Haverhill's Tilton Public School. The goal for Phase 1 of the program was to match 25 youth in the fourth grade with one-to-one mentor with future program planning to expand in follow-on phases over the next several years. The program is overseen by a Program Director who is accountable to the HYMN Steering Committee, a committee comprised of a wide-range of community representatives from both the public and private sector.

The HYMN program is a one-to-two year mentoring commitment with matches meeting for at least one hour per week on site at the Tilton School before, during or after school. The program began October 2010. Fourth grade mentees were identified at the end of the academic year by third grade faculty who identifies students using a set criteria and recommendations for students who would most benefit from this effort. Mentors are recruited from the City of Haverhill residents, local and regional businesses as well as from other resource pools, such as retired teachers and members of local service organizations. Mentor and mentee relationships continue to grow and expand into the next school year, as the Haverhill Youth Mentor Network begins its' new round of mentor-mentee match-ups with 25 incoming fourth grade students.

The Haverhill Youth Mentor Network (HYMN) is a program component of Team Haverhill. Team Haverhill is an independent, volunteer action group dedicated to making Haverhill a better place to live, learn, work and play. This effort has fulfilled Team Haverhill's purpose to foster civic dialogue, organize hands-on projects, create a more informed public and advocate for positive change. Creating systemic support for the school community through community-based partnership efforts has brought schools, volunteers, and community entities together under a common goal: Support for Haverhill's Youth.

Value of School and Community Collaboration

Through his analysis of the current challenges that struggling students and school administrators face, Price (2008) contends that,

> it's time to realize that when it comes to educating youngsters who struggle in school, educators cannot succeed on their own. In order to accelerate the pace of improvement in large populations of youngsters who chronically perform below par, we must augment the accountability and reform initiatives currently focused on school systems with initiatives aimed at stoking a *heightened desire for achievement* on the part of these children, their families, and community groups. In short, what's missing from the school reform playbook is an emphasis on motivation: sustained and effective encouragement for these underachievers to succeed. And conspicuously missing from teams of reformers that must figure out how to do this is the community-the proverbial village, in its myriad organizational forms (p.15).

In order to effectively support struggling students, communities must galvanize support for struggling students to address students' needs for positive student achievement and to advocate for strong educational and community-based endeavors. Collaboration and action planning between schools and community organizations and agencies will fill the void left behind from current educational reform measures and will create opportunities for student motivation and achievement. Overall, Sanders (2003) states, "community involvement in schools is an opportunity for a more democratic and participatory approach to school functioning—one that can serve to enhance students' achievement and well-being, build stronger, schools, assist families, and revitalize communities" (p. 14). Building a better community through school-linked support builds the capacity within the schools to offer stronger support to students and families as well as building the capacity of the community itself.

Educational reform measures place reform solely on the schools, in an effort to address student achievement. Missing from educational reform measures is the expectation for parents and the community to work together in support of children. It is clear that schools alone cannot effectively perform this function, as schools do not have the autonomy to fully engage the child when the child is not in the school-based setting. Parental involvement and community involvement are valuable components of a child's out-of-school life, and collaboration among these entities will enlist a healthier and more comprehensive approach to student achievement.

Many community organizations set goals toward advancing the community in a variety of ways. As Price (2008) states, "If communities are aggressively mobilized, and their energies are productively focused, they can transmit pro-achievement values to counteract student negativity toward and disengagement with school" (p. 21). Aggressive community mobilization to affect student engagement and achievement requires legwork on the part of school administrators in an effort to enlist a community's help in to the public school setting. In many instances, school administration must engage the community and elicit support from the community.

Developing Community Understanding

Many educational leaders must become community activists to get the message of student need out to community members. As it may be challenging for school administrators to openly advocate for community support, school administration must look to create a system of cultural and community scaffolds and supports that tie community members and their strengths to school-based educational initiatives in an attempt to create safety nets for disadvantaged students. Identifying the specific needs of the student population for the community is a step forward. Communities must fully understanding of *"the who"*, *"the what"*, and *"the why"*, when it comes to addressing positive student development. While it is clear that engaged students will better support the community and eventually the nation, community organizations must first learn and understand the challenges that disadvantaged and disengaged students face and the economic future that disengaged students *will* face if community organizations do not rally to support educational initiatives. Author of *The Last Dropout: Stop the Epidemic* (2007), Bill Milliken relates a conversation with Paul Houston, the previous leader of the American Association of School Administrators, in which Paul advises business owners to champion the cause for community collaboration with schools asking them to "...speak out and take action on behalf of the community involvement with our kids' education" (p. 114). Milliken credits Houston with this mantra:

awareness, advocacy, and action (Milliken, 2007). To create a system of awareness, advocacy, and action, community leaders must be brought into the fold. "Local business leaders and other power brokers must first become *aware* of the true problems confronting their school system; then they must firmly claim a role as *advocates* for the right kind of change. Last, they can take appropriate *action* to support a coordinated community response to the needs of children-and their teachers (p.114-115). In order to make efforts such as this to happen, community and school-based dialogues must occur to set the wheels of community and school collaboration into action. To reform education at the community level, community and business leaders can advocate for the support students need and enlist the community's help to activate initiatives.

Determining Goals for Positive Student Development

The educational leader of a school system or a principal can successfully enlist the help of the community through engagement with community groups and participation in informational meetings held to purposefully identify the needs of the school system. Indicators for performance, lack of performance, and system-wide data can be used to highlight the school system's and students' needs. Many types of challenges exist that leaders must be careful to address to ensure a quality and cohesive program. According to Mavis Sanders's (2001) article *Schools, Families, and Communities Partnering for Middle Level Students' Success*, "these challenges encourage school leaders to go beyond traditional practices and understandings of school, family, and community partnerships and to be more responsive to all families, including those under social and economic stresses, those with physical disabilities, and those from minority cultural backgrounds. These challenges also encourage school leaders to identify and develop strategies and practices to promote stronger connections with community agencies and organizations, and to reach out to and involve "hard to reach" families" (p. 7). Collective thinking, used to address the true needs of the student population and families, will build a strong structure from which an intervention or program concept idea can take shape. Yet another idea for cohesive collaboration in schools comes from Joyce L. Epstein's (2001) article, *New Directions for School, Family, and Community Partnerships in Middle and High Schools* in which the author shares Mary Anne Burk's research on school-based partnerships and identifies that collaboration between community leaders and middle and high school leadership provides insights and ideas for schools to engage parent and community volunteers in ways that support schools and benefit students. Epstein (2001) states "research corroborates Burke's points that volunteers can help schools and students reach important goals, such as improving attendance, increasing reading and spelling skills, and developing art appreciation. She advises schools to (a) recruit widely to increase the number of volunteers, involve diverse families, and extend the skills and talents available to assist the school and students; (b) prepare volunteers with targeted training so that their efforts are effective; and (c) prepare teachers to work well with volunteers. Principals of middle and high schools should support the organization, training, and purposeful assignment of volunteers as part of a comprehensive program of school, family, and community partnerships" (p.4). Creating collaborative structures requires school administration to be knowledgeable about the needs of the school's students, the goals for the intervention, and the means by which this intervention will take place.

Informational school and community leadership meetings may also target human capital goals commonly held by schools and educational reform. College and career readiness goals may also be discussed in an effort to rally support around school system goals. In addition, school leaders may share specific goals for student emotional and social well-being and significant areas of support needed for students in literacy and math. Leaders may also choose to relate this information in an effort to showcase goals for 21st century learning and Common Core Standards goals and expectations. By creating a team of educational supporters, school leaders can actively create opportunities with businesses, community service agencies, and youth service agencies. By creating a goal-oriented approach or action plan, schools and community resources can be triangulated to address positive student development.

Once the goals by the community and school teams have been set, the collective team can identify the schools or students most in need of services. Using national, state, and district data to support decision making, team members will analyze and create a coordinated response to address specific areas of student achievement in need of remediation and support. The ownership and responsibility for this type of grassroots campaign will reside solely with the team. As stakeholders in the campaign, team members will bring ideas for programmatic and intervention supports to students in the form of an action and implementation plan.

Choosing a site and format for the implementation of the action plan will consist of determining the students and schools that will benefit most from the campaign. A systematic use of data and inquiry will support the decision-making process in this regard. It is crucial that the use of data facilitates the clarification and identification of areas of student need necessary to best target student achievement, motivation, and engagement. The use of data allows for the identification of the school or specific student need in that data informs the intervention. Choosing the best possible intervention, through data, allows for an accurate and appropriate creation of support systems to be used with students. In addition, data informs a student's or school's needs and will allow for true support rather than a remediation or intervention that may seem redundant or needless to the student.

Becoming agents of change and advocates for positive student engagement and achievement will require volunteers and donations of some type whether it be time, money, or materials necessary to achieve the intended goals. Community leaders can support campaigns in many ways. Most beneficial at the onset of program coordination will be *committed time* to the project's creation and organization. As time develops, money and volunteers become increasingly important as the plan must flow from the idea-planning stage to the idea- implementation stage. Creating attainable goals will be challenging, yet rewarding once the implementation is set to begin. Monitoring the program's implementation will also be critical in the program development. Some communities and teams may choose to enlist a program director as an overseer for the overall strategic implementation of the project.

Oversight of programmatic organization, volunteer recruitment, and funding resources will also become significant in the overall implementation of the team's ideas. To ensure success, monitoring the detailed and specified plan for program support and organization will remain necessary throughout the program development. Working together, community and school leaders can call on each other for strategies of and for implementation. Because this type of planning and collaboration is required for successful implementation, participating in the steps toward the goal will motivate the team to create quality learning and achievement supports that will undoubtedly, for the impacted students and dedicated team organizers, last a lifetime.

References

Epstein, J. L. (2001). *Introduction to the special section: New directions for school, family, and community partnerships in middle and high schools.* NASSP Bulletin (85) 627, 3-6. doi: 10.1177/019263650108562701.

Karlstad & Mann. (n.d.). Team Haverhill: Vision. In *Team Haverhill.* Retrieved January 10, 2011, from http://www.teamhaverhill.org/vision.html.

Massachusetts Department of Elementary and Secondary Education. (2010). Massachusetts Department of Elementary and Secondary Education. In *Haverhill Level 3 Review.* Retrieved January 10, 2011, from http://www.doemass.org/sda/review/district/reports/level3/10_0128.pdf.

Milliken, B. (2007). *The last dropout: Stop the epidemic.* New York, NY: Hay House, Inc.

Nilsson, E. & Nicol, J.. (n.d.). City of Haverhill. In *City History.* Retrieved January 10, 2011, from http://ci.haverhill.ma.us/resources/history.htm.

Price, H. (2008). *Mobilizing the community to help students succeed.* Alexandria, VA: ASDC.

Sanders, M.G. (2001). *Schools, families, and communities partnering for middle level Students' success.* NASSP Bulletin 85, 53-61. doi:10.1177/019263650108562706.

Sanders, M.G. (2003). *Community involvement in schools: From concept to practice.* Education and Urban Society. 35, 161-180. doi:10.1177/0013124502239390.

Author Note
Julie DeRoche, CAGS

Julie DeRoche is the Director of Curriculum and Instruction for Georgetown Public Schools in Georgetown, MA. Prior to assuming this position, she served in a variety of other positions during her 15 year career in education to date including Title 1 reading tutor, middle school English and Social Studies teacher, Middle school English curriculum coordinator, Adjunct English faculty at NECC, andK-12 English Curriculum Supervisor. Julie holds a BA in English and Secondary Education, an MS in Reading and Literacy from Wheelock College, and a CAGS in Educational Leadership from American International College. Julie's doctoral work is focused on at-risk student writers and teacher perceptions of best practices in writing instruction.

NOTES

CHAPTER TEN

Securing Student Success: The Increasing Role of Local Private Foundations

By: Nadine B. Binkley

Introduction

More and more public schools and public school districts are doing what private schools have always done – formed foundations to raise money for both large ticket and small ticket items. This is a relatively new phenomenon. For many years, public education has held tightly to public finance and rejected private funding for all but a few needs, fieldtrips, supplies, entertainment and school social events, paid for with money raised by the school's PTO. However, as the economy has worsened, and accountability has increased, local private foundations have formed as a way to fund more essentials of education: computer labs, professional development for teachers, curricular development, new programs, extended day activities, and even teaching positions. This change has not been without great thought and discussion on the part of parents, the business community and educators.

This chapter will explore some of the questions raised by stakeholders as foundations morph to take on new roles and responsibilities. It will integrate two cases in which school districts have grown to rely on the work of private individuals working through a local foundation, to influence educational change: a new foundation in a small poor, multicultural, urban community and the evolution of a long-standing foundation in a wealthy suburban area. This chapter will explore how foundations have evolved, the extent to which foundations are influencing education in those districts, as well as the boundaries that schools systems have felt compelled to put on the use of money raised by private foundations. This chapter will also explore how districts and foundation board members view the work of the foundation in supporting student achievement.

The Evolving Role of Foundations

For many years educators have questioned the support of public education by foundations. On the one hand, publicly funded schools have often struggled under low-funding formulas and looked to other sources to provide enrichment for students. However, as major foundations began to target school systems as recipients of, sometimes, a large sum of money, that money was met with joy and skepticism. In 1969, Diane Ravitch in her article "Foundations: Playing God in the Ghetto", discussed the unrest which arose when funding by the Ford Foundation in New York City schools was aimed at facilitating decentralization of the schools and a move toward community control over those schools (Ravitch, 1969). She continued to discuss the uncertain role of foundations in public education in her 2010 book, *The Death and Life of the Great American School System: How Testing and Choice Are Undermining Education* where she states "There is something fundamentally antidemocratic about relinquishing control of the public education policy agenda to private foundations run by society's wealthiest people." (Ravitch, 2010, p. 200).

Stephen Mark Dobbs, an advocate for public funding of arts education, explores this issue in depth in his article in the Yale Law and Policy Review entitled, "Arts Education in Schools: Private foundations and public responsibility". Mr. Dobbs discusses the influences that foundations have on public entities. He states that particularly when public agencies have relinquished or abandoned their fiscal responsibility for schools, private foundations and other sources have stepped in to help. "There is a strong social and economic dimension to philanthropy that encourages private sector support for public causes" (Dobbs, 1989, p. 433). While that help is often needed, there are serious consequences that may arise from the acceptance of these funds. One of those consequences is that as the financial picture becomes bleaker, the public sector may rely on the private sector more. This may, in turn, provide the public sector with an excuse for not providing necessary funding (Dobbs, 1989, p. 434) or of viewing those programs paid for by private funds as dispensable. Dobbs goes on to strongly state, "Students should not be subjected to the vagaries of on-again, off-again programs, no matter how well-intentioned." (Dobbs, 1989, p.435) when foundations have no obligations to fund a program over a long period of time (p. 437).

Private foundations have their own agenda. That agenda may coincide with that of the school district, or it may be counter to the school district's agenda. Mosley and Galaskiewicz (2010) write that foundations "shape knowledge and preferences for policy solutions by funding specific kinds of research, driving community development initiatives, and supporting selected forms of social services." (Mosley and Galaskiewicz, p. 1). And Nathan Saunders, General Vice President of the Washington D.C. Teachers' Union in 2009-2010, cautions, "'educators need to look carefully at the larger implications of allowing private foundations such a major role. This is a significant moment not just for teachers, but for public employees,' Saunders said. 'This is heavy medicine.' ' It may be a very dangerous road to go down in which district officials and unions have to give up a stake in setting education policy to an additional player, a stake which may be hard to take back'" (Bink, 2010)

The challenge of the school district is then to work closely with the foundation to ensure that both foundation and school share similar beliefs about allocation of resources and that a working partnership is formed with open and honest communication about how money is used and the short and long term goals of resource allocation. The board of the foundation may be a stable board that is consistent in its funding decisions. Or there could be a built in rotation of board members, which means that as the face of the board changes, so may be what the Board funds. Dobbs comments, "Private foundations are free to finance what they believe deserves their attention, whether or not support is forthcoming from other sources. Although such latitude may be offset by the fact that choices are often determined by a board of directors attempting to represent (in an often undefined fashion) the "community interest," this is still a "limitation" to those who disagree with a foundation's policies and the direction it takes in its funding" (Dobbs, 1989, p. 437).

Although there are cautions to be taken when accepting funds from private foundations, there are many positive reasons to do so. David Arons reports in his essay "Public Policy and Civic Engagement: Foundations in Action" that foundations play important public policy roles through several means: convening critical stakeholders, building coalitions and funding necessary research (Arons, 2007). As well, Dobbs writes, "Ironically, private sector interests often are more concerned with promoting equal educational opportunity than are public agencies" (Dobbs, 1989, p. 434).

The Work of Foundations – Case Studies

Case Study I - Promoting STEM initiatives

Concord, Massachusetts is beautiful old New England town filled with the history of the American Revolution. Its residents are for the most part affluent and well educated. According to the 2000 census, the median income for a household in the town was $115,897, and the median income for a family was $135,839. The Concord Education Fund was started in 1994 with the following mission, which is still in effect today. "The Concord Education Fund (CEF) is an independent organization that avidly supports the pursuit of excellence in the Concord Public Schools and Concord-Carlisle High School, by granting funds for the development of curricula, programs, and initiatives designed to enhance the experience of education of students and teachers.

In the pursuit of excellence, CEF encourages on the part of grant applicants thinking that is creative and sound; quality that is exceptional; and personal vision that goes above and beyond the norm. Curriculum, programs and initiatives supported by the CEF, spanning all academic disciplines and levels, serve to deepen and broaden the experience of education. Through its work, the CEF strives to continue the growth of self-sustained excellence throughout the public schools in Concord."

Michelle Ernst, one of the two co-presidents of the fund reported that originally the foundation was a way of giving teachers a mechanism for teacher-driven grass roots programs. Teachers would submit proposals for projects they would like to do with their students and the foundation would choose the ones the Board wanted to fund. This was always done in conjunction with district administration. The first year of the fund, they were able to fund twelve grants for a total of $18,000, they now raise a quarter of a million dollars yearly. The foundation is run by a board of twenty people who each serve two-year terms, with a maximum of three terms. Ernst says that some of the Board members are still attached to the original concept, but most have moved on. For this reason, every year the foundation funds some teacher grants, but the real money goes to their STEM initiative called STEM Academy (Science, Technology, Engineering, Math Academy). The STEM Academy grew out of a close working relationship with the superintendent. They approached her with the idea of exploring more experiential learning in science at the high school. As Michelle put it, "we have enough AP [advanced placement] courses for everyone. What we did not have is the fun part of science and engineering. We wanted to get our kids excited about technology and engineering." Four years ago, after discussing their idea with the superintendent, a group of Board members met with the high school science teachers and asked, "if teachers could do anything, if money was not an issue, what would they do?" This led to a project that originally was called Hooked on Science and then morphed into the STEM Academy. The Board worked with the superintendent and the director of operations to take over a no-longer -used auto body shop in the high school. They put in comfortable chairs and couches, and converted much of the area to a big science lab that was outfitted as a robotics lab among other possible uses. The idea would be that students could come there to sit and watch and would hopefully be lured into the activity. They also paid for professional development for teachers, paid stipends to teachers to participate, purchased equipment and curricular materials, bought tee shirts and pizza for students when appropriate and paid for entry into robotics competitions. They are looking forward to adding biotechnology, environmental field studies and continuing with robotics. A next project in the STEM Academy is building a car that runs on used oil, perhaps from the local Dunkin Donuts.

The next venture of the foundation is something that they are calling Tech Bridge. They recognize that the budget development cycle does not allow for technology purchases as quickly as the technology changes. This fund will allow teachers to request equipment when there is a piece of technology that they need to improve the learning experience for students. As Ernst put it, "We are there to throw money at the problem." She continued, "This town has resources. There should not be programs that the schools want but cannot get because of the budget."

The foundation began the STEM Academy project with a single donation of $200,000 from a family in the town. They run one event per year, a dinner and auction, but most of the quarter of a million dollars they raise each year comes from individual donations. This year for the first time they have a sponsor. Cambridge Savings Bank has agreed to sponsor them. Ernst was a little nervous about this. Concord is a town with deep traditions and change is not always easy. She is not sure how people will react to seeing an advertisement in the foundation newsletter.

Ernst talked about the successful collaboration of the Board and the superintendent. The superintendent reviews all grant applications and the Board has made the decision not to approve any that the superintendent thinks are inappropriate. That said, the Board is always struggling with what the school district should pay for and what they should pay for. They are careful not to take over the public responsibility. However, they also recognize that budgets are tight and one solution has been to cost share with the district. They may split the cost of professional training for teachers, or of curricula materials. The bottom line is that the foundation does not want to be just a supplement to the budget; they want to make a difference in the lives of students. Improving student achievement results is not something that they talk about. Concord is a town where many students go to the best universities and where standardized test scores are high. The underlying goal of the foundation is to provide experiential learning to help make learning more fun for students. In the case of the STEM Academy, Ernst said, "we asked the science teachers to dream big, to fantasize about what the program could be. And they did."

The Superintendent of Schools, Diana Rigby, lauds the work of the Concord Education Fund. She confirms Ernst's view that the district and foundation work closely together to ensure that what the foundation supports coincides with the direction in which the district is headed. Rigby reports that the work of the foundation has helped to move the district to a technology rich experience for students in which they are allowed to explore and actively participate in the changing world of technology. The uses of technology brought to the district through the foundation have certainly added to the rich program that Concord runs to ensure high student achievement in a varied learning environment.

Case Study II - Providing Needed Technology to Schools

Leominster is a small city of approximately 42,000 people, located in central Massachusetts. Once known for making bone or ivory combs and ivory piano keys, it later becoming the self-proclaimed "Pioneer Plastic City", producing, among other plastic objects, those tacky pink flamingos that you see placed on lawns to help celebrate the inhabitants decennial birthdays. It is also known as "The Home of Street Hockey" because of its contributions to the game. According to the 2000 census, the median income for a household in the city was $44,893, and the median income for a family was $54,660.

The Mayor traditionally supports the school system's budget with close to the minimum amount mandated by the Commonwealth of Massachusetts. This amount did not offer the schools the funds that were needed to provide the kinds of educational opportunities for students that many parents wanted and many students needed. So in 2006, with the hiring of a new superintendent, the school board asked that she look at alternative forms of funding. The superintendent moved quickly to form an independent foundation, putting a board of powerful business people and politicians in place to oversee the work of the foundation. The foundation was formed in early 2007.

The mission of the Leominster Education Foundation is "to provide support for exemplary educational programs within the Leominster Public Schools that are beyond the normal scope of public funding."

The Board consists of nine members with the superintendent elected as President. In addition, there is a Chair, a Clerk and Treasurer. One of the first decisions of the Board of Directors was to determine what its fundraising focus would be. The Superintendent engaged in an effort to get feedback from staff, administrators, parents and the community on what they thought were the most pressing needs of the schools. The most common response was for technology at all grade levels. The Board adopted this goal looking to provide each of the seven Leominster schools with at least one mobile computer lab equipped with a classroom set of laptop computers, an in-focus projector, and a wireless hub.

The work of raising money was divided into two parts. Board members would identify donors and make an "ask." They would also support the efforts of the Advisory Committee, a group of parents who would organize fund raising events. The Advisory Committee tried a number of ideas, finally settling on three yearly events: a fall wine tasting, a Dining Out for Education day in which restaurants in Leominster agreed to donate up to 20% of their net for the day to the foundation in return for extensive advertising, and a golf tournament. Over the course of it's 3 ½ years to this date in existence, the foundation raised enough money to provide 4 mobile computer labs to schools.

The role of the Board did not work so well. With the economy crashing around the same time that the foundation was getting on its feet, there were few donations from individuals or companies, and those that came in were not large. Because the Superintendent is a member of the Board, she monitors the needs of the schools and communicates those needs to the Board. Thus, the Board and the district were in agreement on goals.

Schools that received the mobile computer labs report that within the first year of having it, the use of technology by teachers in enhancing teaching and learning has increased significantly and the assignments have moved to stretching students thinking, thus positively influencing student achievement.

The Superintendent has recently retired. Shortly before her retirement date, the person who had been the long-time chair of the wine tasting event stepped down. As well, the person who chaired the "Dining Out for Education" event stepped down. In this case, it appears that the Superintendent may have been the person holding the foundation together. In a city school system where the relatively small number of engaged parents are tapped for many school-based fund raising events, it may be difficult to sustain a long-tern district initiative such as a foundation.

Conclusion

The two foundations illustrated in this chapter demonstrate the evolution of community support for school districts from the traditional fundraising to support small teacher grants and provide enrichment activities for students to community foundations that have chosen to tackle important issues in teaching and learning; issues that have the opportunity to positively effect student achievement. In both locations, the foundation worked closely with the school administration in order to work in concert with district goals. Local foundations can be very effective in positively influencing the work of public education when those foundations work in concert with the school district to ensure that the goals of the two organizations complement each other. When that occurs, the winners are the students who benefit from a well-focused approach to their education.

References

Arons, David. (2007). "Public Policy and Civic Engagement: Foundations in Action." Pp. 69-74 in D. Arons (Ed.), Power in Policy: A Funder's Guide to Advocacy and Civic Participation. St. Paul, MN: Fieldstone Alliance.

Bink, Adam. (April 8, 2010) Private foundation money in public education. *Open Left,* Retrieved from http://openleft.com/diary/18187/private-foundation-money-in-public-education

Dobbs, Stephen Mark. (1989) Arts Education in Schools: Private foundations and public responsibility", Yale Law & Policy Review vol 7 no 2 pp 419-441

Ernst, Michelle (2010, September 8), Co-President of the Concord Education Fund, Interview

Mosley, Jennifer E., and Joseph Galaskiewicz. 2010. The role of foundations in shaping and responding to social welfare policy change: The case of welfare reform. In American Foundations: Roles and Contributions, ed. Hemlut K. Anheier and David C. Hammack, 182-204. Washington, D.C.: Brookings Institution Press.

Ravitch, Diane, "Foundations: Playing God in the Ghetto", Center Forum 3(May 15, 1969): 24-27

Ravitch, D. (2010). *The Death and Life of the Great American School System: How Testing and Choice Are Undermining Education.* Basic Books.

Rigby, Diana (2010, September 3), Superintendent of Schools, Concord, Concord-Carlisle, Telephone Interview

Author Note
Nadine Bonda Binkley, Ph.D.

Nadine Bonda Binkley served as Superintendent of schools in Leominster, MA and before that in Peabody, MA. Prior to assuming the position of superintendent she served in a number of other teaching and administrative positions in MA, CT and British Columbia, CA, including mathematics teacher, department head, assistant principal, principal, and assistant superintendent. She is the author of several publications. Presently, Dr. Binkley works as a consultant in school assessment and accountability and teaches in the doctoral program at American International College in Springfield, MA. She holds a BA in Mathematics Education from Regis College, a M.Ed. in Mathematics Education from Boston University, a CAGS in Educational Leadership from Boston University and a Ph.D. in Curriculum and Instruction from the University of British Columbia.

NOTES

CHAPTER ELEVEN

Community Involvement and School Safety: Thoughts on Streamlining the Process

By: Warren Corson III

Introduction

With record national and state level governmental debt, ongoing wars and higher than normal unemployment and a decade or more of steady reductions in federal and state funding for school districts, there is a need to become increasingly creative in developing programs that meet the needs of our students and community in ways that do not increase costs nor needlessly add to the work of often already overworked school personnel. This chapter seeks to provide information related to school safety while presenting a "non- model" approach that melds new mindsets and approaches to increase community and student involvement without further personnel expenses that are often associated with new program models.

Employing a program model can be a good starting point to addressing a defined problem. They provide guidance, principles as well as a set of clear definitions, function and scope. They can help provide uniform services and are often an aid in training new staff and insuring quality and consistency. Unfortunately, they also can provide dogmatic approaches to situations as well as a "one size fits all approach to problem solving." At other times models can lack the flexibility required to grow and adapt to changing needs, student make up and environmental issues. Models can be dynamic to be sure but they can also become stagnant, dated and ineffectual if they lack the ability to allow those who use them to adapt them to changing times and needs. They can be expensive to maintain or at times become cumbersome. Even a potentially effective program can lose its ability to serve those in need if the personnel charged with using the program do not feel included in the decision making process, design and or implementation. The author feels that it is imperative that the teachers, staff and administrators be included in the process of design and implementation of any new programming. The US Dept. of Education (2010) Built for teachers discusses the need for fewer restrictions in order to provide more fluid changes and empowerment for local programs to have more control and choices.

One of the tenets of behavioral therapy is that people are bothered not by things but by how they perceive them (see Ellis, Beck etc.). In that vein, students, teachers, parents, the community at large and other interested parties can experience change not through costly programming but through assisting them in changing their perceptions of the school and community in which they live and work.

The Partnership for Family Involvement in Education published Investing in Partnerships for Student Success: A Basic Tool for Community Stakeholders to Guide Educational Partnership and Development and Management in 1999. The publication seeks to provide a tool to build and manage partnerships between schools and community stakeholders. One of the key goals of this tool is to recruit, organize and manage a community partnership between Education, businesses, family members and other community stakeholders; it is through such a collaboration that much can be accomplished in order to improve education, safety and programming that is both within and without the normal scope and practice of educators but that may be within the boundaries of those who form the collaborative. This tool includes a means to help recruit and organize the stakeholders through the use of an included template for formulating the partnership as well as techniques for creating a vision for the partnership and related issues. While this model is indeed comprehensive and undoubtedly useful to many, the author is concerned at the level of bureaucratic responsibilities, meeting requirements, measurement and report requirements that were built into this model. The hours required to perform these measurements are potentially very expensive, time consuming and could limit the effectiveness and responsiveness of the overall goals.

It must be noted that these issues are not limited to this one model but instead are found in many if not most models; the reader should not infer that this model is inferior to others. The inclusion of measurement, reporting etc. are indeed a necessary part of education and are in many cases required in order to secure funding and to be found in compliance but have we at times lost sight of our goals in order to focus on documentation and systems process related issues? Have process and systems become more important than product? It is the opinion of the author that more emphasis should be placed on effective interventions and less on cumbersome documentation requirements. Occam's Razor teaches us to use the least cumbersome approach to problem solving as it is often times found to be the most effective; perhaps simplifying the documentation requirements will enable more effective interventions?

Violence has been a part of our culture, heritage and upbringing. War has claimed large segments of generations throughout the world; no one is immune. It has become ingrained in our psyches, infiltrated our lives, and in the process desensitized the youth of the world. The effects of war seem to have somehow touched every generation. Children see their older loved ones marching out to war, many not returning alive, others permanently disfigured and or emotionally devastated. On the home front we have seen the rise of inner city violence, drive-by shootings and gang wars that are waged where our children are playing, where we live.

Much has been said of the easy access of guns and of the seemingly endless means by which criminals are able to purchase illegal weapons. Violence has been embraced and in many ways glorified by certain segments of the media. While violence has always been part of the media, with the increasing abilities of the media to broadcast crime scenes, breaking events etc., we as a population are able to get a feeling that we are there.

Some movies portray violence as either a regular fact of life, or glorify the offenders. Some of the popular music includes the glorification of deviant lifestyles, the objectification of women, violence, drug use and abuse, etc. To many, it would appear that acting badly is the cool thing to do.

While few would suggest that censorship is the answer, most agree that something must be done. While there is no legitimate research that this author is aware of that conclusively links music or television to violence, there is in this author's opinion, a growing need for effective intervention strategies. Children need to know the consequences of living deviant lifestyles. They need to be educated on other ways of living, the finality of death, and the reality that is caused by violence or violent lifestyles. This can be done via including daily classroom education with every day, practical examples of the consequences of one's choices, both positive and negative. One ready built example would be the inclusion of contemporary events being compared to historical events that are already part of the curriculum. Perhaps having children see the parallels of events unfolding today with those of the past can prevent issues from reoccurring needlessly.

Famed FBI profiler John Douglas is but one expert who disclaims that media violence causes any person to commit violence although it may give those who are planning to commit violence a source for ideas (Douglas & Olshaker, 1999). Moreover, the authors cite that there have been no cases in which media violence has been blamed that the defendant has been found innocent (Douglas & Olshaker, 1999).

School Violence

As with most things in life, in order to be consistently effective over the passage of time, individuals, institutions and society must find ways to prepare for and possibly reduce the threat of violence. Simply developing a plan to react to violence only is not an effective idea, as it will do little to nothing in terms of raising awareness and prevention. Therefore it is the opinion of this writer that effective plans for dealing with school violence include a system of raising awareness and instituting well thought out prevention strategies. This strategy should include a plan that allows for schools to be able to alter the district wide plans to suit the need of each individual school (USDE (3) 2007).

An interdisciplinary committee representing all stages and phases of school life should be included when formulating strategies, accessing needs and developing a comprehensive prevention plan. This committee can be used to help get a total picture of campus life, the areas of concern, as well as gaining the perspective from the staff members that usually have little to no input in the decision making process. This committee will include kitchen staff, grounds people and maintenance workers (USDE (7), 2000) as they many times get different views and see students in areas and behaviors that may not be easily assessable to teachers and administrators. Years ago when this author was working at a transitional living facility, the maintenance supervisor shared an insight and offered an intervention strategy that had up to that point eluded those on the clinical team. It does not take advanced degrees to make valuable contributions to prevention protocols.

A safety minded school has systems in place to deal with the mental, emotional and behavioral issues of the students they serve (Cornell, 1999). One example would be for the school psychologist working along with the assistant principal to develop an anti-bullying and intimidation mindset and atmosphere among staff and students. This mindset would include counseling, education, intervention as well as the requisite awareness and prevention components. Education would include ways in which people could identify the signs and potentiality of hostilities before they progress too far.

In reviewing the current literature available on safe schools, trends are found in the recommended characteristics that define a safe school. Effective prevention, intervention, and crisis response strategies operate best in school communities that address the following: Schools need to have a system designed to identify problems and assessing the advancements made toward substantial solutions (USDE (7), 2000). This may take form in the interdisciplinary committee or parent, teacher and administrator run boards. The school will promote familial involvement at many levels including meaningful situations beyond the usual superficial means adopted by many schools in the past. Family support groups, activities, networking and activities that are of local significance would be a few such examples. Family shall be defined to include those members that are close to the students regardless of blood or legal ties. By including families, school systems will be more easily involved with the community at large, which is imperative in the development of establishing strong links with the community. Including local businesses and other interested parties can also help ensure a continuity of quality interventions that eclipse the physical confines of the school itself.

Relationships between staff and students need to be positive (Skiba, Peterson, et al, 2001) as is the need to treat students with equal respect (regardless of age, race, background, socioeconomic status, or reputation (both family and individual). With an open and comfortable relationship established between staff and students, teachers will have an easier time discussing safety issues and concerns (USDE (7), 2000). It also will serve as a way for the teachers and other staff to model ways for the expression of feelings in a safe environment. Citizenship and character development would be emphasized as well (USDE (10), 1998).

The FBI reports that 1 in 5 violent crimes occur in the 4 hours following the end of school. This statistic had lead to an increase in after school programs. There is a need for programming that maintains a focus on academic achievement by supplying adequate resources for all programs, that have an established system for the referring of children who are suspected of being abused, neglected or at risk and provides the great deal of support needed by the students when making the long and hard transition from adolescents to adult life and employment. Sadly many programs are either being cut or under threat of being cut due to lack of funding due to budget reductions related to the recession.

Principles for Identifying the Early Warning Signs of School Violence

There are many sources for information on the early warning signs of school violence. While most information is in agreement, some are at odds with one another. No one source should be viewed as having the superior or preferred information as the author feels they are all vital in establishing an effective view of the situations we are dealing with and trying to learn to prevent.

When addressing concerns about school safety and the identification of early signs of potential violence, the school clinical staff (counselors, social workers, and school psychologist), administration and staff must keep certain factors in mind. It should be noted that many children would show one or more of the established warning signs without being a potential perpetrator who needs intervention. Simply having some factors that appear to be a problem does not mean someone will commit violence, just as there are some that do not fit any or most of the patterns but who have indeed committed crimes. When making evaluations and observations it is imperative to keep things in a developmental and situational context, and here is where regular education of all parties who are involved with children is key. It is important that we keep stereotyping out of our evaluations. Simply because a person does not fit our ideas of a productive student does not make that person a risk. Baggy pants, which have been associated by many with gang bangers, and trench coats that were once associated with the gothic and "Emo" lifestyle, should not be the reason someone is marked as being at risk. As with therapy, education and all around good professionalism, we must remember to "do no harm."

At risk students often have been observed as being socially withdrawn with excessive feelings of being isolated and alone (Witkin, Tharp et al, 1998). Such students may feel rejected by society at large, their community, (Cornell, 1999) and family in general; and may be or have been the victim of violence (USDE (6), 2000). Moreover, they often times have feelings of being "picked on" or "persecuted" (Reaves, 2001); and potentially show a superficial interest in school and have poor or sporadic academic performance (USDE (6), 2000).

In terms of writings and drawings (or other artistic expressions), violence and anger are often the central theme (Skeesis, 1999). Impulsivity, chronic hitting, history of intimidation, bullying, violence or other aggressive behavior as well as expressions of uncontrolled anger are also frequently present (USDE (6), 2000). At risk students often have a history of discipline problems that may include drug (including alcohol) use, intolerance, prejudicial attitudes, gang affiliation as well as the expression of serious threats of violence (USDE (6), 2000).

Inappropriate access to, ownership of, or known use of firearms (Musil, 1998), when combined with aforementioned behaviors, are grounds for concern. Students who have been found to have serious fights with peers and or family, who destroy property or exhibit self-injurious behaviors including suicide threats, should be noticed as potentially at risk. Finally, severe rages for no apparent reason as well as detailed lethal threats of violence are also concerns.

Students who show a "triad" of behavior (excessive bedwetting beyond the normal age, cruelty to animals and fire starting) should be evaluated for psychological services and referrals made as indicated. Immediate reaction and the implementation of an intervention plan is warranted if the student is found to have a weapon and has threatened to use it, the student has given a detailed account on how he is going to hurt themselves or others (USDE (8), 2000).

Strategies for Proactive Interventions

Intervention takes form in a plethora of techniques, methods and ways. Some techniques work directly with the issues, while others work behind the scenes and are designed to set the foundation for making lasting change. Some examples include the education of students on positive social interaction, providing intensive but individualized intervention for students with moderate to severe behavioral issues as well as providing comprehensive services to students designed to provide a foundation for preventing or reducing violent or abhorrent behavior (Skiba, Peterson, et al, 2001). Another technique is by having an established plan for special education evaluation referrals (USDE (5), 2001).

It is important for students to learn that they are responsible for their behaviors; this can be established by sharing responsibilities through a partnership between with the school, home and community (USDE (5), 2001). Ideally, a partnership with parents should be established. This partnership includes educating the parents on ways to detect early warning signs and ways they can seek and get help for their child by emphasizing communication from all parties (Cornell, 1999). Training for parents and students on the protections, limits and parameters of confidentiality is needed in order to develop an atmosphere that encourages trust and communication.

In the author's experience, many if not most schools have internal school resources; however, many problems can occur when trying to coordinate these resources between departments. Because of the "red tape" that is commonly inherent in coordinating interdepartmental interventions, some students may never receive the care they need. For this reason the simplification of staff requesting processes for urgent services is needed. With the simplification protocols in place interventions can occur when they are needed: as soon as at all possible.

In order to develop and maintain optimal levels of interventions, funds must be allocated to train not only the parents and students, as well as to keep staff knowledgeable of the latest findings and most effective techniques (USDE (5), 2001).

The development of 24 hour anonymous phone lines where students can express their concerns, share information on potential violence and share suspicions has also been suggested (Toppo, 2001).

Maintaining Safety on School Grounds

Safe schools require more than special programs and community involvement; they require safe grounds and facilities as well. Improving safety requires many root level strategies some of which may be harder for some facilities than others depending on extraneous factors such as the crime rate of the general community, gang infiltration etc. Safety audits can be performed in order to establish a base on which to build. It is recommended that these audits be performed through a collaborative effort between school security and law enforcement experts (USDE (5), 2001). This audit should include a plan to monitor routes used by students to get both to and from school. Local police can assure safety by having officers monitor these routes on a daily basis. The use of trained and qualified volunteers can help fill the gaps that are often found along commonly used walking routes that are beyond the ability of Board of Education staff and local police. A point person for each school could serve as the area coordinator but would not have to be a staff member. For supervisory needs, retired citizens and homemakers could be invaluable. The utilization of modern technologies such as cell phones, texting and possibly social networking sites could be utilized to provide instant notifications of coverage needs. Hot spots and other concerns for safety should be available to the public though there is a potential that such knowledge could be exploited by those that these interventions seek to stop.

Just as law enforcement agencies have a policy of placing their patrol officers in conspicuous places in order to deter crime, having a visible adult presence throughout the school reduces abhorrent behavior (Toppo, 2001). This presence during critical times needs to be consistent and is recommended to also include the school grounds as well (USDE (6), 2000). Students who wish to engage in rule breaking can select areas that offer reduced visibility; therefore it is recommended that such areas be off limits to students. This can be assured by the installation of cameras or regular checks by security personnel (Toppo, 2001). Most schools today have installed cameras in key locations but it has been the author's experience that in smaller or under-funded school systems there are often no dedicated personnel to monitor the camera monitors; this leaves a great deal of potential protection being lost. In a few reviews conducted by the author, the office administrative assistants were in charge of reviewing the monitors while they performed their normal tasks. While they were often busy taking care of the administrative needs of the school and had little "free" time to address the monitors, to make matters worse, the monitors were installed behind their desks so they could not view the monitors at all while they were performing any other tasks! What could have been a huge increase in safety had become little more than a very expensive backdrop in the office. A much better system would have been to install the monitors where they could be viewed while performing their normal tasks or better yet, having dedicated personnel viewing the monitors. Here again, the community could play a key role as unpaid volunteers could be sought and trained in ways to utilize the monitors fully. These volunteers could then alert security should there be a need. Paid staff could be utilized should large gaps in the volunteer schedule be present. As is common practice in security, the timing of the security officer's checks should not follow a consistent pattern such as every half hour, but instead be staggered so it reduces the chances of these areas being used between checks. Similarly, security rounds should not follow a pattern of the order of rooms being checked, but have room checks following a random pattern. That is to say, the security officer should not follow a set path or room check for every review. For instance, if the officer started with the auditorium area on one check they would be best served by starting with another section on the next check so as to make it harder for those who may be trying to commit negative acts from "knowing" where and when the security officer will appear next. This lack of ability to work around the officer can in and of itself serve as a deterrent to all but the most determined individual.

Access to the building and grounds should be supervised as well. This can be accomplished in part by having exit doors that are not closely monitored, being equipped with mechanisms that will allow people to egress the building only but not allow ingress. Some schools also have a policy of closing campuses during lunch periods so as to reduce the chances of having non-authorized persons having access to the student body (USDE (8), 2000). Here again the use of cameras, monitors, and community volunteers could play a crucial role.

Research shows that schools with smaller populations and reduced class sizes often have lower crime rates. Therefore it is imperative for administrators to do whatever is in their means to limit the size of classes and overall student body population. Other techniques for lowering the size of groups involve staggering lunch periods and if possible the dismissal times as well. The limiting of scheduled time between classes reduces the opportunities for deviant behavior as does the modification of traffic flows.

Many schools now utilize Resource Officers who are Police officers that are permanently assigned to a given school. Schools may also have installed metal detectors (Toppo (2), 2001). While metal detectors may reduce the amount of weaponry that is present in schools at any given point, it provides little safety from students who enter the schools armed and with the intent to shoot (Toppo (2), 2001). Many cases of school shootings illustrate the fact that these gunmen make little effort to conceal their weapons, but to begin shooting when they have a target in view. It can also create a bottleneck around the detectors that could increase the chances that school shooters will be more successful in a confined space (Toppo, 2001).

Some recommend the adoption of mandatory school uniforms; Three percent of public schools were using them in the 1996-1997 school year (USDE (6), 2000). It remains unclear how such a policy would reduce violence other than possibly reducing the wearing of gang colors that may allow for the identification of rival gang members. This, however, would have no effect on the common practices of gang sign language or tattoos to signify ones gang affiliation.

Establishing Disciplinary Policies

As is the case with effective parenting, consistency in rules and discipline are required in order to maintain a safe school environment (USDE (6), 2000). One way to ensure consistency in the disciplining of students among differing staff is to develop a comprehensive school wide disciplinary plan, and the education of all staff on said policies (USDE (5), 2001). These rules should be posted and made available to students in order for them to become familiar with the rules and to be aware of the consequences if they should violate them. Staff, students and families should be as involved as possible in the development of fair rules (USDE (7), 2000).

Rules should reflect the cultural values of the community while remaining true to educational goals (USDE (6), 2000). Consequences should be commensurate with the offense; a policy of "letting the punishment fit the crime" ensures that students will not be disciplined any harsher than necessary. When disciplining it is imperative to combine positive strategies on learning and maintaining appropriate behaviors (Canter & Garrison, 1994).

Some suggest the implementation of a zero tolerance policy for students who bring weapons or drugs (including alcohol) to school (USDE (7), 2000). Others suggest that these measures are ineffective (Skiba, Perterson et al, 2001). Although this policy is necessary to ensure safety, common sense should not be abandoned. For instance, a second grader who violates the spirit of this policy by bringing a squirt gun to class should be educated on the rules; he does not deserve to be suspended or expelled. Remember the maxims of keeping things in developmental perspective and to let the punishment fit the crime. Students who have been suspended or expelled have not lost their right to education, therefore ongoing student support must be provided such as alternative schools that are equipped to deal with potentially violent individuals.

Effective Crisis Preparation

Ensuring safety in an educational setting includes the planning and preparation for the unwelcome possibility that a major crisis will befall your school. As with most things in life, reaction times and effectiveness depend on being knowledgeable of ways to respond in order to keep things as manageable as possible. One publication that may be an effective tool for those concerned would be Tips for helping Students Recovering From Traumatic Events (2005) which provides information for parents, Students, counseling staff, teachers and coaches. Procedures for dealing with crises need to be developed (see earlier description on the formation of a committee). The results from the committee will be made into a document that will be given to all staff in order to educate all individuals of their duties in particular, and of the reaction plan itself (USDE (10), 1998). Regular in-service training for all staff is recommended (USDE (10), 1998), as is the regular training of volunteers and community helpers. This training should include hands on practice of responding to imminent signs of violence. Members should become well versed on ways of effectively communicating in a given situation, know the procedures for evacuation and maintaining the safety of students. One of the most important aspects of this process is the establishment of securing immediate external support. Police, medical and fire personnel need to be contacted as soon as possible in order to aid in calming the crisis (USDE (10), 1998).

After a Major Crisis

Work is far from over just because the assailants and physically injured or murdered victims have been removed. In many ways this is the time when school psychologists, counselors as well as other mental health workers begin work in earnest. While these workers have been active in all the stages of intervention and training, it is after the tragedy that an organized crisis support team is most needed. The possible use of qualified volunteer crisis professionals should be considered and a list of willing professionals should be made, kept updated and regular contact from the coordinator be maintained. Paraprofessionals both paid and volunteer could be utilized to help regulate the flow of individuals needing services as well as a host of other activities from assisting with food, beverage, blankets, seating etc. as needed, will help minimize post incident chaos and help restore a sense of normalcy and order to the situation.

Counseling staff has the responsibility for helping more than students and their families. They need to assist staff and teachers to work through and understand their reactions to the crisis and to help them to understand and deal with the issues of adjusting back to a level as close to their pre-crisis status as possible.

As is to be expected, students and families will have differing needs and issues with adjusting. Parents need to understand children's reactions to and issues surrounding the violence. Temporary crisis facilities need to be set up to offer these services in the community as soon as possible after the crisis. Ideally these services should be supplied within a day or so of the crisis (Jimmerson & Brock, 2001). Here again is where planning can be key. A list of community resources ranging from property owners willing to donate the use of large rooms, auditoriums and other suitable locations in times of crisis as well as a list of likely needed items can help relieve issues often inherent in the aftermath of dangerous events. A plan for quickly accessing these items for distribution and the ability to allocate enough labor for distribution needs to be part of training and planning as well. As Hurricane Katrina has illustrated, simply having stockpiled supplies without a coherent plan for distribution and management leaves little hope that the survivors will get the resources they need in the most critical period after an event. If there are not enough potential volunteers, donated items and locations, funds should be raised and maintained in order to meet the needs. In the author's opinion fundraising, donations from the community and from manufacturers should be explored prior to seeking funding from the Board of Education, local, state or federal governments.

Shortly after the incident, but after counseling services have been put into practice, victims, families and staff need to be counseled on the reentry of the school environment (Jimmerson & Brock, 2001). This reentry should not take place until after needed repairs from the incident have been completed.

In cases where lethal violence was not used, there is a real need to prepare students, staff, family and the community for the possible return of the student or students who were involved in the crisis (USDE (10), 1998).

Review of Secret Service Opinions on Prevention Strategies Being Attempted by Schools

As with any crisis there often follows a deluge of offers of quick fixes that promise to make drastic improvements, often at a large price. History has shown that many of these fixes turn out to be anything but. For that reason it is the author's opinion that schools and communities should be optimistic but skeptical in reviewing proposals, especially ones that come with large price tags.

Methods that have been suggested include:
- Metal detectors-while metal detectors may find weapons being held by some students, in the cases of school shooters, they usually make no effort to conceal their weapons or their intent.
- SWAT teams-relying on SWAT teams they have found is not necessarily a reliable strategy as most attacks are completed before authorities arrive (Vossekuil, Reddy & Fein, 2001).
- Profiles-while profiles of those that are in jeopardy may be useful, they are not usually valid for identifying possible school shooters.
- Warning signs-these lists of warning signs may be quite useful at times to detect at risk students but they may be useless in identifying potential school shooters. (See profiles above).
- Checklists (see profiles above).
- Zero tolerance policies-zero tolerance policies may make for good publicity, but they have not been found to be an effective measure towards preventing school shootings (Skiba, Peterson et al, 2001).

- Software designed to compare a student's actions with past attacks- software designed to evaluate student threats have been found to be useless in identifying school shooters as most shooters rarely make direct threats (Vossekuil, Reddy & Fein, 2001).

Researchers recommend principals and teachers follow these principles to improve school climate: 1) listen to children 2) thoroughly investigate children that have come under the attention of administrators (USDE (8), 2000). It is also pointed out that many prevention techniques have been inspired by the Columbine massacre when this incident was an exceptionally rare occurrence (Donohue, Schirade & Ziedenberg, 1998).

Case Study: "Choose To Be A Champion"

In the mid to late 1990's the author was transferred from a clinical day school to an extended day program that treated adolescents with behavioral/ anger related issues. The program held up to 19 children all of whom were deemed at risk and in need of psychological services and milieu therapy. The program prior to the author's transfer averaged multiple therapeutic holds (restraints) per day and utilized a theme entitled "reach for the stars" that allowed each child to earn higher levels as a "space explorer;" each level allowed for the child's paper figure to visit a different planet on the bulletin board. Upon transfer it was obvious to the author that the planetary theme was falling upon deaf ears not only with the children but with the staff as well. Upon asking the ways in which advancements could be made, differing ideas and accounts were proffered; no one appeared invested or interested.

A quick assessment of the program, its effectiveness and goals was conducted. It found that some of the staff of three were burnt out with the program and had lost their desire to be there; of the children involved some were interested in getting better, others saw the program as nothing more than a formality that they had to work through in order to get more time to themselves (either by successfully completing the program or through exhausting insurance benefits). There was no involvement or ownership: this program was ineffective as it had grown stagnant.

With the Director's permission, changes were employed almost immediately. Staff was asked what they would like to see changed, what they thought were the programs biggest issues etc., as well as their thoughts on improving it. The children were asked similar questions as well. The author then sought to change the mindset of all involved. Education concerning therapeutic holds was one of the first initiatives implemented. It appeared upon review that such holds had become the first line of defense/ reaction as opposed to one that would be used only if such things as redirection, containment, de-escalation etc., had failed. In its first week a dramatic decline in holds was noted, the program later averaged between 3-7 holds per month with the same children and type of children in place. Of that number the majority came from responding to the same children who needed to be moved to residential programming but who were being held in the program until beds were available.

Looking around the program there was a built in theme noticed in the t-shirts of the children; they all were wearing wrestling related clothing. The author started researching professional wrestling, both the television programming and the performers themselves in order to find components that could be utilized for a new program theme. The "Choose to be a Champion" program was soon launched. The Choose to be a Champion model used paradoxical techniques in order to reach the children how to reduce violence. Here violence, or rather choreographed violence was being used in order to teach the children not to be violent. Through contact with the major wrestling promotions in the US, the author was able to get items donated that could be used as prizes once the children made marked improvements. Utilizing books and "behind the scenes" resources and websites, information pertaining to the wrestlers and how things were choreographed were shared as part of the educational piece. Children were educated in the need to keep wrestling and other types of violence in the appropriate place such as a wrestling or boxing mat/ring. They were educated in the fact that the language used on these shows was not appropriate for normal use and that the hatred many of these performers showed was actually just acting. Examples of "hated enemies" who where great friends in real life and even in at least one case, best men at each other's weddings! The result of this education was a real reduction in violence and inappropriate talk directed at peers.

Instead of planets, the children could earn belts-United States was for those who had been violence free for a given period of time, World was for those who had a few weeks more of violence free time and the Tag Team championship was for those who had shown an increase in their ability to work cooperatively with others for sustained periods. Children did not challenge others for their belts and instead worked on improving themselves- there were often multiple champions in the program at any time. A volunteer from the community designed certificates that were given to children when they earned a belt and a local printing company printed a box of certificates. When children earned belts, replica metal belts were brought in that the children could wear and have a picture of them wearing the belts taken.

In order to help educate the parents and other staff who were concerned with the use of wrestling to teach children not to be violent, regular in-services were scheduled. These meetings also served as a great resource to encourage volunteers. There were some setbacks such as when "Rowdy Roddy Piper" donated a stack of promotional pictures and the Director pulled them from the children's prize area because he did not think it was appropriate for the program to give out photographs of "a man wearing a skirt" to the children. Educating the Director on the difference between a skirt and a kilt worn by a Scotsman proved fruitless and the photos were removed. Some failures should be expected in trying something new however.

When the author left the program they were in talks to get some of the major league wresters to come in to give a talk on Respect, Education, Achievement and Leadership which was a theme that the then WWF had developed as part of their Get Real program. This program has been modified and utilized in both clinical and public school settings since its inception. One example of its modification was the de-emphasis on wrestling as the product became more adult orientated and the movement to a more generic use of the word champion to define becoming the best person you can be- living your dreams positively.

Conclusion

In times where funding is tight and school days are expected to cover an ever growing list of topics there is a need to incorporate new techniques in existing programming as opposed to trying to introduce new program models which require dedicated staff and blocks of time. Real change does not always require funding or additional staff; changing the mindsets of those we serve as well as those who serve can produce dynamic results without overworking already stretched staff.

Through reaching out regularly and working with community resources, much can be accomplished. The utilization of local resources from area business' groups and homemakers, new ideas, resources, techniques and volunteer labor sources can immerge. Reducing red tape through streamlined communication and approval systems can greatly reduce response rate and keep a program/ school working effectively and efficiently. Instead of designing new programs, the development of an evolving program mindset can allow for rapid, custom approaches to local issues without the need to reinvent or re-conceptualize the overall goals of the programming.

In attempting to improve safety it is important to learn from the past for both examples of effective and ineffective techniques and modalities. The secret service and other agencies have shown us ways to improve services without following new techniques and programming blindly. We have learned that we must avoid programming that is designed in such a way that it is allowed to become stagnant; that is to say, we must design a means of intervention that will allow itself to evolve with the growing needs of those we serve, unencumbered by a overbearing demand for process over the need for quality product. Perhaps the best way to prevent violence is to increase positive communication in the classroom, school and community and to remember that simply discussing the issues we face is not enough; we must actually listen what is being said and then act accordingly.

References

Canter, L. (1994). *Preventing conflict and violence in your classroom: scared or prepared?* Santa Monica, CA: Lee Canter & Associates.

Cornell, D. (1999, May). *Psychology of school shootings [23 paragraphs]. APA Public Policy Office* [online]. Available: (WWW) http://apa.org/ppo/pi/cornell.html

Donohue, E., Schiraldi, V., & Ziedenberg, J. (1999). School house hype: school shootings and the real risks kids face in America [65 paragraphs]. *Justice Policy Institute* [online]. Available: (WWW) http://cjcj.org/jpi/schoolhouse.html

Douglas, J & Olshaker, M (1999). *The anatomy of motive.* New York: Pocket Books.

Jimerson, S. R., & Brock, S. E. (2001, May). NASP/CASP respond following school shootings. Communique, p. 6.

Musil, R. (1998, May). School shooting spree in oregon is symptom of larger public health problem [3 paragraphs]. *Physicians for Social Responsibility* [online]. Available: (WWW) http://psr.org/school_shooting.htm

Reaves, J. (2001, May). School shooting highlights issue of parental responsibility [10paragraphs]. *Time.com* [online]. Available: (WWW) http://time.com/time/nation/printout/0,8816,101641,00.html

Skeesis. (2000, December). Monsters among us...the tragedy at Columbine high [18 paragraphs]. *Columbine High School Tragedy Web Ring* [online]. Available: (WWW) http://angelfire.com/tx2/coroner/columbin.html

Skiba, R. & Fontanini, A. (2001, May). Bullying prevention: early identification and intervention. **NASP Publications**.

Skiba, R., Peterson, R., Miller, C., Boone, K., McKelvey, J., Fontanini, A., Strom, T., & Simmons, A. (2001, May). The safe and responsive schools project: comprehensive planning for school violence prevention. Communique, p. 16.

Toppo, G. (2001, March). Schools tighten security, open fears [19 paragraphs]. *Associated Press* [online]. Available: (WWW) http://...center_package.html?FRONTID=NATIONAL&PACKAGEID=schoolshootings&STORYID

US Department of Education. (2010). Built for teachers: how the Blueprint for Reform empowers educators. 1-19.

US Department of Education. (2007). Crime, violence, discipline, and safety in U.S. public schools. Findings from the school survey on crime and safety, 2005-06. *National Center for Education Statistics*, 1-13.

US Department of Education. (2007). Practical information on crisis planning: a guide for schools and communities. *Office of Safe and Drug-Free Schools.*

US Department of Education. (2005). Tips for helping students recovering from traumatic events. *U.S. Department of Education*, 1-11.

US Department of Education. (2001). Tips for creating a safe school. *Community Update*, 85, 2.

US Department of Education. (2000). *Indicators of school crime and safety (NECS-2001-017)*. Washington, DC: Office of Educational Research and Improvement.

US Department of Education. (2000). *School safety: a collaborative report* (NLE 2000-4403). Washington, DC: Office of Educational Research and Improvement.

US Department of Education. (2000). *Safeguarding our children: an action guide* (2000 466-713). Washington, DC: US Government Printing Office.

US Department of Education. (1999). *Investing in Partnerships for Student Success: A Basic Tool for Community Stakeholders to Guide Educational Partnership and Development and Management.* Washington, DC: Office of Educational Research and Improvement.

US Department of Education. (1998). *Early warning, timely response: a guide to safe schools* (USGPO 1999-722-690/94397). Washington, DC: Office of Special Education and Rehabilitative Services.

Vossekuil, B., Reddy, M., Fein, R. (2001, March). Evaluating risk for targeted violence in schools: comparing risk assessment, threat assessment, and other approaches. *Psychology in the Schools*. 157-172.

Witkin, G., Tharp, M., Schrof, J., Toch, T., Scattarella, C. (1998, June). Again [26 paragraphs]. *US News* [online]. Available: (WWW) http://usnews.com/usnews/issue/980601/1shoo.htm

Author Note
Warren Corson III, Ph.D.

Dr. Warren Corson III who is known as "Doc Warren" by most clients and many colleagues, is a lecturer and Licensed Professional Counselor, a Certified School Counselor in the state of Connecticut. He earned his Ph.D with a specialization in Counselor Education & Supervision from Union Institute & University and is an Approved Clinical Supervisor. He is the Clinical & Executive Director of Community Counseling Center of Central Connecticut Inc. (www.cccofcentralct.org,which is a not-for-profit organization he founded in 2005. Dr. Corson III is currently designing a model for a therapeutic farm that he hope to locate in Wolcott CT (Pillwillop Farm); and he is the President of the Connecticut Mental Health Counselor Association (CMHCA) (2011-2012) and is a blogger for the American Counseling Association (listed as "Doc Warren" on the ACA website).

Correspondence concerning this chapter should be directed to the author at: docwarren@docwarren.org.

NOTES

CHAPTER TWELVE

Building Real Relationships in a Rural Setting

By: Neil Gile

Introduction

While there are recognizable benefits to living and working in a rural community, there are disadvantages as well. The Appalachia Educational Laboratory (AEL) (2000) expounds, "While the tradition of close relationships between rural schools and communities has deep root, the forces of economic globalization, school consolidation, and teacher and administrator professionalism divided schools from communities during much of the twentieth century" (p.12). The challenge for rural communities is to find a balance between the two rapidly diverging themes. The question becomes, how do educators and community members maintain the unique and wonderful qualities that define rural communities, yet embrace the changes of modern times that are impacting their community?

The need for building strong effective collaboration between the community, family, and school is critical in terms of promoting positive student development; moreover, such collaborative ventures are at the crux of overcoming the many variables that inhibit rural schools from being successful. Botelho (2005) points out that when there is significant presence of family support, the child(ren)'s achievement is improved. Without a committed and unified effort by the parents, community members, and teachers, rural schools are in jeopardy of failing. Boyer (1995) expresses his concern and sums it up well: "What's becoming clear is that it's not the school that's failed, it's the partnership that's failed" (p.49).

Based on the research, it is clear that parent and community involvement play a major role in increasing student performance and development. Olson (1990) asserts "studies indicate that once one-third of the school's parent body are reasonably active, all children start doing better" (as cited in Caplan, 1995). When parents, teachers and community members are actively engage in effective collaboration, they develop a stronger sense of support for everyone. Botelho (2005) captures the importance of establishing strong effective relationships: Children need families and schools that care about them. A child's development, achievement and lifetime outcomes are greatly enhanced when all work together as partners. Families cannot do it alone, schools cannot reach targets on their own and children cannot thrive when adults cannot respond to their needs (p.6).

Inhibiting factors

Having a clear contextual understanding of the inhibiting factors that impact rural school districts is necessary when considering the promotion of positive student development. This requires one to look at the big picture and to appreciate the intricacies found within a given community. The sense of isolation experienced in rural communities is perhaps one of the more significant inhibiting factors to promoting a successful schooling experience for students. Capper (1993) asserts that "Isolation restricts rural schools and communities from making use of urban-based resources that might enhance educational programs- museums, research, libraries, and colleges and universities" (as cited in Maynard and Howley, 1997, p.2). Consequently, students in rural elementary schools are exposed to the minimum required curriculum because of the limited funds, which limit enriching learning experiences; thus parents choose to search for school districts that offer a more comprehensive learning experience. Stephens (1983) summarizes that "the recent loss of population and the financial difficulties of many rural regions will also complicate efforts to close the education and training gap that currently exists in much of rural America" (p.75). In addition to the fact that students are at a disadvantage, the parents find themselves in an equally precarious situation due to the lack of employment. An unfortunate outcome is that parents leave rural areas in search of employment that may not exist in the rural setting. Given the fact that rural settings cannot compete with urban settings when it comes to employment opportunities, parents have little choice but to leave that area in search of more prosperous employment opportunities elsewhere. Caplan (1995) emphasizes, "Other parents may be unaware of their role in their child's education or may be too consumed by trying to meet their family's basic needs" (p.5). Financially, it may not be feasible for a family to continue to reside in a community that does not pay on a similar scale to its counterparts in suburban and urban areas.

As families leave and student enrollment declines, a rural school district's ability to maintain appropriate funding to support students is compromised; thus creating a snowball effect that eats away at a school budget, which is already bare bones. According to Harmon, Gordanier, Henry, and George (2007) the majority of a school district's budget (80- 90 percent) is consumed by the day-to-day facility costs, teachers' salaries and benefits, and other essential business related items, which leaves limited funds for improving instruction and learning. Simply put, there is not enough money to address all the needs.

When looking solely at the community makeup, there are other inhibiting factors that impact the students' learning. In some cases, rural families place a low value on the education of their children. Maynard and Howley (1997) speculate that parents in rural setting have on average a "lower educational attainment than their urban and suburban counterparts" (p. 2). As a result, parents neglect to recognize the importance of education for their child(ren). With this in mind, some parents do not have the necessary tools to support their child(ren) at home. "For some parents, a lack of confidence in their own basic skills may be a problem or a previously negative experience in school might stand in the way" (Montana State Department of Public Instruction, 1989, p.11).

The Montana State Department of Public Instruction (1989) identifies the fact that some parents in rural communities are lacking in educational experiences or have had negative schooling experiences may be intimidated by school leaders and teachers. Hole (2006) describes this perception as the "Expert Syndrome" (as cited in McEntee, 2003, p. 69). Capper (as cited in Maynard and Howley, 1997) furthers this notion by stating "parents may feel intimidated by school procedures and expectations" (p.3). The fact that teachers have had formal education to teach implies that they know more than the parents. Regardless of the perception, whether it is positive or negative, the sense of intimidation plays a role in the school's inability to establish positive relationships between home and school.

It is equally important to recognize the fact that teachers, just like parents inhibit the ability to form effective collaborative relationships. Not all teachers embrace the thought of parents being part of the classroom experience. In some instances teachers feel "overwhelmed and at times undermined in their dealings with parents" (Botelho, 2005, p. 2). This lack of trust inhibits the ability to establish working relationships between the home and school.

Overcoming Barriers

It is recognized throughout the research that increased and effective collaboration between the family and teachers results in higher achievement. "The work by Epstein (1984) indicates that there are positive, significant changes in reading achievement from fall to spring in those classrooms where teachers are leaders in terms of involving parents" (Montana State Department of Public Instruction, 1989, p.1). The priority of any rural school should be to gain a better understanding of the context in which the families live. Botelho (2005) expresses the need for teachers to take the time to get to know the parents in order to better understand the students. By doing this, the teacher is able to align his or her aspirations for the child with the parents. "Family involvement helps both teachers and parents realize their common goal of high achievement for all learners" (Botelho, 2005, p. 3).

Epstein (2009) stresses the need for a philosophical overlap between the family and school. A better understanding must be developed by both the family and school in order to develop a stronger bond between both. In order for this to occur, there needs to be a shift in thinking on behalf of both parties. This requires the family to think about how to better integrate the school into the home or by thinking of the family as a *school-like family*. This promotes the message that the school is an extension of the family, and the child is also a student; thus the family is supporting the school's mission. Conversely, the school needs to think more in line with the family or as a *family-like school*. By doing this, the school recognizes the fact that each child has unique qualities predetermined by the family that are special. This is the beginning steps to building effective collaboration between the family and school.

Schools must undertake a critical analysis of the community's strengths and weaknesses relative to the families residing in the community. Asking critical questions that uncover the underlying values of the community leads to a heightened awareness of factors that impact the families and children. According to the AEL (2000), the initial step "requires planners to think beyond just the school district. You must also consider where people work, shop, go to church, and go to relax." (p.12). By better understanding the context where the children reside, the school is able to address the specific attributes unique to that community. Caplan (1995) acknowledges the importance of recognizing the families' background and culture: "When families feel that the cultural values of their homes are not respected, they often respond by withdrawing support from the school" (p. 15). It is crucial for the school to pursue a sound comprehension of the community's makeup.

A fundamental element to improving effective collaboration is establishing a common goal, which, ultimately, leads to building positive relationships between the families and school. Botelho (2005) embraces this point: The threads of caring families, caring teachers, school administrators, and educational policy makers need to be woven together to knot a warm blanket that nurtures and provides safety, security, and challenges, thus enabling all kids and all families to reach their highest and best achievements (p.6).

The school must focus its attention on bringing families and teachers together for the common good of the children. If this is missing, the efforts to promote collaboration between the parties is all for not. "The school is now seen not as a substitute for the family, but as a partner to the family" (Caplan 1995, p. 1). When there is a strong partnership between the school and parents, Caplan (1995) reports that there are many positive benefits, such as better student motivation, self-esteem, and behavior. Additionally, this promotes the school in a positive light because the parents become advocates for the school. This is especially significant when rural districts are faced with lean budgets and need to rely on the community for financial support. "Actively involved parents can be vocal advocates for schools at referendum time" (Caplan, 2000, p. 3). With this in mind, it is critical that the overarching theme be kept in mind: building effective collaboration between the home and school hinges on the development of positive relationships. "The inarguable fact is that students are the main actors in their education, development, and success in school. School, family, and community partnerships cannot simply produce successful students. Rather, partnership activities may be designed to engage, guide, energize, and motivate students to produce their own successes" (Epstein, 2009, p. 10).

The school must demonstrate a transparent effort to bridge the gap between the home and school. Time and effort must be dedicated to reducing the level of intimidation and inadequacy felt by the parents and community members. "We need to dispel the myth that we are somehow the experts and that is our job to provide all the answers to the questions. In terms of the children, the parents are the experts" (as cited in McEntee, 2003, p. 69). As a result, parents and community members become more comfortable with working with the school. Ways in which schools can achieve this is by providing opportunities for parent to be engaged in meaningful decision making relative to the needs of the students. Establishing a nurturing environment for student learning that is embraced not only by the teacher but the parents as well is a critical step in the right direction (Hole, 2006). The task then becomes focused on involving "parents and others interested in the education of our children" (as cited in McEntee, 2003 p.68); it takes a communal effort to support high academic achievement. Hole (2006) discusses the practice of involving the parents in the process of critically examining student work. Through this collaborative exercise, both parties are engaged in meaningful dialogue that highlights the standards and expectations of good work.

In attempt to overcome the division between home and school, The Montana State Department of Public Instruction (1989) implemented a comprehensive model that focused on increasing collaboration between the two parties. The model emphasized the importance of starting with parent and community focused workshops. Workshops emphasized building esteem, confidence, and promoting student achievement. This approach fostered a learning environment that nurtured the adults and began to build a rapport among the participants.

AEL (2000), Maynard and Howley (1997), Caplan (1995), and The Montana State of public Instruction (1989) have all implemented similar methods to overcome the barriers of building effective collaboration between the family, community and school. They express the need to establish family-school networks that have the goal of supporting the community. The first step is to address the differences in perception between the home and school. Schools must expose parents and the community to the standards that are taught in the school; thus resulting in a symbiotic relationship between the home and school and creating meaningful learning experiences. This is accomplished by the schools providing opportunities for parents to learn teaching strategies that can be implemented in the home. Botelho (2005) expresses the need for parents to have an increased awareness regarding their child relative to schooling. They should have an appreciation of fact that there are many people involved in their child's upbringing that can either promote or hinder the learning experience.

By establishing networks consisting of outside organizations, such as, social workers and family engagement teams, parents and teachers are given an opportunity to collaborate in a venue beyond the school. Granted, the topics focus on schooling; however, this occurs in a neutral setting that is focused on the parents' needs. "This effort requires a great deal of skills on the part of the social worker to reach out to families and assist them in navigating the formal and informal aspects of public education" (Botelho, 2005, p. 4).

Literature suggests that a key component to improving student performance is linked to active community involvement (Blair, 2001; Pitzel et al, 2007; Reagle, 2006, Williams, 2010). "Changing schools requires a different type of commitment from everyone involved with education. Community members, as well as parents and educators need to be connected to schools and be aware of what is happening in schools" (Reagle, 2006, p. 26). Williams (2010) asserts "full-service community schools may well provide the greatest opportunity for quality education and success in rural communities where resources are few" (p.3). Time and time again, the term community is associated with effective reform in rural elementary schools. At the heart of an elementary school is the community. The concept of community is focused on building a support the leads to the development of the whole child. Furthermore, the process of reform is a collaborative effort that requires a reciprocal understanding between both the school and community. Pitzel et al (2007) support this notion by stating, "Any attempt at school reform must be linked with the concurrent revitalization of the communities in which the schools are located" (p.5). The emphasis of building a strong bond within the community of cannot be minimized; rather, the emphasis needs to be maximized in attempt to implement effective change. There needs to be a stronger recognition of the influences that a community has on schooling. Embracing the strengths of the community needs to be priority and infused throughout the school.

Williams (2010) discusses the concept of embracing "community schools" to overcome the challenges found in rural settings. A community school is a school that works with local agencies and community-based organizations to provide an environment that has a uniformed set of goals that address the needs of the whole child. Also, Williams describes the need to heavily involve all parties of a community in the effort of providing a stronger schooling experience for the youth and children of a rural community. "This deeper sense of community may make community schools unrivaled in their potential to provide quality education for all children, whether rural or urban" (p. 10). In order for this to occur, there are six key components to developing a community school: 1) Preparing the children to learn, 2) Extended learning opportunities, 3) Increasing parent and community engagement, 4) Strengthening families, 5) Strengthening community, and 6) Sustaining rural schools through economies of scale (Williams, 2010, pp. 11-15).

Often times, there is a dichotomy between the community and school. In rural communities, where the struggles to meet the needs of students within the context of school continues to grow, effort must be put forth to reconnect the two parties; moreover, there needs to be a heightened awareness relative to the importance of the community. Hubbard (2009) discusses the idea of utilizing the strengths of the community to better support the students. In particular, he questions the traditional schooling model and how it focuses too much on grade levels and not enough on the community. A better approach would be to look at education relative to the community or neighborhood. Children, outside of school, gather in groups not developed by grade levels; they interact frequently without hesitation in social groups that are not focused on grade levels. "When this happens out of school, we call it "family" or "youth group" or "neighborhood," and we can see it regularly at the neighborhood swimming pool, ice skating rink, movie theater" (Hubbard, 2009, p. 746).

Through the process of building strong community relations, it becomes clear that the educational experiences that extend beyond school must be relevant for the students to be successful. Wagner and Kegan (2006) elaborate on the idea of making learning relevant to each learner: "Relevance, then, is essential for students to understand the purpose of learning and be motivated to achieve rigor" (p.42). Information being taught must have a direct connection to the real world. Teachers must look at the manner in which instruction is delivered. Material must be adapted to make it meaningful for students.

Many successful rural elementary schools have applied this concept by implementing community service learning experiences and/ or have provided students with opportunities to learn beyond the traditional school calendar. Pennington (2001) writes about the benefits service based learning has had on a rural town in the western portion of Texas. Balmorhea, Texas has a k – 12 student population of 230. The students, through the process of service learning, became active participants in supporting the community on many levels. The results were twofold: 1) students become more connected with the community through the real life learning experiences, and 2) student test scores improved with the revitalize sense of purpose (as cited in Blair, 2001). "Researchers have underscored the importance of out-of-school learning noting that two-thirds of the achievement gap between higher-income and lower-income ninth graders is attributed to the cumulative effect of the differences in summer learning experiences during the elementary school years" (Williams, 2010, p. 12). Esptein (2009) adds to this point by expressing the need to provide parents with opportunities to work with their child(ren) beyond the school day. She introduces the concept of creating interactive homework assignments. These types of homework assignments are intended to engage the parents and children in schoolwork. "Elementary school students' math achievement test scores increase significantly when their teachers assign interactive math homework" (Epstein, 2009, p. 19).

The need to have a more involved parent constituency cannot be emphasized enough. In a rural elementary school, the parents' perspectives and opinions matter greatly. There needs to be more outreach on behalf of the school to better incorporate parents in the reform process. Parents need to be involved in the process of their child(ren)'s education. This is a challenge, especially in a rural environment, where parents are typically nonexistent for reasons having to do with obligations that are often out of their control (e.g. work hours).

Conclusion

The process of promoting effective collaboration is messy and can be overwhelming. With that said, much thought and care must go into developing a plan of action for implementing such collaborative efforts that will endure time and the challenges faced along the way. It all begins with the school clearly understanding of context of the community. Asking the right questions regarding the needs of the families and community is key because those identified challenges must be addressed through engaging the parents and community members. If there is not a clear understanding of the issues, much time and effort is meaningless and misguided.

Building effective collaboration between parents, community members, and school comes down to building relationships. All must parties must acknowledge the other's perspectives. This builds an awareness and empathy, which is the initial step in the process of establishing positive relationships, which promotes positive student development. The benefits of this process are boundless: a) the children see the community working together for their benefit. It shows that the community as a whole cares about them. b) It is an investment in the children's futures, which has a direct benefit to the community. Through this collaborative experience, the community is investing in the sustainability of the community. c) The parents are experiencing a certain level of enlightenment, which promotes a sense of pride about being part of the community. This could potentially maintain the population and improve the quality of living conditions found in rural communities.

References

AEL, I. V. (2000). *[Rural School Administrator's Resouces.]*. Retrieved from EBSCOhost.

Blair, L., & Southwest Educational Development Lab., A. (2001). *Changes & Challenges for Rural Schools*. SEDLetter. Retrieved from ERIC database.

Botelho, E., (2005). School-family partnerships: Sharing responsibility for student achievement. Retrieved from http://www.ritap.org/ritap/content/ri_innovations_spring05.pdf.

Boyer, E., (1995). *The basic school: A community for learning*. San Francisco, CA: Jossey-Bass.

Caplan, J. G., & North Central Regional Educational Lab., O. L. (1995). Parent Involvement 101: A Guide for Rural Educators. Rural School Development Outreach Project. Retrieved from EBSCOhost.

Epstein, J., (2009). *The school, family, and community partnerships: Your handbook for action*. (3rd ed.). Thousand Oaks, CA: Corwin Press.

Harmon, H., Gordanier, J., Henry, L., & George, A. (2007). Changing Teaching Practices in Rural Schools. *Rural Educator, 28*(2), 8-12. Retrieved from ERIC database.

Hubbard, R. (2009). Tinkering Change vs. System Change. *Phi Delta Kappan, 90*(10), 745-747. Retrieved from ERIC database.

Jennings, N. (1999). Reform in Small Places: Examining Two Rural Schools' Implementation of State Reform. *Journal of Research in Rural Education, 15*(3), 127-40. Retrieved from ERIC database.

Maynard, S., Howley, A., & ERIC Clearinghouse on Rural Education and Small Schools, C. (1997). *Parent and Community Involvement in Rural Schools*. ERIC Digest. Retrieved from ERIC database.

McEntee, G.H. (Ed.). (2003). *At the heart of teaching: A guide to reflective practice*. New York: Teachers College Press.

Montana State Univ., B. n., & Conrad Public Schools, M. T. (1989). *A Model for Rural Schools To Involve Parents in the Education of Their Children*. Retrieved from EBSCOhost.

Pitzel, G., Benavidez, A., Bianchi, B., Croom, L., de la Riva, B., Grein, D., et al. (2007). Rural Revitalization in New Mexico: A Grass Roots Initiative Involving School and Community. *Rural Educator, 28*(3), 4-11. Retrieved from ERIC database.

Reagle, C. (2006). Creating Effective Schools Where All Students Can Learn. *Rural Educator, 27*(3), 24-33. Retrieved from ERIC database.

Stephens, E., & Appalachia Educational Lab., C. (1988). *The Changing Context of Education in a Rural Setting. Occasional Paper 26.* Retrieved from ERIC database.

Wagner, J., Kegan, R., Lahey, L., & Lemons, R.W. (2005). *Change leadership: A practical guide to transforming our schools. California:* Jossey-Bass.

Williams, D. (2010). The rural solution: How can community schools reinvigorate rural education. Retrieved from http://www.americanprogress.org/issues/2010/09/rural_solution.html.

Author Note
Neil Gile, M.Ed.

Neil Gile has been an elementary school principal since 2007. Currently, he is the principal of Wolf Swamp Road School in Longmeadow, MA. Prior to assuming this position, he spent five years working as an administrator of a rural school in Monson, MA. His educational career dates back to 1997 where he first began teaching in Charlotte, NC. While there he assumed many roles ranging from classroom teacher to science coordinator of a kindergarten through fifth grade building. He holds a BS in Mathematics, Science and Technology and a M. Ed. in Educational Administration from Springfield College. Currently, he is working on his Ed. D. in Supervision and Leadership at American International College.

NOTES

CHAPTER THIRTEEN

Using Technology to Foster Purpose and Community in the School Setting

By: Meryl L. French

Introduction

The first decade of the twenty-first century has passed. The Internet is the constantly updated all-purpose resource of the digital age (Junco & Mastrodicasa, 2007).

Probably more than any other innovation, technology has revolutionized what is known as "community." Indeed, when checking the (online) dictionary for meanings of the word, along with the traditional definitions of community including "people in area; people with common background; nations with common history; society; interacting plants and animals " is "same as virtual community." The relatively newly-coined term "virtual community" is immediately recognizable as a reference to computer-generated social networking sites such as Facebook.

While the media is laden with many unfortunately factual stories about how technology has disturbed and distressed 'real' relationships, another perspective deserves mention. Technology, when used strategically and meaningfully, can and *does* enhance community. And a strong community supports positive student development. Today's students were born into a wired world, using technology for a high volume of communication. The effective school will meet the students "where they are" (Junco, 2010). Resisting technology is not a reasonable option. This chapter will describe specific uses of technology in the school setting that serve to inform and connect students, families, faculty and staff, and the public, thereby promoting community and positive student development. According to Ginsburg (2010), building resiliency young people is prompted by the meaningful and authentic opportunities for the development of competence, confidence, connection, character, contribution, coping, and control. Considered use of technology can be a useful factor in successfully promoting each of those goals.

Website

Probably all public and private schools as well as institutions of higher learning now focus on the creation and maintenance of a comprehensive website as the primary source of information for the school community. From the philosophical to the practical, school websites provide quickly accessed current information, with the ability to limit access to particular and confidential portals as desired.

A school's website has the potential to offer an interested audience accurate, targeted, easily accessible information. A superior school or school - district website will achieve four goals suggested by McKenzie (1997):

offering visitors a substantial introduction to the mission of the school, streamlining data searches to other worthy websites, presenting publishing opportunities for students and staff, and providing curriculum-enhancing local, community information. Further crucial benefits of well-designed and maintained school websites include the advantages of maximizing two vital resources: environment and time. Limiting printed communication reduces paper waste and permits parents to seek out and read applicable information when time permits. The fact that information is not lost in a backpack is an additional boon. With an increasingly high number of dual-working couples (Leedy, 2010), and divorced couples approximating 50% of marriages (Calo-oy & Calo-oy, 2010), websites provide efficient access to both parents at any time. Not surprisingly, communication and community "share similar Latin roots, carrying with them the fullest senses of "one, together, share" (Syme, 2010). Indeed, to ensure community, communication is essential, and technology-fueled websites are proven and efficient bridges.

One school website designing company states its mission as "to empower educators and education institutions with affordable web based technology that stimulates community involvement using tools that enhance, not encumber their work and profession" (wildfireweb, 2009). Another option suggests that teachers and students create and manage a website together (Follman, 2007), an activity that can further foster internal community while simultaneously enhancing external.

Communication Among Staff

While sensitive situations and topics demand in-person discussions, and it is impossible and ill advised to replace 'real time' connections, faculty and staff are grateful to have the nuts and bolts of school information disseminated via email rather than by convening extra meetings. Updates to schedules, absentee lists, protocols for formal assemblies, even recommendations for websites and resource materials can easily be shared online. Such mindfulness serves to increase time for meaningful community building.

In the arena of professional development, technology offers a timesaving, green and effective learning experience: the webinar. For teachers, seminars that in prior years might have been scheduled in distant locations can be reinvented (or supplemented) as "webinars", in which subscribers can attend and even submit and respond to real-time comments and questions, forming a society of virtual learners. The more such offerings, the wider the boundaries of the community can go.

Communication between Students and Staff

Faculty and student interactions can be substantially enhanced by email, as well. Within increasingly densely scheduled days, students can ask for or receive essential information, permitting an assignment to move ahead on a productive track. Moreover, in a middle or high school setting, a teacher can check in on the well - being of an introverted student who might feel intimidated by a face-to-face inquiry. The encouragement such exchanges of information provide is immeasurable. For some people, concerns are more comfortably admitted in writing than in person, and email permits swift exchanges. Indeed, in a blog titled *Social media in higher education,* college professor and social media researcher Junco comments in a September 2010 post on the importance of utilizing technologies that are meaningful to today's students, and "using technologies to enhance...face-to-face-interactions" with current technologies which are "...more interactive, engaging, and democratizing" (Junco, 2010). Junco advocates using social media in "educationally relevant ways" and notes the substantially effectiveness of e-mail as a way for the introverted student to connect to the teacher and become more engaged in class (Junco 2010).

Address lists can be compiled to target specific clusters, including grades (i.e. sophomores), classes (World History, for example), athletic teams, community service clubs, and more, permitting all members of a particular group to receive the information regardless of attendance in school on that particular day. Digital natives (Prensky, 2001) are notorious for being "always on" (Baron, 2008), and will read and internalize what might not be heard. Another way to reach the student audience is via an online "conference." Beyond email postings by the instructor, a student enrolled in the conference can reply, comment, post and communicate on the replies, comments and postings of all the fellow members. Such a conference appears as a separate folder on an email account, increasing the likelihood that posted messages will not be overlooked in a crowded inbox. Students report being "proud" to be part of a conference; there is a feeling of exclusivity without the hurtful component (Jones, personal communication, 2010). The academic community is thus enriched.

For the homebound student, technological options can help expand borders and make a profound difference. Schools can video and stream classes to a student recovering from an accident or serious illness, permitting the student to stay on track and also stay connected to classmates. The child suffering from leukemia will be far less isolated if still a 'virtual' part of the class. And the lessons in empathic community-mindedness for the children in the conventional classroom cannot be overstated. For the classroom students, resilience, positive development and character – building are prompted by such opportunities to connect and to be genuinely supportive, while for the home-bound child, coping is facilitated by the connection to community.

For students in need of additional credits for graduation, but unable to attend traditional school, online courses can provide the essential flexibility. Concurrently, course work can be completed, convalescence can be managed, or a job can be maintained. "Seamless" is a word often used by people recommending a specific technological application; for schools and associated constituencies, *seamless* can be a technologically fueled reality that permits productive participation in the range of activities, indeed in the communities that comprise an individual's unique circumstances.

Assistance with Harassment

Another problem with which technology can help relates to bullying, an unfortunate reality in many schools. According to an article in *The Washington Post* published in March 2010, one third of students admit to having been bullied at school, an estimate that is likely low (Strauss, 2010), as corroborated by another source's earlier statistic of closer to 75% (National Center for Victims of Crime, 2005). Regardless of the number, a frequently offered explanation for *not* reporting bullying behavior is fear of reprisal on the part of the victim. Emailing a teacher or administrator is one proven approach for the target of bullying to feel safe discreetly reporting the harassment.

A protocol recently implemented in a United States school district further suggests a dedicated phone number that can be texted on a cell phone at the moment in order to prompt the immediate intervention of the administrator and/or police officer receiving the message (Dominick, 2010; Hawksworth, 2010). While admittedly, technology may fuel bullying in certain situations, because of the ubiquitous use, the very same technology can be harnessed for help. Students should recognize that there is a community at large primed to help. Interestingly, a recent Blog post suggests that if a dedicated phone number is not feasible, "create a Twitter account" to reach a wider audience of adults to help (CroWolf, 2010). Coming together to the aid of someone in need is a proven community-enhancer; technology offers myriad opportunities.

Recent coverage in an account in *The Zimababwean* further dramatically illustrates technology's usefulness as a portal for support. Evidently, a young woman was tied up and robbed. With a laptop open on her bed, the injured party competently succeeded in using her toes to contact a friend, tapping out "HELP. CALL 911" (Zimbabwean, 2010). Help came. Technology provided an avenue for control and survival for the victim.

Email (Staff and Parents)

For parent-teacher communication, technology can provide clear, comprehensive information to all members in a constituency. Akin to systems for students, parents can be organized by grade or other meaningful demographic for the timely dissemination of relevant information. Even more, schools can subscribe to services permitting parents a far closer view of their children's academic life than was possible in pre-technology eras. Companies such as Blackboard® have software that can enable parents and guardians to view their child's real-time assignments, grades, special activities and more. A student's single test that brings down an otherwise stellar average will be recorded along with the stream of A's that were undoubtedly immediately reported by the student. Waiting for report cards to convey the status of an uncommunicative and/or troubled student is no longer necessary, thus improving the opportunities for the parents to productively intervene and support the child's efforts. Cooperative and communicative adults in support of students is key to enhancing positive student development. Additionally, schools can upload videos of student performances, administrators' speeches, and can post essential and evolving announcements. For parents unable to attend a special school event, such options provide opportunities for the otherwise absent guardians to feel and be a part of the community (Blackboard®, 2010).

School closings or other urgent notifications are expedited by technology. Many schools now have an automated email and/or phone system that permits a message to be sent to all families (or all targeted families) at once. With the ability to reach every parent and guardian immediately and simultaneously, every member of the community understands that every *other* member is in possession of the same information, a fact that facilitates still further communication.

Every school year inevitably brings some sensitive and difficult news. In situations such as the death of a member of the staff, salient information can be distributed so that all affected will learn of the situation, the details and the plans as quickly as possible. Moreover, links can be established on which comments can be posted, sites similar to what many funeral homes offer with online condolence and guest books. Such links can be kept 'live' indefinitely, permitting ongoing access to comments and photos, including details that might expand understanding and appreciation of the honored individual. Members of the school community feel sustained by the words of colleagues and students and upon convening at a memorial service and at school, the shared online support will have further strengthened the bonds of the affected community.

Students as Instructors

Being able to contribute, having a purpose, is widely believed to be *the* essential ingredient for a satisfying life. In former years, teenagers were genuinely needed as members of a community. In agrarian, pre-industrial cultures, children worked side-by-side adults, and young teens performed essentially the same roles as adults (Grenier, 1989). Later, internalizing roles as "an integral part of a community...being genuinely useful" (Pipher, 1994), young people were able to recognize, perform and gain satisfaction from the essential roles they played. Interestingly, the identification of adolescence as a discrete stage of life came as a result of industrialization. Feeling and actually being needed comes less naturally in a more affluent society; technology provides the venue. How might young people born in this unparalleled period of technological history be offered opportunities to be and to feel genuinely needed?

Today it is not uncommon for adolescents and adults to experience communication breakdowns, even impasses. Turning the tables and having youth play the roles of experts to adults eager to learn provides a historically unique and essential bridge of communication and connectivity.

The children born in the years since the advent of the world wide web in 1989 and the first Internet browser in 1993 (Griffin, 2000), known as digital natives (Prensky, 2001) or the "net generation" (Rosen, 2010) have known no world without the Internet. Older generations compare life before and after the influx of technology, and may struggle with the changes to communication and the work force. Like fish who do not see the water because that is all that they swim in (Rana, 2007), the population growing up immersed in technology "... are defined by their reliance on technology, their use of technology, and particularly their propensity for multitasking technologically; they are also defined by the fact that they use a variety of media to communicate with the world, with their friends and even in the business world" (Rosen, 2010).

In the early days of introducing computers in education, technically conversant students often served as trouble-shooters in classrooms, offering a necessary service and gaining substantial satisfaction and self-esteem in return. These students, not incidentally, were often less comfortable with typical adolescent social chit-chat; technology offered an alternative way 'in.' Today, fluent digital natives can serve as interpreters of things technological for parents, teachers, and adults in the wider public, gaining a personal sense of purpose in the process and fostering a public sense of community.

Courses can be devised in which students learn about the effects of technology, incorporating a youth participatory action project. Students learn about research techniques, while studying themselves. In so doing, students can come to understand, for instance, the effect of technology use on brains, on concentration and on sleep (Small, G., 2008) and can report findings to the wider school community. Such studies can be supported by organizations such as The Center for the Study of Boys and Girls Lives (CSBGL, 2010). Students empowered as researchers can serve a community brilliantly while learning about research methods and being self-reflective. "The primary goal of ... education is not merely the successful completion of ...degrees. It is the formation of a generation of people that clearly understands their unique contribution and genuinely desire to use this uniqueness for the common good" (Shushok & Hulme, 2006).

Conclusion

Technology provides more equitable access to information than ever before in history. This virtually universal access and communication broadens and deepens understanding, propelling community where community may never have existed. Time saving and 'green,' technology's tools can be thoughtfully utilized when promoting both positive student *and* community development. Harnessing technology and making systems work for the improvement of school communities is not only possible, but proven. Digitally fluent students can serve as the catalysts for understanding the machinations of today's machines. Given such respect, other essential lessons may fall on more receptive ears. The bonding of generations as well as communities is possible. Purposeful connection is technology's challenge and opportunity.

References

Baron, N.S. (2008). *Always on: Language in an online and mobile world.* New York, NY: Oxford University Press, Inc.

Best Online Memoorials (2009). Retrieved on October 8, 2010 from http://www.bestonlinememorials.com/

Blackboard (2010). *Learn for K – 12.* Retrieved on October 8, 2010 from http://www.blackboard.com/Solutions-by-Market/K-12/Learn-for-K12/Video-Courses.aspx

Calo-oy, S. & Calo-oy, B. (2010) Retrieved on October 8, 2010 from http://marriage101.org/divorce-rates-in-america/

CroWolf, S. (2010). *Putting the bullies on notice.* Retrieved on October 8, 2010 from http://sayencrowolf.net/2010/09/things-that-piss-me-right-off-special-edition-putting-the-bullies-on-notice/

CSBGL (2010). http://www.csbl.org/.

Dominick, K. (2010) *Text a tip line to stop bullying.* Retrieved on September 28, 2010 from: http://www.wwlp.com/dpp/news/local/Text-a-tip-line-to-stop-bullying

Follman, J. (2007). *Building a school website.* Retrieved on September 28, 2010 from: http://www.wigglebits.com/

Ginsberg, K. R. (2006). *A parent's guide to building resilience in children and teens: Giving your child roots and wings.* Elk Grove Village, IL: American Academy of Pediatrics.

Grenier, G. J. (1989). *Inhuman relations: Quality circles and anti-unionism, in American industry.* Philadelphia, PA: Temple University Press.

Griffin, S. (2000). *Internet pioneers.* Retrieved on December 2, 2008 from http://www.ibiblio.org/pioneers/author.html

Hawksworth, E. (2010) *Texting part of Massachusetts plan to stop bullying.* Retrieved on September 28, 2010 from: http://www.myfoxdetroit.com/dpp/health/texting-part-of-massachusetts-school-plan-to-stop-bullying-20100825-wpms

Junco, R. (2010). *Academic advising social media, and student engagement.* Retrieved on October 8, 2010 from http://blog.reyjunco.com/academic-advising-social-media-and-student-engagement/comment-page-1#comment-86

Junco, R. & Mastrodicasa, J. (2007). *Connecting to the net generation: What higher education professionals need to know about today's students.* Washington D.C.: NASPA

Leedy, B. (2010). *Stop the paper madness.* Retrieved on September 28, 2010 from: http://www.schoolwebmasters.com/index.cfm?pID=3799&blog=3

McKenzie, J. (1997). *"Technology & learning"* Vol. 6, No. 6. Retrieved on September 28, 2010 from: http://fno.org/mar97/why.html

National Center for Victims of Crime (2005). *Teen tools: Bullying and harassment.* Retrieved on September 28, 2010 from: http://www.ncvc.org/tvp/main/aspx?db

Pipher, M. (1994). *Reviving Ophelia.* New York, NY: The Berkley Publishing Group.

Prensky, M. (2001). *Digital natives, digital immigrants.* On the horizon. MCB University press. Vol. 9, No. 5, October 2001. Bingley, UK: Emerald Publishing Group Limited.

Rana, S. (2007). *Do fish see water.* Retrieved on October 9, 2010 from http://ezinearticles.com/?Do-Fish-See-Water&id=423704

Rosen, L. (2010). Retrieved on October 9, 2010 from http://news.cnet.com/Net-generation-comes-of-age/2008-1022_3-6195553.html

Shushok, Jr., F. & Hulme, E. (2006). *What's right with you: Helping students find and use their personal strengths*. About Campus, Vol. 11, No. 4, pp. 2- 8. Hoboken, NJ: John Wiley & Sons.

Small. G. (2008). *ibrain: Surviving the technological alteration of the modern mind.* New York, NY: Collins Living.

Strauss, V. (2010). *Making strong anti-bullying programs mandatory in schools.* Retrieved on September 28, 2010 from: http://voices.washingtonpost.com/answer-sheet/bullying/make-strong-anti-bullying-prog.html

Syme, J. (2010). *Communications and community.* Retrieved on September 28, 2010 from: http://daybook.davidson.edu/?p=2301 wildfireweb (2009). Retrieved on September 28, 2010 from: http://webschoolpro.com/about.html

Zimbabwean (2010). *Bound woman used toes to email for help.* Retrieved on September 28, 2010 from: http://www.thezimbabwean.co.uk/index.php?option=c

Author Note
Meryl L. French, MA.

Meryl French has been employed by Greenwich Academy since 1975, serving as a teacher, drama director, Head of Middle School, Assistant Head of School and currently as an advisor for student research projects and consultant to the administration. She earned bachelor and masters degrees in English and education from Carnegie-Mellon University in the 1970's and her Master's of Arts in Counseling Psychology from Union Institute & University in December 2009. In addition to her ongoing role as an educator, she is currently working as a Bereavement Counselor for Hospice.

NOTES

NOTES

Section Three
CASE STUDY SUCCESSES

CHAPTER FOURTEEN

Promoting Collaboration Across Constituency Groups: Lincoln Middle School

By: Timothy Allen

Introduction

Collaboration is at the heart of many fields of work in this growing global economy. Education is no different. In a time when accountability and testing have changed the way students are educated, new programs, systems, and processes are prevalent. However, more than any one system or curriculum, collaboration is the most direct route toward school improvement. Without collaboration, schools are homes to isolated teachers, stagnant instructional practices, and low-level problem solving. When true collaboration is present, schools contain many professionals working together toward common goals.

This chapter will examine the beginning of collaboration at a "failing" urban middle school. Lincoln Middle School is in a mid-size New England city that is in the top one hundred cities nationally for crime rates and poverty levels. There are approximately 700 students from grade 6 through grade 8. The following summarizes important student-demographic information from Lincoln Middle School:

- 93% of students qualify for free/reduced lunch due to low income
- 23.3% of students are special education
- 21.1% of students' first language is not English
- 31% of students are African American, 57% are Hispanic, and 8% are Caucasian
- 50% of students score at or above "proficient" on standardized ELA testing
- 14% of students score at or above "proficient" on standardized math testing

Last school year, due to continually poor test scores, Lincoln Middle School was labeled a "failing" school by the state school board. A new principal was assigned to Lincoln, as well as two new assistant principals. Multiple other staff changes took place as well. The Leadership Team met for the first time in the summer before the school year began. They discussed many aspects of school improvement, including changing the schedule, building teams of teachers, implementing consistent behavioral expectations, etc., but they decided quickly that nothing would be more important than the building of collaboration between teachers, administrators, and families. If Lincoln is truly to improve – and improve quickly – these three stakeholders needed to collaborate to increase student achievement.

Characteristics of a "Failing" School

As Noguera (2003) articulates in the following passage, the relationship between teachers and families can be very negative in a failing school:

In schools where low student achievement has been present for a long time, it is not uncommon for educators to develop a variety of ways to rationalize their students' failure. Blaming uncaring parents, lazy students, or a society that does not provide adequately for the needs of poor children serves as an effective means to avoid taking responsibility for one's role as an educator. Once failure is normalized and the causes of failure are attributed to some set of factors beyond one's control, reversing patterns of achievement can be nearly impossible. (p. 49)

When the new leadership team arrived at Lincoln Middle School, the school faced many of the challenges mentioned above. Discouraged teachers, lack of routines and discipline consistency, stagnant instructional practices, poor test scores, lack of positive family involvement, and many complaints of student-apathy were all present at Lincoln. The question for the new leadership team was how to address all of these issues quickly and effectively. Michelle Rhee (2010), the former chancellor of the Washington, D.C. public-school system, addresses this issue of confronting a magnitude of problems as quickly as possible:

So much needed to be fixed, and there were times when I know it must have felt over-whelming to the teachers because we were trying to fix everything at once. But from my point of view, waiting meant that another year was going by when kids were not getting the education they deserved" (p. 39).

Planning Collaboration

The new principal of Lincoln, Mrs. Collins, realized quickly that there was a lack of communication and trust between school staff and students' families. In order to move the school forward, this needed to improve. Mrs. Collins decided that two steps were necessary. First, systems would have to be put in place in which collaboration could grow between teachers, parents, and administrators. Secondly, collaboration would have to be built through *individual relationships.*

Collaboration with Families

As all of the research demonstrates, increased family involvement in education leads to increased student achievement (Constatino, 2008; Henderon, Mapp, Johnson, & Davies, 2007; Noguera, 2003; Papalewis, R. & Fortune, R., 2002). In one respect, the team wanted to create a schedule of family nights, open houses, and school activities that would invite families in to the school immediately. However, the team also realized that they did not know the teachers of the school very well, did not fully understand their belief systems on family-involvement, and did not understand what the interaction between teachers and families looked like at Lincoln Middle School. The first goal in any collaborative relationship is to establish trust. As Constatino (2008) states, "Relationships cannot exist without trust. At the heart of most disengagement is a lack of trust between families and school personnel. Rebuilding and supporting trusting relationships is essential for engaging families in the academic lives of their children" (p. 9). If the leadership team put teachers and families in the same place on a big scale too early, without understanding the belief system of the teachers and their ability level in dealing with parents, then trust could actually be damaged instead of created. The process of becoming a "failing" school happens over multiple years, which is a long time for the strain in family and school relationships to grow.

The leadership team decided to spend the first four months focused on two elements of engaging families: Working individually, one-at-a-time with families through interaction to rebuild their trust in the school environment and culture; and observing and analyzing teachers' belief systems about family involvement, as well as their skill-level in interacting with parents.

Open house would of course take place, and teams of teachers would be encouraged to host other events, but from a leadership standpoint, the focus would be smaller for the first four months. Collaboration would be built by first re-building families' faith in the school. The team would work to create a school that parents could be proud of and making sure the doors were always open. Completely overhauling the system with parents was not the first priority; examining and addressing teacher-belief systems, as well as dealing with individual parents the right way *was*.

Constatino (2008) identifies four domains of family engagement (p. 25):
- A welcoming environment for families
- Effective two way communication
- The degree of overall engagement
- School support for home learning

Basically, the leadership team at Lincoln Middle School decided to address the first two domains of family engagement in the first four months, then turn their attention to the last two when they had more information available. This would be done by regaining control of the school, demonstrating this fact to families as often as possible, and engaging as many families as possible on an individual basis.

When creating a welcoming environment for families, many small, but important changes had to take place. The first focus of the team was the main office. This is the place all families first visit and it sets the tone for their interaction with the school. Through conversation with office staff and teachers, it was clear that the culture of the main office needed improvement. Too many students were often in the main office, or in the hallway outside the office. Parents' first view of the school often included the chaos of middle school students who were in trouble, or having emotional moments. This stemmed from the fact that there were two offices connected to the main office, one of the principal and one of an assistant principal. While the principal needs to be in the main office due to constant interaction with administrative assistants, assistant principals are more needed in the hallways near classrooms. They need to be a constant supportive presence for teachers and students. The team decided to move the assistant principal's office out of the main office and into the academic hallway. This meant that the main office would no longer be a waiting area for students that were in trouble, in conflict, or in the midst of an emotional moment. Most importantly, the main office would now present a calm, professional environment for families and visitors of the school.

The next question was what to do with the vacated office. After many options were presented, Mrs. Collins and the team decided to create a conference room. A conference table with comfortable chairs was purchased, as well as a water cooler. The room would be used for meetings with parents in order to, once again, present a calm, professional environment. In this quiet area, school personnel would be able to focus on meetings and families would appreciate the undivided attention.

Anyone with urban middle school experience knows that the walkie-talkies often used by administrators, counselors, and office personnel can be a constant reminder of how busy everyone is and how needy the students can be. When parents are in the main office, they hear the administrative assistants' walkie-talkies and when the discourse is chaotic, they can again lose trust in the functionality of the school. Especially frustrating for parents is when they hear that there is a fight in the hallways or in a classroom. While the goal is for fights *never* to take place, in a middle school like Lincoln, where gang involvement and poverty are prevalent, fights do occur. As another method of maintaining a calm environment for parents, administration developed a code name for fights. Never would someone come over the walkie-talkie and say, "There's a fight in room 116! There's a fight in room 116!," inciting anyone that can hear a walkie-talkie (including students) to become upset. Instead, the first person who knew would simply say, "Charlie Jones is in room 116." A small change, indeed, but this was another important change for Mrs. Collins when it came to providing a positive environment for parents.

When trying to improve communication with parents on an individual basis, parent conferences are extremely important. Whenever possible, allowing parents to meet with all of their child's teachers at one time allows them to fully understand the school's expectations of their child, as well as ask questions which should be answered by all teachers (Papalewis & Fortune, 2002). Mrs. Collins and the team decided to change the school's schedule so that teams of teachers could be available to meet with parents as a group twice each week. The conferences were scheduled by the guidance counselor and attended by all of the child's teachers, the guidance counselor, and sometimes the assistant principal. Parent conferences with teams of teachers took place in classrooms. This allowed parents to see their child's learning environment and feel comfortable with where they spent six-and-a-half hours each day.

Other methods for improving and increasing school and family interaction were also implemented. Each student was given an agenda book for recording homework. Whenever possible, teachers explained to parents that it was important to check the agenda book each night and both teachers and parents used the agenda book to correspond with one another. Teachers were encouraged to make positive phone calls to families as often as possible. A local professional basketball team donated season tickets and each game was distributed to students that showed strong work ethic, also increasing positive interaction with families. Finally, administrators and counselors started visiting families at home when their students were struggling and families could not make it into the school.

Mrs. Collins understood negative interactions with parents would be handled by the assistant principals or the teacher or department. Within these negative interactions, relationships between families and the school would either improve or worsen. Mrs. Collins made sure she had two assistant principals and a teacher of deportment that worked well with parents. The teacher of deportment was fluent in Spanish and a former principal of a school in Puerto Rico. He was able to significantly improve the school's interaction with Latino families. Both assistant principals understood the nuances of working with parents through difficult situations. As Payne (2006) presents, the following techniques are needed to work well with parents of students in poverty (pp. 13-16):

- Greet parents as Mr. or Mrs. at all times.
- Identify your intent in the meeting and make sure that your non-verbal cues reflect this intent. Parents from poverty form their opinion of you based on your non-verbal cues in the situation.
- Use humor, but never sarcasm.
- Deliver bad news through a story, rather than stating the bad news directly.
- If you're comfortable using casual register, use it, if you're not, don't!
- Be human and don't be afraid to admit that you don't have all of the answers.
- Emphasize that there are two sets of rules: one for school and work and another outside of school and work.

Mrs. Collins' assistant principals dedicated themselves to the list above, working to positively engage parents as often as possible, even when discussing negative situations regarding their child. Despite the changes noted, there were many challenges with families in the first four months at Lincoln Middle School. Administrators and teachers often realized that many parents harbored great distrust toward the school, even amidst the changes. Any bad news that needed to be delivered to parents was often met with comments such as "This is why I never wanted my kid to come to that school!" or "This is why I hate Lincoln. I need to get my kid out of there!" All school staff quickly became experts at explaining to parents that the school had changed drastically since the previous year. Parents were constantly reminded that new personnel were ready to work *with* them to ensure a high quality of education for their child. When parents were extremely upset, they were quickly invited to come to the school and to meet with whomever necessary. The goal was to increase face-to-face interaction between parents and staff, as well as increase the amount of time that parents spent in the school. In turn, trust could be built in order to break down the defenses caused by the years of failing.

It must be noted that working with families is a constant endeavor. In an urban school, this endeavor can be the most positive part of the day, or the most negative. It was no different at Lincoln in the first four months of change. Families from poverty carry much stress, as well as many different feelings toward school. There were moments when parents of students whom had difficulties in previous years championed the effort of the staff in creating a new environment. There were also moments when school staff felt completely hopeless in their interactions with parents. One afternoon, an hour after school was dismissed, the assistant principals of Lincoln had to break up a fight in the front of the building in which the family of one student (six adults total) were beating up two other students.

This story is only meant to highlight how complicated the relationship between schools and families can be in an urban, failing school. The assistant principals were nervous for themselves in this moment, but were more nervous for the students facing such an attack. At the end of the day, here was just one more school-family relationship that needed some mending, as so many others did as well.

As for the leadership team's examination of the staff's belief system in regard to parents and families, the results of four months of observation were primarily positive. Many teachers reached out to families on a daily basis, truly viewing them as key partners in the pursuit of academic achievement. The entire eighth grade teaching staff even put together a parent night that went far beyond traditional open houses. The teachers called parents individually to invite them to the event, planned a multitude of activities, and collaborated with students to create a night that would be enjoyable and educational for all.

There were, of course, some instances in which parents became upset with teachers. Usually this was due to simple breakdowns in communication between teachers and parents, as well as parents that were still harboring extremely negative feelings toward the school. There were also instances in which teachers became lost in their frustration with students after having negative experiences with their parents. But overall, the staff proved that they were ready to move forward on a larger scale with family engagement.

To engage families long-term, more must be done at Lincoln. According to Constantino (2008), "In order for any organization to benefit from family engagement, a belief that family engagement will improve student achievement must be present" (p. 19). Lincoln Middle School has this belief, but there is no prescribed form of familial involvement (Papalewis & Fortune, 2002). What is most important is a dedication by both schools and families to working together to improve student achievement (Papalewis & Fortune, 2002). Moving forward with family engagement after the first four months, the team's goal became to start building the social capital of parents. Social capital refers to building the knowledge, unity, and involvement of large numbers of parents. Building social capital in parents can lead to significantly increased engagement and increased student achievement (Constantino, 2008; Noguera, 2005). The Leadership Team met in December and decided to form a committee of teachers in January dedicated to moving this initiative into the next phase. The Leadership Team was clear: collaboration with families had improved, but there was much more difficult work ahead if family engagement was going to reach a higher level.

Conclusion

By focusing on collaboration between the school and families, the school culture at Lincoln Middle School has started to improve in just four months. As Constantino (2008) states: "In the early days of any organization, people set the tone, shape, and direction of the organizational culture. As the organization matures, the culture shapes the people" (p. 18). Such is the process being started at Lincoln Middle School. With an increase in student achievement being the goal, teachers, administrators, and families are working together to create collaboration that promotes student improvement. More than any other factor, the growing collaboration between parents, teachers, and administrators will ultimately determine whether Lincoln Middle School is able to improve.

References

Constantino, S. (2008). *101 ways to create real family engagement*. Galax, VA: Engage! Press.

Evans, R. (2001). *The human side of school change: Reform, resistance, and the real-life problems of innovation*. San Francisco, CA: Jossey Bass.

Gray, S. P. & Streshly, W. A. (2008). *From good schools to great schools: What their principals do well*. Thousand Oaks, CA: Corwin Press.

Hargreaves, A. (1997). *Rethinking educational change with heart and mind: ASCD Yearbook*. Alexandria, VA: Association for Supervision and Curriculum Development.

Henderson, A. T., Mapp, K. L., Johnson, V. R., & Davies, D. (2007). *Beyond the bake sale; The essential guide to family-school partnerships*. New York, NY: The New Press.

Ingram, A. (2010). Springfield Public Schools: Creating a culture of educational excellence. *The District Management Journal*. Winter, 2011 (6): 14-22.

Noguera, P. (2003). *City schools and the American dream: Reclaiming the promise of public education*. New York, NY: Teachers College Press.

Papalewis, R. & Fortune, R. (2002). *Leadership on purpose: Promising practices for African American and Hispanic students*. Thousand Oaks, CA: Corwin Press, Inc.

Payne, R. (2006). *Working with parents: Building relationships for student success*. Highlands, TX: aha! Process, Inc.

Phelps, P. H. (2008). Helping teachers become leaders. *The Clearing House*, 81 (3): 119-122.

Rhee, M. (2010, December 13). What I've learned: The challenges facing our schools. *Newsweek*, 36-41.

Reeves, D. B. (2006). *The learning leader: How to focus school improvement for better results.* Alexandria, VA: Association for Supervision and Curriculum Development.

Rhodes, J. E., Camic, P. M., Milburn, M., & Lowe, S. R. (2009). Improving middle school climate through teacher-centered change. *Journal of Community Psychology* 37 (6): 711-724.

Wagner, J., Keegan, R., Lahey, L., & Lemons, R.W. (2006). *Change leadership: A practical guide to transforming our schools.* San Francisco, CA: Jossey-Bass.

Whitaker, T. (2003). *What great principals do differently: Fifteen things that matter most.* Larchmont, NY: Eye On Education.

Author Note
Timothy Allen, CAGS

Timothy Allen is currently the principal of a new middle school in Springfield, Massachusetts. Prior to assuming this position, he was an assistant principal at two large, urban middle schools. He has also been a middle school English teacher, an elementary school teacher in the Bronx, and an English teacher in a juvenile detention center. He is currently an Ed.D student in educational leadership at American International College and he has earned a C.A.G.S. certificate from University of Massachusetts at Amherst in school administration, a M.A. from Columbia University Teachers College in developmental psychology, and a B.A. from Wheaton College of Massachusetts in psychology.

NOTES

NOTES

CHAPTER FIFTEEN

A Case Study in Collaboration: The Orange Elementary School

By: Paul Burnam

Introduction

Hope. It became the word that staff and families from the Orange Elementary Schools used as a unifying theme for working together. It provided the foundation for what has become a six-year process for schools, families, and community agencies to rally around. It spawned a belief that whatever else has happened to parents, grandparents, and great-grand parents, life could be different in the future for our children. For the past seven years, the Orange Elementary Schools have been striving to address many of the underlying factors that have precluded hopes and dreams from being part of a child's upbringing. We have been collaborating with human service providers and State agencies to address these underlying factors, and to support systems changes in the social and economic culture of the region. We are striving to make hopes and dreams a regular component of family life and futures. We are striving to move hope to expectation. As one author so appropriately stated, "Hope is a muscle!" Our efforts, however, are severely under funded and hampered by pervasive poverty and the multi-generational and socio-economic conditions of a poor rural community.

The North Quabbin Area includes the nine towns of Athol, Erving, New Salem, Orange, Phillipston, Petersham, Royalston, Warwick and Wendell, with a combined population of 27,004 (U.S. Census, 2000). The following demographic and socio-economic data on the region comes largely from a systematic community needs assessment conducted by the North Quabbin Community Coalition (NQCC) in 2002. The North Quabbin region is a rural area with two rural economic centers -- Athol and Orange. These two towns have the largest populations in the area and are the most densely populated, but still have fewer than 350 people per square mile. This nine-town region is spread over 344 square miles, with five towns having fewer than 30 people per square mile. There is little ethnic/racial diversity and only a small percentage of new immigrants, with limited English proficiency. Three of the nine towns (Athol, Orange, and Erving) are among the 50 poorest towns in Massachusetts, according to U.S Census 2000 data. The region is geographically isolated and has faced economic depression for over 15 years. Through the first 75 years of the 20th century, agriculture and manufacturing provided the principal employment. In the last part of the 20th century, many of the manufacturing sector jobs were no longer available because of a large plant closing and other downsizing activities. A large proportion of the population has been affected during the past 20 years by unemployment and under employment. People living in the smaller towns still remain isolated from both education programs and other services. Primary data collected from human service providers and adult education providers shows that many current and past students have parents or other family members without a high school diploma. All but one town in the region had an unemployment rate above the state unemployment rate of 4.5% for the first half of 2002 (the year of the comprehensive community needs assessment). In recent years, these trends have remained largely the same. The total number of births to women age 15-19 in the Athol-Orange area stood at 41 per 1,000 for 2006, compared with 21 per 1,000 statewide. Teen data from the 2000 U. S. Census showed, for example, that 19% of 16-19 year-olds in Orange were not in school or had not graduated.

Needs as They Persist throughout Orange and North Quabbin

At present, the region is characterized by an alarming set of demographic statistics. Each individual statistic about Orange, Massachusetts illustrates a specific need. But the full story cannot be seen in the totality of the statistics, which paint a picture of long-term, multi-generational family distress and despair. This despair affects children's readiness for public school and their ability to learn. This despair affects the capacity of the community and its schools to support the health, well being, and safety of children and their families. This despair contributes to a culture that compromises the health and safety of our students, both in and out of school. Only through well-funded, comprehensive services can the underlying causes be addressed so that our children can develop socially, emotionally, and academically and reach their potential. (Ruby Payne, *A Framework for Understanding Poverty*, 1998)

Economically, Orange is listed among the 25 poorest communities in Massachusetts. According to the 2000 Census data, Orange ranked 332nd out of the commonwealth's 351 communities in median household income. Over 80% of the public school budget comes from State Aid and the town is listed among the 10 communities with the least capacity for supporting public education. The unemployment rate consistently runs well above the state average, and typically the available jobs are neither ideal nor career oriented. Many are minimum wage, with low or no benefits. Others are only part-time opportunities. . Among the nine towns in the North Quabbin region, Orange has the highest percentage of adults without a high school diploma (20.4%). The percentage was even higher in past census data.

In the Orange Elementary Schools, approximately 60% of the children receive Free/Reduced Lunch -- one of the federal government's primary indicators of poverty. The Orange Elementary Schools also provide Universal Free Breakfast, primarily to make sure our children begin the day with a healthy meal. Because of the clear correlation between a healthy diet and school achievement, the Orange Elementary Schools place great emphasis on student nutrition and meals. In addition to Universal Free Breakfast, we offer a mid-morning Fresh Fruit Snack, and a nutritionally approved lunch. Further, all children attending our after-school programs (free for low-income children) are provided with a drink and a healthy snack. Finally, as part of our food service program we run a Summer Feeding Program in seventeen different sites, providing breakfast and lunch to many families throughout the community. The end result of all these efforts is that the Orange Elementary Schools offer year-round food programs for children and families.

Collectively, these various programs provide students with the basic foundations for life skills and environmental understanding as well as a framework for lifelong change. At the same time, there are limitations and inescapable realities associated with the poverty and economics of a rural area. The uncertain economic base, combined with high unemployment and underemployment, make our children very dependent on the elementary schools for meals and food. With transportation being a major barrier for many poor families, access to supermarkets and fresh food is very difficult. Consequently, many low-income families are forced to do their weekly shopping at neighborhood convenience stores – with virtually no thought about nutrition and health. There is a perceptible disconnecting between learning, education and activities at school and what is practiced at home. The two worlds can be strikingly different, to the detriment of the children who live in those homes. Research has long showed a high correlation between children with learning disabilities and poor diet. (Mass Department of Public Health, 2002; 2005; 2008)

When looking at statistics regarding children in the Orange Elementary Schools, there is an unquestioned need to formally and structurally address the social, behavioral, and child development needs of the student population. Based on data for the 2008-2009 school year (and continuing at the same projected rate for the 2009-2010 school year), approximately 55% of the student population is living below the poverty level. In addition, approximately 17% of the children (and their families) can be classified as homeless based on the guidelines of McKinney-Vento Act, and 30 – 35% of entering kindergarten students are exposed to violence, traumatic, and violent situations prior to the start of the school year. (North Quabbin Study 2006) Research from the Massachusetts Advocates for Children: Trauma and Learning Policy Initiative and the Task Force on Children Affected by Domestic Violence illustrate the direct impacts of violence and trauma on student achievement. "Traumatic experiences have the power to undermine the development of linguistic and communicative skills, thwart the establishment of a coherent sense of self, and compromise the ability to attend to classroom tasks and instructions, organize and remember new information, and grasp cause-and-effect relationships – all of which are necessary to process information effectively. Trauma can interfere with the capacity for creative play, which is one of the ways children learn how to cope with the realities of their everyday life; and it can adversely affect the ability to have good peer and adult relationships." (Massachusetts Advocates for Children: *Helping Traumatized Children Learn*, 2005)   Additionally, experts in the field of child development, brain development, and families have been working to quantify data and statistics relative to family distress and student learning. "Research now shows that trauma (and domestic distresses) can undermine children's ability to learn, form relationships, and function appropriately in the classroom. Schools, which are significant communities for children and teachers ---the primary role models in these communities---, must be given the supports they need to address trauma's impact on learning". (Massachusetts Advocates for Children: *Helping Traumatized Children Learn*, 2005)

In FY 2007 and FY 2008, teachers in the Orange Elementary Schools were asked to list characteristics of trauma, domestic violence, poverty, and other social indicators affecting learning for the children in their classrooms. Much of the information could be easily obtained from student records (confidential), information from law enforcement, state agencies, and human service and mental health providers. All information was kept confidential. The intent was to develop more accurate profiles of our classrooms and the needs of children. We also wanted a more accurate portrait of classroom needs and the complex social and emotional issues teachers and paraprofessionals must deal with to support student success – academically, socially, and developmentally. The surveying process identified approximately 15 factors related to poverty, domestic distress, and social needs that could be checked for any child. It is also known from research on domestic and family distress that a child with three or more check marks would probably be dealing with serious impediments to learning and success in schools (J. Ristuccia 2007). For most of our classrooms, the survey made it clear that social interventions and programs are an imperative within our schools and classrooms. It also illustrated our glaring need for personnel with the qualifications and experience to effectively meet the social and emotional needs of our children while maintaining a positive learning environment for all. (See Appendix for survey)

Within our schools, these scenarios are often manifested in students' behavior. We can point to examples that occur each and every day: Frequent outbursts - The 'explosive child'; A child's inability to adapt and/or understand the social construct of a classroom or the school; A child who has not experienced enough appropriate social situations to formulate an internal system of right and wrong or even appropriate behavior. The list goes on and on. Far too many of the children entering our kindergartens have not had family and/or social experiences that generate the kinds of internal responses to distinguish differences in social situations. Too many children do not even know how to act developmentally appropriate in a classroom, in the cafeteria, with other children on the playground, in the school library, or in other areas throughout the schools. Just as immigrant children often live in two differing worlds of school and home, many of our children in Orange live under comparable conditions. And the two worlds can often be quite different in expectations, beliefs and values, consequences, and social behaviors.

The cumulative impact of these statistics point to a need within the Orange Elementary Schools to provide an extensive array of school-based services to promote positive mental health strategies. These services will help children cope effectively with these issues, grow and develop in healthy ways, achieve academic and social success throughout the school environment. During the past few years, our schools have collaborated with area mental health providers to improve services to children. We have piloted collaborative programs with State and local agencies engaged with children and family services. We have hosted family programs to nurture family members while also promoting positive strategies for family harmony and literacy. We have established regular meetings with State agencies and area providers to better address the needs of children and their families. We are integral to the newly established Children's Behavioral Health Initiative (CBHI) in Massachusetts, which specifically targets the mental health needs of families and access to services. Many of our school-based professional development programs address issues related to trauma, explosive children, positive behavior in school, Responsive Classroom, and specific trainings on the individual diagnosis for extreme behaviors.

The Philosophy and Culture of the Schools

The Mission Statement for the Orange Elementary Schools includes the following three goals. We believe that our challenge is to operationalize programs and services for all children. We recognize the difficulties our schools and families confront daily. We always maintain high expectations for all children regarding academic and social performance.
1. All children can and will be successful;
2. All our programs and activities must be designed with best practices for children;
3. We must maintain unconditional respect and acceptance of all children.

Developing the Competencies to Effectively Support all Families, Especially At-Risk Families

Within the Orange Elementary Schools, a great deal of time and energy has been expended on Professional Development activities and programs so teachers and staff can be effective teachers of our academic curriculum. We have had a longtime focus on specific academic subject matter programs as well as effective instructional practices for teaching children. Since the adoption of Education Reform legislation in 1993, the expectations associated with successful student performance on MCAS and other standardized assessment measures have been part of the culture of education and learning throughout Massachusetts.

Every year, professional development time is devoted to student achievement, academic subject matter and achievement expectations. Children are prepared to know and understand the curriculum materials while also becoming successful test takers.

Concurrent with this approach is the essential need to support children and families who are not socially and/or emotionally equipped for success in our schools. Given the long-term economic realities facing Orange and the entire North Quabbin region, there is a strong need to help all children develop the competencies and strategies to be successful in our schools. The achievement of this objective is extremely complex and difficult and often takes a two-pronged approach. A considerable amount of training and staffing resources must be available throughout the schools to effectively meet the social/emotional needs of children so they may find academic and social success. Additionally, resources need to be available for serving families so they may grow in their capacity to also assist children.

Cultural Context of Rural Multi-Generational Poverty and Social Needs

Rural poverty is very different from urban poverty. The causes, implications, resources, programs, local impacts, immediate services, and context all vary from urban area to rural locations. In brief, poverty in urban locations can often be seen as temporary, situational, and serviced by a wide array of agencies, programs and local resources. Rural poverty, according to Ruby Payne, is much more multi-generational, chronic, closely tied to mental health issues and low literacy, and often accompanied by a lack of local resources and services. In rural poverty, solutions are often quite easy to determine. However, because resources are not available -- and frequently have not existed for a considerable period of time --

the solutions are not simple to implement. Nor are they well accepted or valued.

One common indicator of success in our programs is increased interaction, added trust, and stronger relationships with families. During the past several years, our schools have maintained a strong commitment and focus that values parental participation and builds trust. Regardless of background, parents and guardians are actively recruited for participation and input into programs and services.

Impact of State and Local Budgets on School-Based Services

In 2003, the Orange Elementary Schools had six full-time counselors. With two counselors per building, there were professionals in each school building to deal with the counseling, therapy, and social-emotional needs of students, while also being able to address the unpredictable outbursts and 'explosions' (*The Explosive Child,* Dr. Ross Greene, 2001) that often occur with a population of children with significant therapeutic needs. During this time, our district was able to provide in-class social skills programs and activities for children and staff. We were able to help children identify their challenges and work towards establishing and introducing strategies for effectively coping with, and overcoming, some of these concerns. We were able to provide in-school consultative services between counselor and teacher to develop and promote behavior programs, or at least plans, to deal with disruptive behaviors. However, severe budget reductions during the past six years have reduced this model to only two full-time counselors. The recognition of the need to collaborate with area human service providers, mental health specialist, and state agencies became a priority for our capacity to meet the social and emotional needs of children and their families.

Addressing Mental Health Problems: Prevention, Detection, Intervention and Treatment

The Orange Elementary Schools have been active participants in the North Quabbin Community Coalition, an umbrella activist group providing human service and mental health coordination to North Quabbin communities. During this time, we have expanded our linkages and relationships to include smaller coalitions of area community mental health agencies, State agencies, and behavioral specialists addressing specific mental health needs of our children and families.

We have established case coordination strategies and service models with mental health providers, state agencies, and the schools. As a result of a state class action suit, our region presently has funds for emergency mental health services, Family Stabilization Teams, and Intensive Case Coordination programs. A collaborative infrastructure of schools and area providers has finally been established to deliver the long-term system of care that many of our families will require if change is to occur. The crisis services – coordinated through schools and area providers - have included Community Based Health Initiatives, Mobile Crisis, and Behavior and Mental Health Screenings. Grant funds would enable us to further expand these linkages and develop a much more efficient service delivery model, with screenings and crisis response protocols assigned to appropriate professional staff.

In public schools throughout the country, there is a generally acceptable norm for appropriate school and classroom behavior. Schools and classrooms regularly begin their school year by establishing and reinforcing a set of acceptable practices for children's behavior – together with a set of consequences for unacceptable behavior. Administration, staff, and school committees form policies and procedures regarding these school practices. In that respect, the Orange Elementary Schools are like schools throughout the state and nation. Our school year begins with a concerted effort to establish a common understanding of expectations. Traditionally, school districts have used a variety of strategies and methodologies to deal with children's behavior. Most are based on accepted principles of child development, group interactions, individual expectations, and established sets of behaviors, norms, actions, and consequences. Most of these policies and procedures are also based on knowledge of child development and a common understanding of expectations for all children. Yet, it is very common to see far too many children entering our doors without the experiences or supportive environments to foster successful interactions and behavior in our schools. It is very common to see far too many children entering our doors with violent and traumatic upbringings. These experiences have altered and skewed their set of norms regarding the behaviors that will foster successful, positive interactions and relationships. They have also had a negative effect on students' assimilation into our school environment. It has also become very common for the Orange Elementary Schools to spend an inordinate amount of time and energy intervening in the social milieu of our student body to ensure children receive the academic instruction and supports that will foster success throughout their public school careers.

The district has been sponsoring Professional Development opportunities for staff in Responsive Classroom. This scientifically based approach fosters teaching skills that emphasize social, emotional, and academic growth in a strong, safe school community. Developed by classroom teachers in 1981, the approach consists of practical strategies for helping children build academic and social-emotional competencies day in and day out. Based on evaluations of the model to date, schools are reporting increased student engagement and academic progress, along with fewer discipline problems. With the commitment to Responsive Classroom growing, Fisher Hill Elementary School currently has a principal with extensive training and leadership in its strategies. In addition, a Study Group has been formed to provide leadership toward becoming a Responsive Classroom School. The model has proven successful in improving social development, academic progress, school-home partnerships, and school climate and culture.

During the 2009 – 2010 school year, the Orange Elementary Schools received funding to support training and implementation of Tools of the Mind for both Pre-K and Kindergarten classrooms. This literacy-based program is also designed to develop children's cognitive skills of executive function, self-regulation, memory and focused attention. Our district is very excited about the potential for children's social and academic success through this model.

Innovative & Promising Practices

Tools of the Mind and Responsive Classroom are among the programs that are critical to the success of all children in the Orange Elementary Schools. For the past five years, our district has supported teachers and support staff with professional development activities relating to the tiered levels of Responsive Classroom expertise. Despite diminished funds, about a third of our teaching staff has had the opportunity to complete at least Level I of the Responsive Classroom training.

For our Pre-School and Kindergarten classrooms, Tools of the Mind offers a strong research-based early childhood program that builds foundations for school success in preschool and kindergarten children by promoting intentional and self-regulated learning. Tools of the Mind is an early childhood education curriculum based on the work of L. S. Vygotsky – a social psychologist who views learning as active play that is socially mediated by teachers and classmates. The curriculum seeks to develop cognitive skills such as self-regulation, deliberate memory, and focused attention, while also cultivating academic skills such as symbolic thought, literacy, and mathematical understanding. The curriculum views play as the leading skill-development activity for young children and emphasize the teacher's role in supporting the development of mature, intentional dramatic play. A growing body of research indicates that many children are not ready to learn when they start school --not because they do not know their letters or numbers but because they lack the critical ability to self-regulate their social, emotional and cognitive behaviors. Current research shows that self-regulation – often called executive function – has a stronger association with academic achievement than IQ or entry-level reading or math skills. Historically, we were not sure of the needs of these children, or what an effective intervention strategy should be. Additionally, children were often mislabeled as special needs when in essence the issue was knowledge and skills.

Research indicates that interventions at the early childhood level can have a positive influence on self-regulation and the development of executive function in the early years and beyond. Findings from classrooms utilizing Tools of the Mind demonstrate far longer time on task, fewer discipline and referrals for children, and far fewer classroom disruptions from teacher instruction and interactions with the children. A 2009 research study from Rutgers University (Barnett, et. al; *Educational Effects of the Tools of the Mind Curriculum, 2009*) confirmed these findings in a three-year study. In a Tools Classroom:

- of self-regulation from being regulated by others, to engaging in "shared" regulation, to eventually becoming "masters of their own behavior;"
- Children gain control of the social, emotional, and cognitive behaviors by learning how to use a variety of "mental tools;"
- Teaching of early literacy and mathematics emphasizes building underlying cognitive competencies such as reflective thinking and metacognition;
- Children practice self-regulated learning throughout the day by engaging in a variety of specifically designed, developmentally appropriate self-regulation activities;
- Children learn to regulate their own behaviors, as well as the behaviors of their friends, as they enact increasingly more complex scenarios in their imaginary play in preschool and in learning activities in kindergarten.

Why are these programs important to Orange? Regulating behavior follows naturally from the ability to regulate one's feelings. If a child recognizes her/his feelings, and can choose the right and appropriate response to a situation with the right intensity, appropriate behaviors are more likely to follow. A child is in control of her/his behavior when she/he connects the behavior to the underlying feeling and experiences that drive it. The child must also be able to make her/his emotional and behavioral response fit within socially acceptable expectations (e.g. classroom/school building norms). Interpreting and understanding these classroom expectations can be further complicated when they differ from the norms of the culture of the students.

For a child exposed to violence and trauma, many behaviors result from survival-driven motivations: fight, flight, freeze. The child is often unaware of the fears that trigger these survival instincts. On the surface, the aggressive, withdrawn, or argumentative behavior may appear unwarranted for the situation or motivated by manipulation or conscious desire to antagonize. Thus, a teacher can be more effective by appreciating patterns and learning the situations that set off a child. Armed with these critical skills, the teacher can help a child become more aware of how to remain in control of her/his behavior. It can also help teachers design a behavior management system that is sensitive to the underlying issues driving problem behaviors. It is our contention that a program like Tools of the Mind would provide the framework for child and teacher development and success. Tools of the Mind would provide children with the skills for success, skills for understanding situations so that self-regulation skills would become an effective strategy for long-term social and academic success in and out of school.

School Practices that Encourage and Support, while Valuing Family Values and Traditions

The Responsive Classroom approach is a way of teaching that emphasizes social, emotional, and academic growth in a strong and safe school community. Developed by classroom teachers, the approach consists of practical strategies for helping children build academic and social-emotional competencies day in and day out. Educators using these strategies report increased student engagement in learning, stronger academic progress, and fewer discipline problems. The approach is informed by educational research and follows seven guiding principles:
- The social curriculum is as important as the academic curriculum;
- How children learn is as important as what they learn: Process and content go hand in hand;
- The greatest cognitive growth occurs through social interaction;
- To be successful academically and socially, children need a set of social skills: cooperation, assertion, responsibility, empathy, and self-control;
- Knowing the children we teach – individually, culturally, and developmentally – is as important as knowing the content we teach;
- Knowing the families of the children we teach, and working with them as partners, is essential to children's education;
- How the adults at school work together is as important as their individual competence: Lasting change begins with the adult community.

The Responsive Classroom approach has had a very positive impact on both the social and academic growth of children. A longitudinal study by Dr. Sara Rimm-Kaufman of schools currently practicing Responsive Classroom approach highlighted six key findings about children and teachers:
1. Children showed greater increases in reading and math test scores;
2. Teachers felt more effective and more positive about teaching;
3. Children demonstrated better social skills;
4. Teachers offered more high-quality instruction;
5. Children felt more positive about school;
6. Teachers collaborated with each other more.

Goals, Outcomes, and Hope

Through the collaborative efforts of our schools, and our focus on literacy and well-being as crucial to a child's success both in and out of school, our goals are to enhance change and change models through the strengths of our children. Our goals are to support our efforts with families through the demonstration of positive change and the success of children. Our goals are to empower children and their families through the clear recognition of the strengths within and throughout each family. Confronting and overcoming generational issues and distress is a daunting challenge. Seeing and realizing the potential through children illustrates that potential in positive and non-threatening strategies. Our possibilities are about watching children grow and develop in very positive and strength-based ways. Our possibilities are through supporting adults and their families to recognize and support the success of their children. Our possibilities are to demonstrate to adults and their families the potential for recognizing hope when our children are succeeding academically, socially, and emotionally.

As we can demonstrate the academic progress and growth of all our children, as we can demonstrate the diminishing of behavior and disciplinary problems in our schools, and as we can work with our students to master the skills for lifelong success, our goals for promoting hope will become more of an expectation than a dream.

References

Barnett, et. al; (2009) – Rutgers University, *Educational Effects of the Tools of the Mind Curriculum,*

Greene, R. (2001 – 3rd Edition) *The Explosive Child.* New York, Harper Paperbacks

Massachusetts Advocates for Children. (2005) *Helping Traumatized Children Learn: A Report and Policy Agenda.*

Massachusetts Advocates for Children. (2007) *Educational Rights of Children Affected by Homelessness and /or Domestic Violence.*

Massachusetts Department of Public Health. (2002, 2005, 2008) *Survey of Characteristics of At-Risk Children in Massachusetts.*

North Quabbin Community Coalition (2006) Dr. Rebecca Bielecki, editor. *Assessment of Social and Economic Factors of Families in North Quabbin Communities* (Unpublished)

Payne, R. (2003 – 3rd Edition) *A Framework for Understanding Poverty.* Houston, Tex. Aha Process Inc.

Payne, R. (2000) *Bridges Out of Poverty: Strategies for Professionals and Communities.* Houston, Tex. Aha Process Inc.

Rimm-Kaufman, S. (2008). The Responsive Classroom Efficacy Study. US Department of Education, Institute for Education Sciences

Author Note
Paul Burnam, EdD.

Dr. Paul Burnam recently retired as Superintendent of Schools in Orange, Massachusetts where he spent the past eight years. He has a thirty plus year experience in education - including school adminsitrative positions, the Massachusetts Department of Education, Adjunct Faculty at UMass/Amherst, and educational research positions overseas. His BA, MEd and EdD are all from the University of Massachusetts. In addition, Dr. Burnam has received numerous education awards and recognition for his work with underserved populations, disadvantaged students, and adult learners.

NOTES

NOTES

CHAPTER SIXTEEN

Free Union Country School:
A Portrait of Community Caring

By: Sarah Goodbar

Introduction

Progressive education is a large field encompassing a host of theories and goals (Kohn, 2008), which aim to make schools more democratic and child centered (John Dewey Project). One of the core tenets of progressive education is that students be seen as whole people and unconditionally valued members of the community. Thus a reasonable starting point for any progressive school is to invest heavily (in the short and long term) in community building, a tall order in any setting and particularly in public schools where economics, overcrowding, and the loud cry for accountability above all else can hamper even the best teachers' efforts (Top Five Reasons why Public Schools Are Failing Our Children, 2007). There are, however, progressive practices and principals that can enrich any classroom.

The "Responsive Classroom" approach developed by the Northeast Foundation for Children offers an array of classroom tools and school-wide initiatives that help educators turn schools into communities. In a longitudinal study on responsive classrooms, several key findings revealed how they help create community and enrich the learning process. The research indicates that both teachers and children feel more positive about school; that children have increased social skills; that a higher quality education is offered; that teacher collaboration is increased, and, finally, that children do better in reading and math assessments (Rimm-Kaufman, 2004).

Calling a classroom "responsive" generally implies that it is built on community-minded routines, like a morning meeting, cooperative rule creation, positive teacher language, logical consequences, guided discovery, academic choice, working with families, and collaborative problem solving (Responsive Classroom, 2011). Behind these routines we find many progressive assumptions, including the belief that the social curriculum is as important as the academic curriculum; that how children learn is as important as what they learn; that cognitive growth happens most effectively through social interaction; and that knowing the children as whole people is essential to successful teaching (Introducing the *Responsive Classroom* Approach, 2009). Situated squarely within the venerable progressive approach and laden with practical teacher-ready solutions, the responsive classroom approach is gaining traction. My own experience of a school that has fully embraced the responsive approach confirms what the preliminary research suggests. When applied with skill and patience, the principals of the responsive classroom offer children an education of the highest quality.

The Individual in the Community

By the time my daughter was four, I knew I couldn't send her to the local public school, and not just for her sake, either. I had taught in a public school one county away from our home and had struggled with students like her, very smart with ADHD. Bored by the standardized materials, struggling to sit still for hours on end, these "unique" kids were almost impossible to deal with. I didn't want my child to be something that had to be "dealt with" at all. When we decided to keep her in the independent school where she attended preschool, our decision was largely based on class size. In a small school like this, we reasoned, the teachers will have the resources they need to (hopefully) keep her engaged and work with her idiosyncrasies. But size has proven to be the most pedestrian of the qualities that has enabled the Free Union Country School to embrace our daughter. The great achievement of this small, rural school is the authentic, deep community it has created for its students, parents, teachers and staff. It is authentic because the bonds that exist between the people of the school are real and transcend the context in which they were forged. It is deep because the sense of community penetrates to every part of the school and the school day. And because it is an authentic and deep community, the students, participate in that community as whole people, not exclusively as "learners." The importance of this cannot be overemphasized since we all learn differently and with greater or lesser ease. Students at Free Union, valued as whole people, feel loved by their teachers, respected and valued by their peers, and at home in their school. And this, in the words of Carolyn Lawlor, the Head of the School, allows each child to start each day "fully available for learning."

The Classroom Community

At Free Union, community among students is fostered within the classroom, across grade levels and school wide. Each classroom day begins with a morning meeting in which students greet their teachers and classmates by name (there are several warm or humorous greetings the kids learn to use), share any important news and talk about what the day will hold. The morning meeting is a cornerstone of the Responsive Classroom approach. In practice, morning meeting ensures that a school is not the one place in our culture where even the courtesy of a cordial greeting is denied (cf. "Jamar Jones?" "Here."). It also ensures that students reach out to each other (literally, with a handshake) across the social spectrum. "There is," as Roxanne Kriete writes in *The Morning Meeting Book,* "an equity and safety in having a structure for the greeting. . .Within a classroom community, starting a day by hearing your name spoken with respect and warmth is not a privilege which lands upon just the popular few" (2006, p.39).

The morning message, handwritten on oversized paper for all to see, welcomes the children, and tells them what's in store for the day. In my daughter's kindergarten, before the school day begins, kids read the morning message (also an NEFC hallmark) with (or to) their parents. Later, when the message is read aloud at morning meeting (notice how this reading lesson is seamlessly integrated into the social activities that begin the day) every student, regardless of reading level, has the confidence to follow along and add to the discussion. Even attendance is made a matter of substance and a locus for social interaction in the Free Union classroom. Kids hurry over to the whiteboard first thing to answer the question of the day, usually something along the lines of "Do you like snow?" or "Have you ever ridden a pony?" Students velcro their names into the yes or no column, thus creating the attendance list; but this morning question also supplies meaningful fodder for conversation, connects kids to each other, and brings their experiences from outside the school into the classroom.

Within the kindergarten classroom, the children are referred to as "friends." You might hear Alice, the head teacher, give an invitation with this word: "Friends, will you all join me on the rug?" Or you might hear it when a conflict is being processed: " Jen, it sounds like your friend David was looking at that book when you picked it up." This subtle message of fellowship, reinforced countless times a day, works brilliantly because it is age-appropriate (imagine telling an eighth-grader who her friends are) and because a standard of friendliness and camaraderie is set at the beginning of the year that makes this affirmation of friendship essentially valid. But creating an environment of fellowship takes planning and work. In fact, the only time parental involvement in the classroom at Free Union is discouraged is in the first month of the school year when teachers at each grade level hunker down within their classrooms painstakingly establishing and reinforcing the routines that will create a classroom culture that is respectful and friendly.

By the time I had *my* first visit to a morning meeting, every kindergartener already knew, for example, the hand sign for "big-kid connection." This is a silent signal kids can give each other in place of the more familiar outburst of "Hey, he took my idea!" Here's how it works: during a unit on ants, Alice might ask the class, "Who remembers how many eyes an ant has?" When Ella is called on and answers, "Five!" the other kids who also had their hands raised can flash Ella the big-kid connection sign. It's a way of saying, "Wow, look at that: we're both big kids and knew the answer!" Those who didn't get to say the answer aloud now feel a connection to the student who did. They also know that the teacher appreciates what they know, and, crucially, the discussion goes on uninterrupted. This thoughtful tool and countless others like it help teachers at Free Union avoid a competitive model of education in favor of a collaborative one. Although you find conflict and classroom struggles in any school, the impression one has at Free Union is of a disarmingly utopian community of children. But when one digs even a little, it immediately becomes evident that this exceptional community is the result of hundreds of carefully made decisions, and a school full of carefully taught children.

The Community of Students

The sense of respect and fellowship found within the kindergarten classroom is also cultivated between grade levels. Once a week, the whole student body comes together for an all-school morning meeting. These begin, like the in-class meetings, with a greeting. (At the last meeting I attended, it was "backwards greeting," i.e., I was greeted with "Goodbar Sarah, Morning Good!") After the greeting, the teachers went through the grades asking if anyone had anything to share. My three year old stood up before the whole group and shared that she went through a dark tunnel at the Port Discovery Museum. A fourth grader told us that they had sacrificed corn and precious obsidian in their "Mayan Simulation" project. A boy told us how tired he was having gotten only twenty minutes of sleep after being awakened by a nightmare, and a girl said (to my daughters' amazement) that she got a real bunny for Easter. The students listened to each other attentively, clapped when a people finished speaking and were equally eager to share news from their homes and classrooms.

Through this weekly meeting, the same substantive connections that are made within the classroom are made across the school. From now on, my daughters will always be able to point across the playground and say, "Hey, she's the girl who got the real bunny for Easter!" These insights into each other's lives help over time to foster friendships across grade levels. Indeed, students do not sit together by grade at the all-school morning meeting, but mingle freely with kids of different ages. Such across-grade friendships are the result of several carefully implemented educational approaches taken by Free Union. First and foremost is the buddy program, the Free Union tradition for which I consistently hear the most exuberant praise from parents and children alike.

From the first days of school, preschoolers are paired with an older buddy from the 2/3 classroom. (I'll have more to say about multi-age classrooms below.) Kindergarteners and first graders are paired with buddies from 4/5. These buddies work together on projects, make special gifts for each other, and play and read together on a weekly basis. The specific pairings of students across grades are not taken lightly. The faculty work together to find buddies whose personalities will be complementary or whose interests align. When I asked one of the teachers about the program I was surprised to find that these all around buddies were once merely reading partners. The older students, though, were losing interest part way through the year. The fact that the faculty recognized this failing and corrected it, without throwing out the baby with the bathwater, is one of the reasons the school in general is so successful. (Public schools are probably at a higher risk of being fickle in their commitment to innovative programs due to the intense pressure they are under to offer immediate results, the limited resources they have for dealing with inevitable contingencies, and the lack of institutional memory concomitant with higher turn-over rates among teachers and staff.) They held to their commitment to creating a school wide community and added craft times, outdoor time, and free time where the buddies could mix with other kids from both grade levels.

Some years the patience and generosity of the older kids, so evident to the parents and to the younger buddies, emerge naturally, but other years older kids have to be nudged in the right direction, providing this progressive school with a prime opportunity to "[help] children become not only good learners but also good people" (Kohn, 2008 ¶.5). And the benefits of this investment are evident. The mother of my three-year-old's buddy told me yesterday that her older son, now eleven, is still friends with his buddy from Free Union, now a sixteen-year-old high school student. Such lasting friendships are a testament to the authenticity of the bonds forged through the buddy system.

The administration and faculty took great pains to make sure that the program was meaningful and transcended designated "buddy time." Among other things, they planned their recess times to overlap across grade levels, a situation many schools strive to avoid at all costs. Moreover, kids are encouraged to "go find your buddy" at recess, at all-school morning meeting, and at special events like all-school lunches. There is an all-school culture at Free Union that is absent in many traditional schools in which the eldest grade is perceived (by the students at least) to rule the school and the relationship between the little fish and the big is essentially one of cowed intimidation on the one hand and boisterous contempt on the other.

Recess does more than just allow kids of different ages to interact, though. It is a time for kids to gain social skills and confidence. For this reason providing ample recess is a commitment at Free Union. A teacher from a nearby public school complained to a faculty member at Free Union that at recess "the kids have just enough time to create a problem and not enough time to solve it." Free Union aims to give kids the time and space to work through their differences and given the long recess, a great deal of problem solving ends up being done by the students on the playground. This is the social equivalent of immersion language learning, and, like the language immersion method, it is the way in which children naturally learn. But in our increasingly scheduled lives, many kids miss out almost entirely on unstructured time with their peers.

Few people would deny the social benefits of recess, but under pressure to meet local and national benchmarks, many teachers and administrators fail see the academic payoff of such a system. Adding twenty minutes on to recess, it is true, will probably not in and of itself increase test scores, but if long recess is incorporated into a unified effort at creating an authentic and deep community, the payoff is clear, because students enter the classroom as a team, ready to learn, ask questions, and take risks. "There are schools that just care how children perform academically," says Carolyn Lawlor, "but you can't separate what's going on emotionally and socially from what's going on academically. If you're worried no one wants to sit next to you, some of your energy for academics is going into anxiety instead." McKenzie Inigo, the first grade teacher, puts it this way, "All of learning is taking risks, asking questions in order to answer bigger ones; if you're worried, you don't ask questions; you don't put yourself out there."

In kindergarten, the teachers hover close by at recess to help students work their way through conflicts and to remind them of the principals of friendship and equality. Teams are not allowed, nor are special boyfriends and girlfriends or boys-only or girls-only clubs. This sets an important precedent that is especially crucial given the extreme bullying culture in many of our schools. Teachers at Free Union do not wait for behavior to become belligerent. The school mandates an environment of authentic respect for every citizen in the community. I use the word "authentic" again to highlight the fact that the faculty is committed to ensuring that the behavioral goals of the school are not just rules to be followed, but principles to live by. The teachers earn the right to hold their students to a high standard of respect by showing their students great respect. Discipline at Free Union is essentially done by conversation and always with the sensible recognition that the student misbehaving is a student who needs help.

As kids get older, they can still bring conflicts to their teachers at Free Union, but increasingly they are encouraged to work through conflicts on their own. In the first grade classroom, a peace table is set up where students sit down and go through a taught process to express their grievances using "I" statements and respectful language. At the beginning of the year, the teacher is there to mentor and facilitate, but by year's end, students will go to the table together of their own accord and sort out their differences. As McKenzie Inigo points out, "you can't prevent conflict, and you wouldn't want to. But you can work with it in a way that is productive."

Combined classrooms are another example of how Free Union creates a community of peers rather than hierarchy of grades. The Free Union model is commonsensical: to begin with, classes are not combined until second grade when normal developmental differences are less extreme than in kindergarten and first grade. All second and third graders belong to one of two mixed-grade homerooms. (The same system in place in the 2/3 classrooms, is repeated in the 4/5 classrooms.) After morning meeting and other classroom business, the students regroup by grade level. One grade heads to math, the other to language arts. After a snack outside, the groups switch. But they don't return to their same teacher for the new subject. Instead, one of the teachers is the math teacher for all students, and the other the language arts teacher. This allows kids to work closely with both teachers and allows the teachers to follow students' progress in one subject area for two years. The grouping for enrichment classes (art, PE, and Spanish) may go by homeroom *or* grade-level and has come to include a special once-a-week PE class that is grouped by gender, which has been very successful. Social studies and science units, meanwhile, are on a two year cycle, so students are combined in other groupings for these units allowing them to mix and remix with their peers and creating a much larger social circle than would have been possible otherwise.

This extremely dynamic structure also allows for every student to be in the position of the new kid in class (as rising second graders or fourth graders) and then the next year to be the experienced mentor. This is one of a number of benefits experienced on the teachers' end of things, but the greatest benefit to the teachers, perhaps, is having another teacher equally invested in the same group of children. Thus two teachers can collaborate, can support each other and troubleshoot without, in the words of Carolyn Lawlor, "being in each other's pockets all day."

Parents in the Community

At Free Union parents are substantively involved in the community. For example, I was recently called on to vote for which fellow kindergarten parent I would like to see represent me in the hiring of a new first grade teacher. The parent representative (along with student volunteers) will sit in on a sample lesson from prospective teachers. (Though not necessarily apropos of this chapter, the concept of requiring teaching demonstrations from prospective employees is something administrators should take note of, especially given the intense debate currently surrounding teacher tenure and what to do about long-time ineffective teachers. How many of those teachers would have been rejected as applicants had they been required to teach as a prerequisite to being hired as teachers?) She will then be part of the community of people helping to decide which teacher is the best fit for the greater Free Union community. Parent volunteering in the classroom is commonplace, and one day a year, parents offer mini-courses to students of all grade levels. Over the years courses have run the gamut from brain function to wind power to hand imprints (care of an orthodontist using the materials for taking tooth imprints) to rock-climbing the exterior wall of the library's fireplace. Each Parent Teach Day, half of the faculty remain at school to facilitate the parent courses while half travel to another school to observe classes as part of the school's ongoing quest for good ideas that work.

Fund-raising is another way in which parents are fundamentally involved in the community. In winter there is a massive wreath-making effort, coordinated by an untiring parent volunteer. Wreaths are then sold to support school initiatives. (This same principle can be found at two other Free Union fundraisers, a silent auction of items donated by families and the Spring Fair. Both of these events have the added benefit of actively welcoming in the larger community in which the school operates.) The picturesque nature of this fundraiser is, of course, not the point. The point is that instead of inviting parents to send in baked goods, or giving students magazine subscriptions to sell, the fundraising brings people together to work for a common goal.

The idea of directly asking parents for help is alien to many school districts. Indeed, it calls into question the accepted notion of what the role of a school, particularly a public school, in the community is. This type of questioning, though, is timely, even urgent. In a culture where many do not want their tax dollars spent on schools, going directly to parents who have a vested interest in their children's school is a logical and an empowering step. If that interest is nurtured it will grow and schools rigidly divided into separate classes of people (students, teachers, administrators, staff, parents) can begin to come together as a single group with a shared purpose.

Administration in the Community

Parent involvement in school life is crucial, but it cannot be one-sided. The school must work for the parents as well. At Free Union, a monthly newsletter comes home electronically with a letter from the head of the school, classroom notes for every grade, pictures, and reminders of upcoming events. The monthly newsletter is supplemented by a weekly email from our daughter's teacher with a brief summary of some of the week's activities and pictures of the kids at work in the classroom and at play outdoors. For the first time in history, thanks to technology, there is an easy and cheap way to offer parents a full-color window into the classroom culture of our schools, and a website updated twice a year really doesn't go far enough. If parents can *see their children* at school, they will already be more involved than they have ever been.

Finally, throughout the year Free Union creates opportunities (community meetings, back-to-school teas, etc.) for parents to interact casually with the head of the school. At Free Union, the head of the school is so invested in the students and in student outcomes that she (along with the 4/5 teachers) travels to neighboring schools each year to meet with the teachers of recent graduates and find out how Free Union kids are adjusting to their new schools. This allows her to have a legitimate sense of how successful the children are in the larger community of schools and gives important feedback on the school's strengths and weaknesses. It also exhibits a peculiar Free Union trait that could perhaps best be called "institutionalized dedication." We have all heard stories of those exceptional teachers and administrators whose extraordinary dedication changed lives in their schools. At Free Union, the dedication of specific individuals has tended to imprint itself over time onto the institution itself becoming first a tradition and finally a legacy that helps to ensure the highest quality of education for future years.

Reciprocity in the Community

A thread that must run through the weave and weft of a deep, authentic community is reciprocity. The ideals of the progressive school and the ideals of democracy echo one another, and while you cannot put most decisions straight into the hands of children, you can ask children to participate in their school (through rule creation, choosing one unit to create per year, etc.) and, importantly, to recognize that giving to a school is as important as receiving from the school. Gift giving is important at Free Union. The library, for one, has a very successful Birthday Book program wherein a family may donate a book to the library at the beginning of the year in honor of the child's birthday. There is a ceremony during the week of the actual birthday with a special song and a small treat and then a nameplate is placed in the book. The library has grown through this program, but equally important is the sense of ownership the children have in their library as they look forward to the new books they will see each year and as they note the birthday nameplates from past years. A growing portion of the library consists of books kids can look at and say, "Hey, this is here because of me."Gifts are often given to the classroom on birthdays, and at the end of the year, the graduating fifth-graders present a parting gift to the whole school. Years ago the main building of the school had to be reached by a series of boards balanced on cinder blocks until one year the fifth-grade class (along with their parents) laid a brick walkway leading to the door. Such a spirit of reciprocity is at times taken to extraordinary lengths. One of the parents involved in that walkway project, for example, has been *volunteering* as the 4/5 PE teacher for around twenty years. That kind of parent involvement, of course, is exceptional, but I would argue that the closer a school gets to achieving the ideals of a deep, authentic community on all levels and throughout the school year, the more likely that school will be to find such outstanding human resources at its disposal.

Free Union also offer its students a chance to extend this spirit of fellowship beyond the school grounds in the annual Service Day, during which each grade level works on a project to benefit the greater community. Parks are cleaned up, a small cemetery on the premises is maintained, placemats are made for retirement communities, breakfasts cooked for a women's shelter. This is one of the ways Free Union fulfils the progressive call for social justice, in which, to quote Alfie Kohn, "students are helped to locate themselves in widening circles of care that extend beyond self, beyond friends, beyond their own ethnic groups, and beyond their own country" (2008, ¶.8)

The School Family

Every school year at Free Union ends with a lovely, traditional graduation ceremony, but the close of the school year is also marked by an all school camp-out at a nearby camp ground. The camp-out epitomizes not only the sense of community that has been created at Free Union, but also the school's dedication to preserving that community above all else as the school grows and changes. It is easy to see how a school that originally consisted of nine families might have initiated such a tradition. But it has taken great effort to continue the camp-out as the school has grown. However, at the end of the day, it is just one last testament to the great achievement of this school. We bought our first family-sized tent for this occasion and I can't thank the school enough for giving us the excuse to do so. It is a school that pushes its parents to be better parents, that pushes its students to be better friends, that pushes its teachers to be better mentors.

During that long spring day (of homemade ice cream, swimming, and skits) and into the night (of marshmallows, glow bracelets and guitar-playing) parents and teachers, students and administrators all come together as the Free Union family. This happy ending to the school year is not bestowed on us with a magic wand as in a fairy tale; it is the hard-earned reward for a year full of planning, trial and error, cooperation, volunteerism, reciprocity, and respect. If a school wishes to stop being just a school and to become a deep, authentic community, those are the ingredients it will need.

References

Introducing the *Responsive Classroom* Approach. *Origins: a website for educators.* 2009. Retrieved from: http://www.originsonline.org/rc_index.php

John Dewey Project on Progressive Education.(2002). Retrieved from: http://www.uvm.edu/~dewey/articles/proged.html

Kohn, A., Progressive Education: Why It's Hard to Beat, but also Hard to Find. *Independent School.* Spring 2008. Retrieved from: alfiekohn.org/articles.htm

Kriete, R., (2006). *The morning meeting book,* Turners Falls, MA: Northeast Foundation for Children.

Responsive Classroom. (2011). http://www.responsiveclassroom.org/about-responsive-classroom

Rimm-Kaufman, S. E., and Sawyer, B. E. 2004. Primary grade teachers' self-efficacy beliefs, attitudes toward teaching, and discipline and teaching practice priorities in relation to the *Responsive Classroom* approach. *Elementary School Journal,* 104, 321341.

Top five reasons why public schools are failing our children. *Education-Portal.com.* August, 2007. Retrieved from: http://education-portal.com/articles/Top_5_Reasons_Why_Public_Schools_Are_Failing_Our_Children.html

Author Note
Sarah Goodbar, M.A.

Sarah lives twenty minutes away from Free Union, Virginia, with her husband and two daughters. She received her Master's of Arts in English from the University of Virginia and her BA in Languages and Literature from Bard College. Sarah is a graduate of the Latin-Greek Institute of the City University of New York and has studied, as well, at the University of Massachusetts, Amherst, and the Curry School of Education. Before her daughters were born she taught eighth-grade language arts in Madison County, Virginia.

NOTES

NOTES

CHAPTER SEVENTEEN

Did the KIPP Schools Get it Right?

By: Shanda Lazare

> *The philosophy of the school room in one generation will be the philosophy of government in the next.* Abraham Lincoln

Introduction

Have our schools transformed from being community centered to being funding dependent? Those with fewer resources tend to have less educational options and less community and governmental support. In the midst of parents struggling with this dynamic, we will also explore how this lack of funding and local government support may or may not translate to a youth's ability to learn in such a potentially stressful environment. Finally, if a school in a low-socioeconomic area were to have the funding it needed and produce exceptional scores on state exams while supporting the family through accessing resources to lessen their struggles, what would be the outcome? One of the KIPP (Knowledge Is Power Program) schools and the Harlem Children's Zone have attempted to address these questions. We will also explore how some communities may respond to changing the "traditional" approach to educating youth.

Is Good Education Only for the Privileged?

In March of 2011, the Boston Globe printed an article by James Vaznis called *"Taking a Chance, Making a Choice"*. The Globe followed and documented the process of 13 families registering their children for school and the choices that they made based on the schools that a lottery randomly picked for them. Many of the families, after their child did not get into their predetermined schools of choice, left the city of Boston, MA. "According to School Department data, more than half the children who did not get the kindergarten or preschool programs they wanted ultimately left Boston schools," (Vaznis, 2011). Many of the families, that do not have the resources to move, are forced to have their child attend their non-preferred local public school. Which begs the question, "If they don't want their kids in that school, why do my kids have to go there?"

Gone are the colonial days when there was only one school for the town that all of the children attended. This timeframe was illustrated in the 1976 television series, Little House on the Prairie (IMDb, 2011), which chronicled the life and adventures of the Ingalls family in the 19th century American west. Children of all ages were grouped into one room and learning was a community effort. Moving to a different town, because the parents did not like the school, was not an option. There was generally one school that had one teacher. This teacher was typically female, not married and relied on the generosity of the townspeople to provide her with housing and food. The townspeople worked together to ensure that the schoolhouse was maintained and that wood was provided to keep the schoolhouse warm during the winter months (School, 2001). The members of the town took ownership for their school. Much has changed since those days.

Now, families are looking for the best education for their children based on state driven performance scores. However traditional public schools, particularly in urban settings, have historically low performance scores that correlate with how they are financed. "Whereas public schools are financed through taxation and are tuition-free, private schools depend primarily on tuition, donations, and volunteer or low-priced labor," (King, Swanson & Sweetland, 2003, p. 471). Due to being funded through tax dollars, the financial resources for public schools are limited. This small pool of money translates to the salary of the teachers, the condition of the school buildings, the number of supplies in the classrooms, and other limited or underfunded resources. Private schools have much more flexibility in the financial area translating into higher standards for the quality of the education, educators, and school environment. In response to this, families have been increasingly fighting to place their children in schools with higher achievement scores. "American studies of the criteria used by parents in selecting schools for their children clearly show that academic, moral, and religious concerns dominate. When given the choice, parents tend to select schools that are better than the ones their children attended previously," (King, Swanson & Sweetland, 2003, p. 487). It is unfortunate that some public schools are losing the best and the brightest to higher performing schools.

Socioeconomic status becomes one of the strongest determining factors of who has access to the highest performing schools. Those with lower socioeconomic status have little choice as to which schools they can attend. Those with fewer resources tend to become the victims in an underfinanced educational system.

How Does Living with Poverty Impact a Child's Education?

Poverty can produce a host of external challenges as well as internal struggles. Parents in urban settings can have a significant amount of stress related to coordinating work and family life. Due to this stress, it can be difficult for parents to focus on and effectively address their child's behavioral concerns and educational development. Brotman, et al, (2011) saw this unmet need and designed a program, called ParentCorps, to support parents with children reaching school age. They provided a series of 13 group sessions for the parents geared towards teaching them parenting strategies. Some of these strategies included establishing structure and routines for children, providing opportunities for positive parent-child interactions during child-directed play, using positive reinforcement to encourage compliance and social and behavioral competence, selectively ignoring mild misbehaviors, and providing consistent, nonphysical consequences for misbehavior. The strategies that are assessed to be most effective and necessary for each family are picked by the parent with the help of a ParentCorps counselor "based on their own family goals, values, and culture," (Brotman, et al, 2011).

Brotman and colleagues created study to examine if supporting the parents in learning and implementing effective parenting strategies had any impact on the child's behavior in school. They had a control group of children that consisted of families that did not have the ParentCorps sessions and an experimental group that did attend the sessions with a total of 171 children involved in the project. All of the families lived in an urban environment in the same school district that covered eight elementary schools in New York. All of the students were registered for entry into Pre-Kindergarten in the fall. The results were encouraging. "By the end of the Pre-Kindergarten year, relative to control schools, children…were rated by their teachers to be better behaved in the classroom and show more social and emotional competencies," (Brotman, et al, 2011).

This group of researchers helped to provide families with a foundation of effective communication strategies to support themselves and their children. The effects were seen by the teachers. What about when the children get to Kindergarten? Without practice and reinforcement, many learned skills can be forgotten with time. What could happen if these or other skills were supported with the families thorough out the child's educational career? What kind of strides can be made?

Community Agencies Supporting the Educational Environment

Grounded in research and supported by public policies and private funding, education and youth development fields are increasingly embracing the idea that multiple learning settings—from schools, to after school and summer programs, to physical and mental health services—can provide more opportunities for and benefits to children than schools alone. (Harvard Research Project, 2010, p. 2).

Supporting a student inside and outside of the academic setting has benefits to the youth. Traditionally, the academic setting has had difficulty managing the needs of their students without community support. An example of this is "the federally funded 21st Century Community Learning Centers program...[They] work in partnership with community... organizations to support children's learning," (Harvard Research Project, 2010, p. 2).

There have been other examples of successful bridges between the school and community settings. One such program is, "KIPP SHINE Prep, a charter elementary school in Houston, Texas," (Harvard Research Project, 2010b, p. 17). The Knowledge Is Power Program (KIPP) was founded in Houston, TX in 1994. It has become a national network of free, open enrollment, college-preparatory public schools with a track record of preparing students in underserved communities for success in college and in life. Its mission is to develop in young people the ability to compete academically in a highly competitive global environment (KIPP, 1994). The strategies they employ have been controversial. The school day is extended (7:30am-5:00pm) and they have other educational opportunities on the weekends and during the summers. Due to teachers typically working nine hours per day, half days on selected Saturdays, three weeks in the summer, and being available in the evenings for phone calls from students asking for homework assistance, the academic rigor and teacher investment are high. They also have the numbers to back up the usefulness of these tactics. In Houston, 90% of KIPPsters are from low-income households and 90% of KIPPsters have matriculated to college.

The KIPP SHINE Preparation school, the nation's first KIPP program according to the Harvard Research Project (2010b), builds community linkages with the local theater, ballet, symphony, and zoo. These promote self-expression and exploration of the arts in partnership with the schools. Lessons plans are built around each location. For example, a plan might be built on a specific animal at the zoo. The lesson plan would include trips to the zoo where the zoo staff who also teach the students about the specific animal and engage in theme related activities with them. "SHINE also partners with organizations, including Communities In Schools and Houston Achievement Place, to support the social and behavioral needs of its students," (Harvard Research Project, 2010b, p.17). The Communities in Schools Organization provides community volunteers and agency support to schools that agree to collaborate with this organization. The program is built on a model of the "Five Basics":

- A one-on-one relationship with a caring adult. Mentors, tutors and parental involvement programs.
- A safe place to learn and grow. After-school and extended-hours programs.
- A healthy start and a healthy future. Mental health counseling, family strengthening initiatives, drug and alcohol education, physical and dental exams, eye care and immunizations, and help for teen parents.

- A marketable skill to use upon graduation. Summer employment programs, college preparation and scholarship opportunities.
- A chance to give back to peers and the community. Community service opportunities. (CIS, 2011)

The Houston KIPP SHINE prep school combined the proven success of uncompromised academic rigor with the support of the nation's largest dropout prevention organization to create an environment for success. Involving the local community can create an environment where the community members embrace and support the success of students that have historically struggled due to their socioeconomic status. With the embedded component of community support, how do the KIPP schools compare to local public education in urban settings?

A KIPP School Success Story: Case Study

The KIPP Schools have espoused to have a high graduation rate (Since KIPP began in 1994, 95 percent of students who finished eighth grade at KIPP have graduated from high school, and 88 percent have matriculated to college, KIPP, 1994) and have the support of the U.S. Secretary of Education Arne Duncan (KIPP, 1994). However, all KIPP schools are opened one grade at a time in urban areas. They do not take over failing public schools. "KIPP's success to date is based on following our model of opening schools with one grade and growing them over time, and our expansion will continue to come through new KIPP schools," (KIPP, 1994). Ross, S. M., McDonald, A. J., Alberg, M., and McSparrin-Gallagher, B. (2007), created a research project to examine the student outcomes of a new KIPP Schools' fifth grade students as compared to the fifth grade students of the neighboring public schools in Memphis, TN.

For the achievement analyses, 49 KIPP: DA [DIAMOND (Daring Individual Achievers Making Outstanding New Dreams) Academy (KIPP:DA)] students were individually matched to highly comparable control students of the same ethnicity, socioeconomic status, gender, and ability, who attended different district schools in the same neighborhood (Ross, McDonald, Alberg, & McSparrin-Gallagher, 2007, p. 137).

Ross, et al (2007) were attempting to examine "whether KIPP:DA students would achieve at higher levels than would matched control students in literacy and mathematics on the state-mandated standardized assessments," (Ross, et al, 2007, p. 140). The educational environment remained the same in the neighboring schools while the KIPP:DA School's educational environment was the dependent variable. Ross (2007) and his colleagues explain that throughout the school year, KIPP:DA was in session from 7:30 a.m. to 5:00 p.m. during the week, 4 hr on Saturday, and a month during the summer. Teachers were provided with cellular phones and were available to students and their families outside normal school hours for assistance with homework or in case of emergency. There was no intellectual or documented achievement requirement for admission to KIPP:DA. However, all students and their parents were required to sign commitment forms indicating their agreement with the educational mission of the school and their willingness to support the school's rigorous requirements for academic engagement and exemplary conduct. Teachers were selected through an extensive application and interview process that suspended traditional considerations such as length of service and allowed the new principal...greater than usual autonomy in staffing. Teachers in this school received higher salaries than their peers in other Memphis City Schools because of greater than usual expectations at KIPP:DA regarding time in the school and after-hours accessibility to students and their parents.

While many of the elements of the experiment could be controlled, many could not. Enrollment in the KIPP school was open and students needed to be recruited. This meant that the principal of the school had to spread the word that a new KIPP school was opening and needed new students. According to Ross (2007), in the principal interview...about half of his students enrolled in KIPP:DA as a result of their families learning about the school through word of mouth or media information and submitting an application. With the desired enrollment quota not nearly filled a few months before school opened, [the principal] went door to door and visited local community organizations to publicize the school. Through this recruitment effort, the remaining slots were filled. Public schools get their students based on youth living within a specific geographical area being assigned to a specific school. This was not the case with the KIPP school. The youth, their families, the principal, community agencies, media advertisements and other sources become the recruiters for this school. One may speculate if those most interested in their child's education may be those with high academic standards for their children. "One might infer, but to an unknown degree, that such families would tend to be more involved in their children's education than those who did not exercise such choice. This factor constitutes a limitation of this...design," (Ross, et al, 2007, p. 141).

Other limitations included not having climate data for the public schools and interviews, surveys, and observations were not done in the public schools. "The reason was that control students were distributed among five neighborhood schools that were not formally participating in the study and that were identified mid year," (Ross, et al, 2007, p. 141). Both of these issues were resolved due to data gathered annually by the public schools in these domains.

Many other factors were explored in this research design. Parents, teachers and students were polled on their perception of the KIPP:DA school's effectiveness. That data can be reviewed in the Journal of Education for Students Placed at Risk, (2007) 12(2), 137-165. What will be discussed in this chapter are the standardized test score comparisons between the KIPP:DA students and the control students. According to Ross (2007), although the two groups scored very similarly on the pretests, KIPP:DA students performed directionally higher than control students on all CRT [Criterion-Referenced Test] and NRT [Norm-Referenced Test] posttests. Moderate to strong effect sizes ranging from +0.24 to +0.63, are indicated. Despite the described emphasis on writing across curriculum, nearly identical KIPP:DA and control group means were obtained on the Writing assessment. This experiment was able to conclude that KIPP:DA students performed better on 4 out of 6 standardized tests. While this may be statistically significant, it cannot be assumed that KIPP schools will have the same impact in other geographical areas. All variables in an educational environment cannot be controlled including the amount and quality of community service involvement. However, KIPP is not alone in adapting an approach that combines community involvement with local schools in a low socioeconomic community.

The Harlem Children's Zone (HCZ, 2009) was founded by Geoffrey Canada in Harlem, NY. The organization began in 1970 and was previously called Rheedlen. Rheedlen was created as "the city's first truancy-prevention program," (HCZ, 2009). Over the years, the staff at Rheedlen began to address other concerning community issues including drug addiction within the families. One of the ways Rheedlen addressed this issue was to rent a school building after school hours as a community center for the city. This allowed for youth and families to have a place to go after school, primarily to provide a safe environment and secondly to engage the youth and families in fun activities. It became a safe-space. The Countee Cullen Community Center became a safe, insulated environment from the danger and chaos of the streets. This progressed, in the 1990's, to the creation of the Peacemakers program. "The Peacemakers program began placing AmeriCorps participants in classrooms," (HCZ, 2009). This was the beginning of the link of community services in the school setting.

In 1997, the agency began the Harlem Children's Zone Project that ballooned to include 100 city blocks by 2001. The goal of the HCZ, directed by Geoffrey Canada since 1990, "is to create a 'tipping point' in the neighborhood so that children are surrounded by an enriching environment of college-oriented peers and supportive adults, a counterweight to 'the street' and a toxic popular culture that glorifies misogyny and anti-social behavior," (HCZ, 2009). This approach has had positive effects. The HCZ's College Success Office (2009) calculated that 626 HCZ after-school program participants are enrolled in college and 254 students were accepted into college for the 2010-2011 year representing 90% of their high-school seniors. With results like this and those from the KIPP schools, why hasn't this community-supported educational approach become more widely used?

Change is a Dirty Word

When confronted with the realities of how effective the KIPP strategy is, one might question why communities do not embrace the KIPP model. Children from underserved populations are academically engaged, become active community members and have a high likelihood of becoming college educated. KIPP schools are public schools which use state money to support underserved populations. Why isn't this catching on like wildfire? The answer, for one town in Tennessee, was "change".

In a 2008 article called Outsourced in the Scholastic Administrator Magazine, the Nashville, TN school system outlined their struggle with low academic performance and their resistance to help. The Nashville Metro Public Schools have 70,000 students spread over a 503-square mile metropolitan area. The district had a history of high dropout rates, underperforming schools, and chronic teacher vacancies and was placed under corrective action under the No Child Left Behind initiative. This appears to be a very clear opportunity for change; however, the people of this metropolitan area struggled with making a decision towards recreating the school environment. "Some people worry about the big 'c' word: Change,' says...assistant superintendent of student services for Metro Public Schools. 'Some people can't get past the big 't' word: Tradition," (Fairbanks, 2008).

Bill Purcell, the mayor, created the catalyst towards community momentum to stem the leaks in their educational system. He repaired the physical infrastructure of the schools and created support organizations that helped to raise millions of dollars for the school system. "One kipp school, delayed due to Tennessee's restrictive charter law, finally opened its doors in 2005," (Fairbanks, 2008). While it still took time to convince the town that outside help was the right decision, the outcome was positive.

Conclusion

In urban settings, best and the brightest tend to leave to go to better performing schools while those without the means to move to better schools are provided a lower quality education. Low-income families in these areas tend to struggle with depression, limited time with their children, and financial constraints. Using social agencies to support families can have a positive effect. The KIPP schools and HCZ were created to address this growing dynamic in many American urban settings. They, in some instances, have partnered with community organizations to connect families with community services dedicated to reducing the number of youth dropping out of school and increasing their social and educational potential. However, many low performing public school districts are resistant to embrace outside agencies coming in to restructure their schools. Is fear of change going to be the reason that urban youth are denied a good education? That is up to us.

Any change, even a change for the better, is always accompanied by drawbacks and discomforts. Arnold Bennett

References

Brotman, L. M., Calzada, E., Huang, K. Y., Kingston, S., & Dawson-McClure, S., Kamboukos, D...Petkova, E. (2011). Promoting effective parenting practices and preventing child behavior problems in school among ethnically diverse families from underserved, urban communities. Child Development, 82(1), 258-276.

Communities in schools-houston. (2011). Retrieved from http://www.cishouston.org/

Fairbanks, A. (2008, September/October). The outsourced district. Scholastic, Retrieved from http://www2.scholastic.com/browse/article.jsp?id=3750153

Harlem children's zone-history. (2009). Retrieved from http://www.hcz.org/about-us/history

Harlem children's zone-history. (2009). Retrieved from http://www.hcz.org/our-results

Harvard Family Research Project. (2010). Partnerships for learning: promising practices in integrating school and out-of-school time program supports (Adobe Reader 8.1), Retrieved from http://www.hfrp.org/publications-resources/browse-our-publications/partnerships-for-learning-promising-practices-in-integrating-school-and-out-of-school-time-program-supports

Harvard Family Research Project. (2010b). Partnerships for learning: profiles of three school-community partnership efforts (Adobe Reader 8.1), Retrieved from http://www.hfrp.org/out-of-school-time/publications-resources/partnerships-for-learning-profiles-of-three-school-community-partnership-efforts

King, R.A., Austin D. Swanson, A.D., & Sweetland, S.R., (2003). School Finance: Achieving High Standards with Equity and Efficiency (3rd Edition). Needham Heights, Massachusetts: Allyn & Bacon.

Kipp: faq. (1994). Retrieved from http://www.kipp.org/faq

Ross, S. M., McDonald, A. J., Alberg, M., & McSparrin-Gallagher, B. (2007). Achievement and climant outcomes for the knowledge is power program in an inner-city middle school. Journal of Education for Students Placed at Risk, 12(2), 137-165.

School: the story of american public education. (2001). Retrieved from http://www.pbs.org/kcet/publicschool/evolving_classroom/index.html

The internet movie database. (2011). Retrieved from http://www.imdb.com/title/tt0071007/

Vaznis, J. (2011, March 13). Taking a chance, making a choice. Boston Globe.

Author Note
Shanda Lazare, MA, LMHC

Shanda Lazare is currently the Clinical Director of the Children and Families Division for the Center for Human Development (CHD) in Western Massachusetts. Prior to this, she has worked in New Hampshire, in the cities of Keene, Dublin, and Manchester, supporting youth and their families who struggled with substance abuse and other anti-social behaviors. Mrs. Lazare is currently a doctoral candidate, studying Leadership and Supervision, at American International College. She has also earned a M.A. from Antioch University in Counseling Psychology and a B.A. from Green Mountain College in Visual and Performing Arts with a concentration in Theatre.

NOTES

CHAPTER EIGHTEEN

New Leadership Charter School

By: Michael D. Moriarty & Jennifer S. Alexander

Background

Located in downtown Springfield, Massachusetts, at the former Holy Name parochial school, New Leadership Horace Mann Charter School (NLCS) was founded in 1998 as an alternative to the public school setting. The vision of the founding board of trustees, educators, parents, and local area business owners was to provide an educational experience in an urban setting for students not only based on academics but character development as well. Graduates of New Leadership would become the future leaders of the community. This vision would be accomplished with a longer school year, smaller class sizes, more time on learning throughout the day, and support from the National Guard to host Leadership weeks focusing on discipline and social development. However, during the school's 14-year history, New Leadership has struggled to achieve it mission.

Being a Horace Mann Charter School, New Leadership has an affiliation with the Springfield Public School system, but is technically deemed its own district. Under a Memorandum of Agreement, New Leadership receives specified services and funding from the Springfield School District. The teaching staff is part of the union under the Springfield Education Association, and the students are residents of Springfield. Originally, Horace Mann Charter Schools were viewed as the solution for the debate of charter schools in Massachusetts according to the Department of Elementary and Secondary Education (DESE). A report by the Rennie Center for Educational research cites this has not been the case for reasons pertaining to political challenges, financial disincentives, and general lack of information. Because of this, Horace Mann Charter Schools have been all but abandoned. Currently, there are only seven charter schools operating in the Commonwealth and the debates still rage on.

For New Leadership, the school has continuously noted a lack of services and funding from the city of Springfield. After moving the school to three different locations, suffering the loss of the National Guard as a partner, and being cited by DESE for faithfulness to the charter, the school has to continuously create new programs to promote character development and academic achievement.

New Leadership serves grades 6 through 12 with open enrollment offered for students in grades 6 though 9. Typically, the school does not accept students in grades 10 through 12 for pedagogical differences. On occasion, there have been exceptions. Despite the school's struggles, there is a waiting list for students to enter at grade 6. Currently, the school has reached a maximum capacity of 500 students.

School Mission Statement

It is the mission of the New Leadership Charter School to develop young people in the sixth through twelfth grades morally, mentally, and physically; and to imbue them with the highest ideals of duty, honor, and loyalty. Graduates will be academically prepared to attend a college or university of their choice. They will embody three cardinal principals of leadership: vision, integrity, and compassion.

Challenges

The population at New Leadership has reached 500 students during the 2010-2011 school year, this represents the maximum number of students the school's charter allows. Students are generally accepted when entering grade six; however, demographic patterns are not always consistent. Although the majority of the students enter at grade six, significant numbers of students are transferring from local schools in grades 7 through 9. New Leadership experienced an unprecedented number of applicants for the 2011-2012 school year totaling more than 230 students for 96 available seats, which represents a ratio greater than 2:1. This increase of interest in the school's program has brought all classes in the middle school to maximum capacity, with class sizes averaging 20 students. Although New Leadership welcomes this great interest, the school is receiving greater numbers of students requiring remediation and ELL support services, all of which necessitates a refocusing and expansion of the school's instructional program.

Applicants entering the sixth grade come from 30 different elementary schools in the Springfield area. This presents a significant challenge for the sixth grade teaching staff. Since the Springfield district boasts 30 elementary schools, each with different administrations, programs, and instructional philosophies, the incoming students have varied educational experiences in elementary school. There is also the potential for a variety of socio-economic backgrounds. Compound this with the various learning styles, opportunities, and the accommodations to meet the goals of each and every student.

The school population consists of 60% African American, 35% Hispanic, and 5% White students. Furthermore, New Leadership is a Title 1 school with more than 80% of its families falling below the poverty line. This leaves administrators and grade level teams with the very difficult task of designing a curriculum that is differentiated, cross disciplinary, and standards based to meet the academic needs of the diverse student body.

New Leadership also focuses on character development that differs in comparison to the local schools. Students are required to abide by a dress code that is very specific and adhere to a set of non-negotiable rules that govern the student body. The non-negotiable rules are aligned to the character development and leadership piece that meets the needs of the social-emotional facet of the child's development. There has been an inherent problem with communication between New Leadership and the community it serves. Often times students live or stay with multiple family members for extended periods of time and on a regular basis, parent phone numbers change or are disconnected. This creates such inconsistency that when communication is finally established, there is an air of frustration between the parents and teachers.

Students have a very difficult time with transition on many levels with varying degrees of intensity. This lagging skill can be simple transitions such as moving from the hallway to a classroom or when walking to other buildings on the school campus. Students coming from an elementary setting struggle with the independence of transitioning to classes.

What instructional program and policies can New Leadership implement that can promote academic learning and a sense of civic duty for all students? How will the program articulate the purpose of education and the pace of public schools in the United States? How will the program bridge the gap between the school, parents, and students?

Effective Strategies

In an attempt to be responsive to student needs, changing demographics, and multiple demands imposed by new state and federal mandates, New Leadership has historically explored new initiatives to meet the ever-changing academic and personal-social needs of the student body. Of these initiatives, one of the most successful programs implemented is the Summer Academy for all incoming sixth grade students. Because of New Leadership's alternative setting to traditional public school education, the administration and board of trustees believe that it is necessary to orientate all new students to New Leadership's unique culture. Students complete a thorough training of the non-negotiable rules, dress code, and mission statement during the two-week program.

The summer academy is also an excellent time to assess the students' prior knowledge of learning standards and identify which students will need remediation through the school's tutorial center during the school year, as well as class placement for intervention services. Parents play a key role in their success during the Summer Academy. They are responsible for ensuring their child arrives on time and is prepared with the required materials.

There has also been extensive research demonstrating student success can be linked to parental involvement. In a *Science Daily* article from the University of New Hampshire, researchers used data from more than 10,000 eighth grade students, parents, and staff surveys about the impact parents have on their child's academic growth. Researcher Karen Conway (2008) suggests "Parental involvement is consistently associated with higher levels of achievement, and the magnitude of the effect of parental involvement is substantial. We found that schools need to increase per-pupil spending by more than $1,000 in order to achieve the same results that are gained with parental involvement" (para 2).

Taking into account the current state of the economy and the number of budgetary cuts in most districts across the country, parental involvement is needed more than ever. Unfortunately, this is not always the case. More often then not, teachers cite that they are not made aware of issues in a child's home life, while parents state that schools lack clear expectations for them and their children.

Author Heather Weiss (2004) stresses the need for services within communities that supports the parents' role in nurturing their children in an article by the Harvard Family Research Project. Family support programs should encompass the development of children past the elementary years and continue into high school. Communities should also recognize and celebrate the achievement of participants in these organizations so that parents feel empowered in a vital role in their child's development. (para. 3) But what happens when the resources are not available for families? Who is responsible for providing these services? A summer academy for incoming new students at New Leadership Charter School resolves some of the above questions and other common issues through a variety of means, to include:

- Clarifying school expectations
- Providing opportunities to meet administrative staff and teachers
- Helping Students learn about the school's mission before the school year begins
- Establishing open lines of communication between parents and teachers
- Allowing the teachers to identify the academic and social emotional needs of students
- Promoting team building and peer relationships
- Reducing the anxiety students may feel when starting a new school

As parents enroll their children in the school during the spring, they are provided with a tour of the school campus, and they meet with a school administrator to learn about the school's expectations, successes, and programs. Information sessions are hosted at the school in evening, so parents are able to ask questions, receive literature about the school, and meet some of the staff members. Families receive a summer reading list. Students are required to read two books during the summer and write an essay for each book. They are expected to turn in the writing assignment when school starts in the fall.

For two weeks in August, 103 incoming sixth grade students attend New Leadership's Summer Academy. Each day begins at 8:00 a.m. and ends at 12:00 p.m. Students follow a routine that consists of an advisory session, leadership class, English Language Arts, and Math.

Student Schedule

Advisory	8:00 a.m.-8:30 a.m.
Leadership	8:30 a.m.-9:40 a.am.
ELA	9:40 a.am.-10:50 a.m.
Math	10:50-12:00 p.m.

The advisory period is specifically designed for students to get to know their new classmates through various team-building exercises. The leadership class focuses primarily on the mission of the school along with the six pillars of leadership and the ten non-negotiable rules of New Leadership. Students also learn the Boys Town Social Skills. The ELA block provides an opportunity for staff members to assess students on reading comprehension and writing skills. Students read short stories, novels, and review standard English conventions. The math block assesses the students' knowledge of fifth grade standards and prepares students for the upcoming curriculum. Students also review math concepts and strategies.

Teacher Feedback

Many staff members feel that the Summer Academy is a huge success.

"Students were more focused when the school year began, and I spent less time on classroom expectations than in previous years." (Miranda Kavanagh, 6th grade ELA teacher). Students also have a clear understanding of the mission and exhibited preparedness, appeared more relaxed and felt less pressure. Alice Rainka, eighth grade ELA teacher, summarize the two weeks as a positive experience for both teachers and students. "I taught the English class for the Academy, and we read *The Lion, The Witch, and The Wardrobe*. We were instructed to teach them as if they were in a normal class at NLCS, so the new students would learn what to expect of their classes in the up-coming school year. We had lesson plans, homework, and classroom rules, just like during the school year. I really enjoyed getting to read a book with the incoming sixth grades, and they seemed eager to jump right in. In addition to the academics, we taught them the leadership principles of the school and the school mission statement. In fact, by the end of academy, nearly every student had the mission statement memorized. I feel like the academy was a great way to get the newest students to the school familiar with the building they would be in throughout the year, some of their future classmates, and the teachers who would be in the building. Coming to a new school is hard enough without knowing anyone or where you are going. Even though I do not teach any of the students I had in the Summer Academy, I still see them in the halls, they say hello to me, and they feel like they have a friend."

Parent and Student Feedback

The two-week academy provides a great opportunity to establish relationships with the parents and students in the sixth grade. During the school year, parents frequently attended Title 1 family events with their children because they established a strong connection to the school and were more likely to participate in after-school events. They became responsive to teacher phones calls from teachers during the school year and felt that they were vested partners in their child's education.

"My daughter had some time to get to know the school and make new friends." -6th grade parent

"The Summer Academy gave us an idea of how much work was required of the students." -6th grade parent

"One thing I learned was the mission statement, and I made some great friends." -6th grade student

The Massachusetts Comprehensive Assessment System (MCAS) data has yet to be released but New Leadership feels that there should be an improvement. Behaviorally, teachers generally feel that students have a better understanding of the school but need more repetition on transitions and conflict resolution.

"Kids knew the mission statement and were aware of the rules but there needs to more structured time on what leadership means and how to transition through their daily activities." Rulon Anderson, 6th grade Science teachers

Reflection

Were the problems identified by the school addressed with the implementation of the Summer Academy? It is important to assess students during this time, so teachers are able to place students in the appropriate classroom setting and refer students to the school-day tutorial center for academic support. Students are identified for Title 1 after-school support services as well. Students who are below grade level in reading comprehension are placed in the Scholastic Read 180 program, and those students who are in need of remediation are identified for additional support services. Read 180 is a computer software program that consists of a comprehensive curriculum, instruction, and assessment used to raise the students' reading level.

Clear Expectations and Communication

New Leadership staff and parents reported that they felt that the Summer Academy addressed this problem. Never before had students been required to learn the mission statement before the first day of school along with the non negotiable rules and pillars of leadership. Teachers noticed that less time is spent on explaining classroom procedures since the students are already familiar with the expectations.

According to the Assistant Principal at New Leadership, there were far less major violations to the Code of Conduct in the sixth grade compared to the rest of the student body. These types of violations involve incidents such as fights, theft, and bullying. However, the number of discipline reports for minor infractions was far greater than the rest of the school. This includes insubordination, accepting "no" as an answer, and resolving verbal arguments with peers. Moving forward, the Assistant Principal would like to see more activities during the Summer Academy that involve conflict resolution and team building activities that promote a sense of belonging within the community.

There is no doubt that time on learning is a key topic in education today with regards to the length of the school day and calendar year. There is also a lot of discussion on the way students learn in school. The academy addresses both areas. New Leadership students typically attend school 191 days in a year. The academy, although voluntary and not part of the regular school year, extends the year during a crucial time for young students when they are transitioning from elementary to middle school. It also allows teachers to practice a "depth over breadth" style of teaching. The longer school year provides students and teachers an opportunity to build solid relationships. As children transition into becoming young adults, they are able to receive the support they need from trusted adults to help them become socially responsible.

Closing Comments

New Leadership continues to gain insight from the Summer Academy. There is tremendous potential and much to be gleaned from this program and the necessary skills that students need in order to become successful in an academic setting. Based on feedback from students, teachers, and parents the school continues to revise the curriculum to improve future summer sessions. There are also plans to have a Summer Academy for all incoming ninth grade students after the sixth grade students complete their program. The goal for the ninth grade students is to ease the transition from middle school to high school and prepare students for the work they must complete in order to pursue higher education.

Authors' Note
Michael D. Moriarty, M.Ed.

Michael D. Moriarty served as a teacher, Science Chairperson and then Vice Principal over the past six years at New Leadership Charter School in Springfield, Massachusetts. He received a Bachelor of Science in Biology form the University of Massachusetts in Amherst and a Masters in Education Administration from American International College in Springfield, Massachusetts. He is currently working on a doctorate in teaching and learning at American International College.

Jennifer S. Alexander, CAGS

Jennifer S. Alexander serves as the Title 1 Supervisor and McKinney-Vento Liaison for the Westfield Public School District, MA. Prior to assuming this position, she served in other teaching and administrative roles such as English Language Arts teacher, reading teacher, Title 1 program coordinator, grade level team leader, and middle school coordinator. She holds a BA in English degree from the University of Washington, a M.Ed in Elementary Education from American International College, and a CAGS in School Administration from American International College. She was the recipient of the Grinspoon Pioneer Valley Excellence in Teaching Award in 2006. Her doctoral studies focus on the impact of family involvement with school-age children.

NOTES

Closing

CHAPTER NINETEEN
"The Welcome Mat is Out": Reflections on What Works in Building Strong School, Family and Community Partnerships

By: Christine N. Michael & Nicholas D. Young

Introduction

In their seminal writing on the value of action research, authors Altrichter, Posch, and Somekh (1993) note a sad trend in education: "between the classroom and the staffroom teachers destroy their most valuable property, the knowledge borne from their experience" (p.176). "In the teaching profession," they go on to say, "there is not a strong tradition of making teachers' professional knowledge public. Professional bodies such as subject associations and the Classroom Action Research Network regularly publish teachers' writing, and the growth of school-based in-service training as done much to break down the unspoken rule that teachers should not tell colleagues about their achievements. Nonetheless, these are all exceptions to the prevailing tradition of teacher privatism. Such a tradition is detrimental to the development of insights on professional practice, to the professional status of teachers, and in the last resort to the quality of educational practice" (p.176).

This chapter, as the closing note to a book that is based upon educators sharing their achievements, attempts to organize those practices around recurrent themes that were embodied in the stories of our colleagues around the country. What we discovered in listening to the success stories was that strategies that built and sustained strong collaborations between schools and families, and schools and communities relied on the following principles:

Creating Collaborative Communications:

One of the most frequently mentioned keys to engage in collaboration building was effective communication with stakeholders. While that took various forms, depending upon the makeup and the needs of each setting, finding a vehicle for keeping information flowing was imperative. As Superintendent Lynne Celli illustrates in the following story, good public relations begin with encouraging constituents to be heard.

"When I began my tenure as Deputy Superintendent in the Lexington, MA Public Schools, there had been a tumultuous 10 years – 7 superintendents in 10 years and much turnover in the central office personnel. When I began as Deputy, the Superintendent, Paul Ash, was also new and we came into the district as a team.

Lexington is an affluent suburb of Boston, MA. This community wanted to be engaged, wanted to be heard, and most of all wanted to be part of the decision-making process. These had not been occurring due to the historical turnover in leadership. Therefore, early on, the superintendent, and I decided we needed a grassroots effort to re-engage the community, and a vehicle to have open and ongoing dialogue as to what the "real" issues in the district were. Further, it was critical to us as the new leadership to send a strong message of caring and careful listening --leadership who wanted input from all constituencies. So what better way to accomplish this, but to engage the presidents of all the PTAs within the district, with the knowledge that these leaders had the pulse of the important issues throughout the district? Hence the formation of the Superintendent/Deputy Superintendent & PTA Presidents' Roundtable. This group met monthly, facilitated by superintendent and me, and many times by me as the superintendent's designee. We would begin each meeting with the important issues of the month, initiatives' updates, budget issues, or staffing updates. The intent was for the presidents to then to bring back all relevant information to their respective buildings to assure that the lines of communication were open and consistent. Each meeting also included important topics on the minds of the presidents that were either district-wide issues or building-based issues. Thus, the monthly roundtable meetings were an opportunity to disseminate information between parties, as well as discuss and agree upon topics for which decisions needed to be made. It is important to note that even though this roundtable was advisory, the discussions informed important decisions that the district faced and the PTA presidents felt a "real" part of this important process.

We determined the success of this roundtable by the level of openness, honesty of discussions and how validated and "part of the decision-making process" not only felt by the presidents by through the presidents to all parents in the district. This vehicle truly became an important, ongoing way to share information on a regular basis, gain input that was so valuable from the community, and most importantly, validated the importance of the family/school partnership."

Paul Andrews, currently the Director of Professional Development and Government Services for the Massachusetts Association of School Superintendents, recalls establishing a communications committee and learning the power of listening:

"On becoming superintendent, I inherited numerous level 3 grievances that got me into the mode of looking at the reason these grievances even got to level 3; I recognized the need for greater communication by me, as the new superintendent, especially with the teachers in the school district. I decided to formulate a 'Communications Committee' that would meet the first and third Thursday of each month. Each school staff (12 schools) would elect a staff person to be on the Communications Committee with the agenda open at each meeting. I would open the meetings and listen to the concerns expressed. On some of the issues I could respond immediately while on other cases, I needed to follow up the concern with other administrators. I did a great deal of listening.

What I found was that the fact that I established an open process and time to communicate "directly" with teacher and school representatives, the staff felt that I cared and in fact that I followed through on the majority of concerns raised with the exception of a few not under my control. I knew that the process was successful when grievances came to an almost complete stop!"

In some cases, the communications need to be focused on a particular audience in order to impart knowledge and reinforce relationships. Frank Vargo, a former school committee member in Leominster, MA, captures this view when writing about his current professional role: *"over the course of my position as a school psychologist for a regional school district, I initiated a schedule of regular and consistent contact with the leaders of the system's Special Education Parent Advisory Council (PAC). In those meetings, the council leaders were able to bring questions, ideas, and concerns from all parents to the council on a monthly basis. My regular meetings with the council leaders allowed me to impart information involving all educational and clinical topics related to special education, and that information was subsequently disseminated and shared with all parents. We also routinely brainstormed together to consider new ideas for programs and strategies that would improve parent and school communications, and provide enhanced services to all special needs students in the district. I also made several presentations each year to the entire council group based on their generated questions, at the parent/council's request."*

Creating Meaningful Roles for Family and Community Members

While communicating effectively with families and community members is an essential component of smooth school functioning, there are many among those stakeholders who seek a more active involvement in the life of the school. In his Shelton Public School District in Connecticut, Superintendent Freeman Burr found an energized parent-community base, but one that needed to have its roles redefined in order to make an additional impact on student development. *"When I began my principalship, I inherited a school with a very active parent and community presence in a diverse, working, middle class community in the west end of Hartford, CT. In looking back, the richness of this experience was that the parent involvement went above and beyond the traditional role of room parents or contributors to bake sales. We were able to utilize these parents as volunteers in our classrooms. Frequently, they spent two or three days per week actively involved in teaching and learning tutoring and support for a minimum of 3 hours per day.*

The two benefits that I believe we derived from this were students in these classrooms enjoyed having another adult in the classroom that they could trust and seek out. In turn these parents built relationships with students (not their own) as well and continue to follow and check in on them in later years. Secondly, the teachers in those classrooms always seemed to be on everyday and wanted to go above and beyond in their teaching and student learning activities. I believe this could be attributed to the fact that the days they had parent support they felt they could do more, thus raising their expectations for students and themselves. Finally, I was amazed at the learning curve of many of the parents as they came to understand our reading and math curriculum through being actively engaged in helping students learn."

In addition to tutoring, serving on committees and councils can be a valuable way for family and community members to support the school—but only if the committees have an actual purpose and real authority to effect change. Paul Andrews created just such a committee when his district needed it:

"As a superintendent in an area near Boston and close to major highways, our community attracted many major and minor business and commercial enterprises. As budgets for many communities were getting less, I determined that there was a need to reach out to business leaders for their support. With the assistance of a cadre of local business leaders we determined those leaders to be reached and held several regular meetings of school and business leaders hosted by one of the major business firms.

Joining in this process were community leaders, as a coalition began to be created both formally and informally. What this process did was to establish communication and understanding between government, industry and the school department.

What grew from this process in addition was a clearer understanding about the importance of a career education focus, with students being provided shadow experiences in local companies and even entry level positions, as well as career fairs and training at the school- based level by industrial leaders and representatives."

Finding a Role for Everyone

As demonstrated in the previous examples, family and community members need to see value in their participation if they are to engage with our schools in meaningful ways. They also must see viable ways to contribute their unique talents and interests if they are to become partners. In speaking about his desire to cultivate community collaboration, former Superintendent of Schools of Wells Central School, Paul Williamson, succinctly summed up his hopes: " developing more of an emphasis on community service." Although miniscule Wells Central School (NY) certainly shared a positive relationship with the surrounding rural town of Wells, Williamson's mission was to build a culture permeated with a sense that all students and community members should join in helping each other. That culture began to expand with the initiation of a mentoring program that included very young scholars as mentors to others, but also tapped the considerable talents of community members who wished to form more personal relationships with Wells students. Community members were recruited to share different talents, ranging from being reading partners, to supplementing the regular curriculum with after-school interest groups, to offering leadership in particular service projects.

Essential in building a service culture was Wells' emphasis on finding a service niche for everyone. Former student Ashley Anderson, now a college student, recalls that just as it was critical to poll community members on what they wished to contribute to the school and what their unique array of talents would be, *"we had to create places for every scholar—even the young ones or ones who weren't very popular—to find a place to shine, to have something that they cared about. In a small school like ours, it is so essential that people don't get left out because each person stands out so much."* It would have been impossible for the school, with its very small staff, to be so inclusive if not for the active participation of so many community members.

Service projects that grew from this brainstorming represented this wide approach to inclusion: a pajama drive for children in need; food drives for the local pantry; collections for soldiers in Kuwait and Afghanistan; and the popular Seniors' Dinner each year. At this community event, *"we plan a dinner at a local restaurant and invite area seniors for a free meal and entertainment. Many of our guests are our own grandparents or grandparents of friends. It is a way that we can honor those who have done so much for our community and us. The scholars cover every aspect of the dinner—from set up, service, clean up, invitations, decorations, and some form of musical, artistic or other activities to entertain the guests. Each year we try to do something different and also include some of the younger scholars so that they can become prepared to be the next generation of leaders themselves."* Senior citizens were so impressed and grateful that they attempted to pass the hat to provide generous tips for the students who had served them; however, when the students stressed that service did not need to be rewarded monetarily, the seniors wrote letters of appreciation to the superintendent and local newspaper instead. This type of public relations did a great deal to build positive regard for the school among others who did not attend the dinner.

Students have been active in many other service activities. Young scholars like the fourth graders are proud because *"We've read 200 books and then Scholastic Books donated up to a million books for needy schools and libraries for every 100 we read. We are collecting juice pouches and get 2 cents each to donate to charity."* When there have been local tragedies (such as a student's house burning down!), everyone pitched in and raised money for the families. Teachers and students also took part in a quilt project for Darfur—an after-school event that brought to mind old-fashioned community quilting bees—after several students were moved by what they learned about the plight of the people of Darfur. This was an idea suggested by several students who were so upset when they saw a show on TV. Even boys felt welcome to come and learn to quilt!

The school garden is another service project that grew out of college and community collaboration with the school. The sixth graders worked with Cornell Cooperative Extension Master Gardener Nancy Welch and loyal community volunteers such as Ellen Craig to utilize a grant that they got from the North Country Healthy Heart Network. Together they learned about soil testing, garden preparation and plant selection. The students then prepared banked planting beds, planted the garden, and protected it with plastic sheeting and floating row covers. Over the summer vacation they got together with community volunteers and tended and harvested the garden. The hundreds of pounds of food produced in the garden went to feed local hungry people who use the town food bank.

Another highly successful project was " A Night at the Museum," based on the popular movie. According to teacher Gail Wilcox," *Our students say that they enjoy this event because " they research a famous person from history or literature. They make tri-folds displaying power points or posters about their person's life. The tri-fold keeps them separated from other students in the gymnasium so as to resemble a museum's different rooms. They dress the era and present themselves as that person. That night, the area is low lit, they'll have a battery-powered candle and when people come in, the attending folks drop a token in their container. The tokens are purchased at the door. When the token is placed in the container, the student comes to life and talks as if they were that person. The money raised is donated to another cause, Project Soil."*

Project SOIL deals with compost toilets for countries without any facilities. It teaches those people how to make and use the waste. Says Wilcox, " *we are modifying that project and making a replica of a toilet and using compost waste from our cafeteria to represent the waste. From that compost soil that develops, we plan to start a garden for each of the elementary grades and use the veggies for the cafeteria. Eventually, the students want to be proficient enough to go to other schools to teach the project as well. The money we raise from the Night at the Museum, and other projects along the way, will help to get us up and running as well as enough to send on to the organization to help worldwide."*

Wells faculty and staff recognize that there are many acts of scholar service that take place outside of the school walls, happening just because scholars care about others in their community. "In school, I'm a leader who helps other people by mentor training," said twelfth grader Jacob Brenan. "But outside school I mow lawns for people, hunt and trap, help people shovel off their roofs and sidewalks. I think there should be more people who do stuff like that." "In a small community," notes Maxine Hoffman, "we don't have the advantages of a larger community so kids do join the fire department, work in the rec leagues, or help with after school activities for community service." In the words of Emily Michienzi, in this little school with an inclusive philosophy, *"we feel important because kids are trusted to help other kids and adults."*

Steve Tullar, Principal of Westminster Schools, in Westminster, Vermont, is on a mission. He is determined to have all children in Westminster be able to make informed educational decisions. His goal is to have children, and their families, know about future educational possibilities--what lies beyond high school--when they are in his K-6 school, long before what tradition has dictated. To this end, Tuller has pulled together key community members, staff, and parents and to create a program called "High Expectations."

"High Expectations" is designed to give Westminster students a vision for their future and an opportunity to look at what options exist beyond high school. Westminster Schools believes that, in order to support all children (regardless of socio-economic status) to reach their full potential, students must be supported by the Westminster educational community throughout their educational career, not simply when they attend the Westminster Schools. To that end, Tullar says, *"this plan addresses the question: How can we, as a responsible and effective educational community, do better at meeting the educational needs of Westminster students from K-12 and beyond?"*

Tullar and his staff articulated a set of long-term goals that were considered non-negotiable:
- 100% high school graduation rate for Westminster students
- 100% of Westminster students will be able to make informed choices about life after high school
- 100% of Westminster students will be able to make informed choices about selecting a middle school and to be engaged consumers and active participants in the their middle school selection process
- 100% of Westminster students will view college and other post-secondary options as a realistic and attainable option.
- 100% of Westminster children will have a "bigger picture" about the purpose of education and the role education plays in their lives.
- 100% of adults who work with Westminster students will believe that all students can and will succeed
- 100% of Westminster students will view Westminster Schools as a valuable resource and support system for them throughout their educational careers

To assist the school in meeting these lofty goals, Tullar hired Virginia Wilkins, a seasoned educational consultant and former teacher, to develop strategies for the initiative. Wilkins focused the community on a number of activities to attain the lofty goals, with sixth graders as their target. They created and used MAP (My Academic Plan) binders with their families, and families and students used their opportunity to select from among several high school options open to Westminster students as a preview of how one goes through the college selection process. A high priority, according to Wilkins, was to get all sixth graders on a college campus, and that entailed inviting families along. When visiting the campuses, students and their families took part in developmentally appropriate, highly interactive activities. They also met with current college students who themselves had graduated from Westminster.

Donna Sheehan, a mother who traveled on the bus with her son's class to spend the day at Vermont Tech said that being invited to join her son and his class on a trip to visit a college campus was one of the best and most important things she, as a parent, could do.

"As a parents you have to support your kids and you have to help them along they way. I did not have that. No one told me about the importance of continuing school after high school, and my father even worked at New York University.

My parents did not really know anything about the college process. So I just went to community college and tried to figure it all out on my own. It is my one regret. If you want to do anything in life, if you want to get ahead, you need to go to school, that is it bottom line."

Donna attended Brookdale Community College for a year and a half, but never finished. She paid her own tuition, but then got a job at a computer company. *"It was the worst thing for me to do. It is my one regret."* In addition to involving parents in academic decision-making and support, Wilkins tapped former Westminster students who are now in college and invited them into the sixth-grade classrooms to speak about their educational journeys from sixth grade to the present. Creating an extensive data base to track Westminster students from their graduation through their post-secondary education also will give the community a sense of what has happened to their graduates and has heightened awareness about the need to stay involved in the lives of these students even after they leave high school.

"The manner in which this project brings the greater community together," Wilkins reflects, *" is fresh and innovative. It has broader appeal to the community than saying ' come into a school and volunteer.' It taps into one's individual talents and at the same time brings the community together around a very simple mission. We want children (and families) in our community to be able to make informed educational decisions. Everyone can wrap their hands around and get behind it. Those of us who no longer have children at the school have a reason to be involved. This project is one that has a multigenerational appeal, from retired folks to current college students and even to current middle school students. The project is stronger when it involves people from different backgrounds and experiences. How we get the community involved? By word of mouth, by talking it up around town (when appropriate), publishing articles in the local paper regularly,*

and local TV station. We let this project percolate organically. It is changing the way we as a community approach education."

Celebrating the Richness of Diversity in the School and Community

Historically, research has shown that mainstream American schools have been reported to be far more welcoming to majority populations than to those in the minority (Schuman, 2004; Sarason, 1990). With demographics rapidly shifting in this century, schools must been inviting places to all in this pluralistic society.

Tom Scott, the Executive Director of the Massachusetts Association of School Superintendents, offered his experiences on how to promote greater community and school connections: *"Our high school had a very successful program called ' Fear No Difference.' This is an annual event which covered several school and community conversations focused on respect for human differences. Using keynotes, panels and activities at school events and evening/Saturday joint school community events we focused on many difficult topics about our community values, behaviors and attitudes. It was extremely well attended and covered broadly by the press. The culmination was a weekend retreat for 100 chosen student leaders and randomly selected students who along with business, government, parent and public safety representatives and selected faculty and administration experienced an intensive two days and nights on the topic of respect for human differences assessing our personal challenges around the topic and what we needed to do as a community to better ourselves. All participants to this experience wore bright yellow "Fear No Difference" shirts to school and in the community on Monday following the weekend experience. These participants became the ambassadors, communicating their experience and being the stewards of this work with classmates and the community."*

In tiny, rural Olathe, Colorado, Student Advocate Stacy Goza and her students celebrate their heritages by inviting families and the community to "Holidays Around the World." This popular event is deliberately scheduled to take place prior to one of the most well-attended activities during the school year: the holiday concert. Working in teams, student groups choose and research a culture and then plan a pre-concert meal based on their findings. They also are responsible for decorating their table and providing the public with information about their chosen culture. Community members act as judges and provide prizes for the winning teams—money to be used for post-secondary education. The event is so successful that *"we usually run out of forks and spoons,"* Goza reports, *"and we plan for 300 to 400!"* In a community of this size, where there are few businesses and agricultural and ranching endeavors dominate the economy, *"it's too easy to think that everyone is pretty much the same. The image of the West is* changing so rapidly, and this is one way to recognize the growth in the number of cultures that are coming here and shaping our community in a positive way."

Giving Back to the Community

One of the most effective ways to solidify strong relations with the community is to cultivate a culture of community service in our schools. In some schools that means a graduation requirement of so many hours of service, while in others, various service clubs or experiential learning opportunities exist. One thing is certain in this day and age: schools must create multiple service opportunities within their programming so that students without means, transportation, or family support to take part in out-of-school service activities can be equal participants in service leadership.

In her chapter on relationships between regional technical schools and the community, Judith Klimkiewicz, the Superintendent of Nashoba Regional Technical School, notes the dramatic growth in positive community relations when her school moved from its traditional policy of building one house annually for a local family chosen by lottery to *"improving community infrastructure via community service projects. Where better to demonstrate that cooperation than to offer our 'cash strapped' communities the ability to get capital projects completed for only the cost of supplies?"* she observed. The gamut of projects has run from construction, culinary, graphic design, and engineering to pre-school classes and health fair services. *"Over the past 15 years we built additions to fire stations, garages for public works departments, constructed pumping stations, and trained town staff on the use of geographic information systems software."* In return, the communities have approved school budgets, approved the establishment of a stabilization project, and supported a 28 million dollar major renovation and addition.

To promote a sense of community, Richard Holzman, the former Superintendent of the Schenectady City School District, reported that he *"implemented an Outward Bound Experiential Education Program that was a precursor to the nationally recognized Expeditionary Learning Outward Bound Program. The genesis of this program grew out of my long-term commitment to experiential education that started in the rain forests of Puerto Rico while I was trained as one of the first Peace Corps volunteers in the early 1960s.*

Students, faculty and parents as stakeholders were involved in planning, organizing and participating in the Outward Bound experience involving community service, rock climbing, hiking, rafting, reading, discussing, calculating, orienteering in both urban and wilderness environments to build competence, confidence and team building, all of which are attributes that are not often nurtured in traditional school environments.

It was implemented as an effort to reach and teach all students in a diverse demographic and was successful in igniting enthusiasm for learning and building trust among the stakeholders where students become teachers and faculty and parents become learners as they grew to appreciate each other's strengths and challenges in their reversed roles. Success was confirmed by the great demand for participation in the program and the fact that the Outward Bound instructor I hired as Director was appointed CEO of Experiential Learning Outward Bound, which is now embedded in schools across the country.

On a smaller scale, little Minerva Central School (population preK-12, 133) located in the Adirondack Mountain region of New York, celebrates an annual Community Service Day, created in part because *"in a small, rural area, it's hard to find enough service projects for everyone to do. Everything is so far away, and transportation is a problem"* Principal Heidi Kelly remarks. Held during their founders' week celebration, Irish Pride Week, every student at the school participates in either a school or community-based project, ranging from working at the local chapter of the American Red Cross with challenged citizens, providing computer tutoring for senior citizens, working in the nursing home, recycling, cleaning up local parks and streams, or becoming a student teacher in a classroom for a week. *"Because the school is really the only community center in town, we are intimately connected to our citizens,"* Kelly observes, *"but we have to be really creative and have a broad definition of service in order to engage everyone in giving back."*

Leading by Example

When he became a superintendent, Stephen Hemman, the Executive Director of the Massachusetts Association of Regional Schools, remembers, *"I was advised by my mentor to be active in the community by attending school events and town events. One of the communities has a town wide craft fair in August. I volunteered to work at the fair and they put me in the food court. Many members of the community saw me and commented that it was great that I was a volunteer at the craft fair. The other community has a town wide fair on Saturday in June I also attended that each year. One year, it was raining and I received a call from an organizer. They asked who they needed to contact for permission to use the school. I indicated that I could take care of their request. I went to the school and opened it for them. I received many compliments for providing such prompt service. Being involved sends a message to the community that I cared and when I needed their support for the education of the children of the district, community members come forward to assist us."* It isn't always the adults who are the leading example; in the case of these two self-described "men on a mission," community-school relationships were revitalized by high school students who care deeply about their school.

Since reopening its doors in the fall of 2006, Manual High School (CO), closed down because it was a failing high school, has been presented with the daunting challenge of reinventing itself and creating a new community-- one where students succeed academically, feel supported socially and emotionally, and have the opportunity to achieve their college and career dreams. Dominique Swain and Kyle Motley, when they were just 10th graders at Manual, were at the forefront of the movement to establish this new school. As the school struggled to re-define itself, the scholars were the ones who planned major events to address two issues they felt were imperative to Manual's future success: community engagement with the school and support for incoming students. They began by hosting a Community Event. Members of the neighborhood surrounding Manual were invited to the school to learn about student groups and initiatives and also to be encouraged to consider opportunities to partner with the school. Students were hoping to change negative perceptions of Manual in the community and solicit support for their drive to make the school a great place in which to study. Kyle describes the community day as *"a fair-like event where we had tables set up with different clubs like telling neighbors what we do to make our school a better place. There were prizes and booths with different community organizations. Most importantly, we asked the community for their suggestions for school improvement and if they are willing to help."* For Dominique, the goal was to *"have more people involved, to showcase our school, and mostly to heal the separation of school and community. We needed more engagement and we needed the neighboring community to open up and become equal partners in educating our kids."* This is an ongoing task that will be fully accomplished, he feels, *"when they know more about who we are now, after re-opening, that we're back, and in a better way. There are so many ways that this community could help us with further academics, athletics, attending our games, mentoring, or helping financially."* The scholars also hosted a pep rally with Manual alumni prior to the fair, hoping that *"they can see where we're coming from, what we're doing right, and get their ideas about how the school can be better, because, after all, it's their school and they want to be proud, too."* A less obvious goal of the fair was that *"we are trying to get more parents involved in college knowledge because most of our parents haven't been to college and really don't know. We want to change parents' minds about the value of going to college and we also want to inspire some parents to think about going to college themselves!"*

With a leadership vacuum in the re-established school, both Kyle and Dominique have filled the void. They have been allowed to practice "more hands on leadership" in this environment and both hold to the notion that if they can inspire both other students and neighborhood students to step up and engage, Manual can become "the place it's supposed to be." "We have to let students go out and fish," says Dominique. *"You know the old saying, 'you can give a man a fish and he'll eat for a day, but if you teach him to fish, he'll eat for a lifetime?' We want to teach the students to fish."*

Seeing Students as Collaboration Builders

As seen in the example cited above, students themselves can serve as the most convincing collaborators, if only adults give them the opportunity to do so. Many of the most effective collaborations with community and family take part when students reach out to these constituents and ask for their participation.

Mention the word "diversity" and South High School in Denver comes to mind. South's student body currently represents over 60 different countries and students speak over 50 different languages. 41% are English Language Learners and 71.2% are on free/reduced lunch. 1% are Native American, 14.4% Asian/Pacific Islander, 23.6% Black/African-American, 32.5% Hispanic/Latino, and 28.3% White. In this mini United Nations, students face tremendous hurdles in taking advantage of post-secondary opportunities. The most frustrating aspect of this challenge is low parent participation in events geared towards college success. Rather than seeing this problem as lack of parental interest, students in a club called College for Every Student knew that their parents simply lacked the knowledge, confidence, and cultural capital to feel able to help their children gain access to college. In a reversal of roles, the CFES scholars proposed empowering their parents as the pathway to college success. The main issue students wanted to address pertained to parents' lack of access to information regarding college. For this reason, they approached building parental buy in by mentoring their own parents about the college process.

At the beginning of last school year, CFES students submitted a grant proposal to State Farm to engage parents. They created a video which was shared with the CFES family of schools via the website. The grant that they won from State Farm allowed them to develop two school-based events designed to give their parents the knowledge that they needed to feel confident in the college application process. In November, over 200 parents attended the first Parent Empowerment session, but not without an incredible effort from the scholars. Scholars used the phones and other forms of communication to make sure that they got the turn out that they needed. "It was so exciting to see parents being more involved in their student's education. It was also great to give them the information they need to help their student," exclaimed scholar Waree Jateny. The reversal in mentoring roles pleased Edith Nyarko: "I loved seeing students being able to give parents something useful. It always seems like it's the other way around."

The first successful event led to a second, focused on the financial aid process—one that can be particularly difficult for first-generation and immigrant parents and their children to decipher. In an atmosphere of comfort, the parents were able to air concerns and get their questions answered. *"It was so exciting to see parents asking questions to learn more about the college process. I realized that parents want to help but they just need more information. I'm glad I was one of the people that offered useful information to them,"* said scholar Lydia Adomako. The event was so well attended that 210 parents and scholars filled out the FAFSA form that evening.

Seeking Support for Scholarship

Jake Eberwein, Superintendent of the Pittsfield Public Schools, located in an urban area of Western Massachusetts, found that tackling an academic challenge was successful only when it became a three-way collaboration. *"Pittsfield developed a school/community reading program at an elementary school that successfully blended community, school and family collaboration. The program was conceived by the school's parent-teacher organization (PTO) in concert with the school council, as a response to concerns about reading outcomes, summer regression, and time (lack thereof) students were spending reading outside of school hours. The program consisted of several key elements that fostered connections between the school, the home and the community. To launch, a goal was developed to increase the number of hours students invested reading during out-of-school hours. A student/family survey was conducted to develop a baseline in order to evaluate the success of the initiative. This data helped the PTO, school council, and principal set out-of-school time reading goals. Second, leveraging the business partner, the PTO and school council hosted a kick-off event during which books were distributed, incentives were offered, expectations were established, and strategies were offered to parents. The event, which I would describe more like a pep rally, also included a local author who conducted a book reading in supporting the "first" book recorded in each student's reading log. Over the course of the next few months, the principal and PTO provided regular updates to students, staff, and families in order to track progress and motivate future efforts. In addition, a book fair was held and several "rallies" helped to recognize students and promote out-of-school reading. The PTO, with the support of the business partner, hosted a "Curl up with a book" program – that allowed families to attend school on a Friday evening in their pajamas, pillows, and blankets. The school also supported a community reading day during which community members visited the schools and read to classes of students. Ultimately, the reading initiative became the school's* academic focus and each event supported reading both within and outside of school hours. As such, the focus became a key element of school's improvement plan and the reading "rap" became a pervasive part of the school's culture. The program was closed at the end of the school year with a rally, acknowledgments and prizes, and data regarding the advancements of students as measured on local reading assessments. Momentum from the school year program led to the addition of a summer program. I believe what is most impressive about this school's efforts and what sets this particular project apart is a) the initiative was linked to student achievement and outcomes, b) clear metrics were set, c) the goals and strategies were pervasive throughout the school community, and d) most of the school's events were tailored towards this initiative with all stakeholders (families and community members) working in concert with school staff. In doing so, and having some fun along the way, the school's reading goals were exceeded and student achievement was positively influenced. While the program was initially developed to raise the amount of out-of-school reading, the school was very pleased when their MCAS results showed improvements in ELA and literacy."

Edward Costa II, the former Superintendent of Schools in East Longmeadow, Massachusetts, and present Superintendent of Schools in Lenox, Massachusetts, created the "Individual Student Success Plan" (see end of chapter) to build a tri-partite support system for all students, in preparation for MCAS testing. His model involves family, student and school, and is built on six components of the ISSP that each school in his district addresses. The triad approach recognizes "all participants (parents, students, and schools) must bear equal responsibility for the success of each plan. Students must design, implement and deliver instructional supports. Students must attend school ready and wiling to try their best and must complete all assignments in school and at home to the best of their abilities. And, parents must monitor their child's work at home, spend time helping their child with directions for homework and communicate with schools frequently."

Finding a Solution that Fits the Community

Delaine Hudson, Director of the Delta Opportunity School in Delta, Colorado, faces some unique hurdles in creating a sense of collaboration between families and communities with what many see as a "last chance" school for secondary students who have not thrived in traditional area high schools. The nearly 100 students who populate her school attend for half-day sessions and then work, often tending to children of their own. The students' parents, many of whom have bad memories of their own educational experiences, frequently remember school as a place that was less than supportive of their needs and aspirations and are reluctant to set foot in DOS's doors. Many students and families struggle with day-to-day issues such as transportation, food, childcare, medical problems and paying the bills, so without creativity and compassion on the part of the staff, school might be relegated to a position of lower importance.

Hudson forges partnerships with her students and their significant others with a "feed the family" approach. Sometimes, quite literally, this entails offering a meal and an opportunity to socialize at school, without any other agenda. "On Back to School Night," as she describes it, *"we didn't do anything really school related, but we invited families to a barbecue and let them just be in our space itself without anything 'heavy.' Our kids are engaged once they start at our school, but it's the families—with their less-than-positive memories of schooling—who need to be enticed into seeing that we're something different, something special."* Many families have never had their children have a success in school, so they expect that any communications from Hudson or staff will be negative. *"The most frequent thing that we hear from parents at graduation,"* Hudson relates, *"is that they never believed that their kids would be successful, that they didn't think they'd ever graduate."* A potential problem with working with her specific parent population, Hudson believes, *"is that it's too easy to sell these parents short, to think that they don't care."* The root cause, she thinks, is that educators often confuse parents' need to prioritize their time around survival issues rather than educational issues leads them to view them as less engaged. *"I rarely have seen a parent of a student in our school who is any less concerned about his or her child than a parent of any other child. We have to tell our parents 'you're one of the family now and we are here to serve you. The welcome mat is out."* This often means that DOS assists parents with their daily needs while simultaneously assisting their children. This also means stretching programming to include a Teen Parents' Group, on line education, the Incredible Years program for infants and toddlers, and a host of other services.

It is also a challenge to sell the school to a community that is used to bonding with its school through traditional activities such as sports, music, and drama. *"We have to put ourselves and our kids out there and let the community see that they're great kids, too"* Hudson says. The major strategy that she has employed to do so is through required community service for all students. While many adults would be hesitant about trusting her population with community projects, Hudson takes just the opposite tack: *"we are everywhere—we mentor severe needs students at a local elementary school, adopt grandparents at a local nursing home, present before civic groups such as the Rotary, Lions and Kiwanis, and hold food drives to support our major project."* That major project—"Food for Thought"—was so outstanding that it won the Chamber of Commerce Volunteer of the Year Award in 2011 for Delta County. *"We knew how important school lunches were for so many of the children in Delta,"* Hudson comments, *"but we didn't know how they were eating on the week end. They often would return to school on Monday morning hungry and unable to concentrate."* With the Backpack Program, eligible families anonymously are able to pick up a backpack full of nutritious food for the weekend each Friday afternoon. The DOS students solicit donations and raise money ($10,000 last year alone) to purchase the food and stuff the backpacks. Over 160 families were fed each weekend last year, and 90 DOS students were involved in the project. *"With a successful community project such as this,"* Hudson reflects, *"we were able to change community relations and allow them to recognize the inherent value of our students. This has brought us to a point of very different community perception of our school and increased their willingness to get involved in a positive way."*

Conclusion

As the chapter clearly illustrates, there appear to be some common practices that underlie successful school-community-family collaboration building. Without a doubt, critical elements such as effective communications, valued roles for volunteers to play, stressing service to others, partnering for scholastic success, collaborating creatively, and engaging students in the process were identified by multiple contributors. The key to building lasting relationships that benefit all stakeholders seems to be each partnership's taking stock of strategies that work and putting their own unique twist on them to better promote positive student development. While every school and community has its own challenges, the pathway to partnership is worth the effort it takes to be paved.

References

Altrichter, H., Posch, P., & Somekh, B. (1993). *Teachers investigate their work: An introduction to the methods of action research.* New York, NY: Routledge.

Sarason, S. B. (1990). *The predictable failure of education reform: Can we change course before it is too late?* San Francisco, CA: Jossey-Bass.

Schuman, D. (2004). *American schools, American teachers: Issues and perspectives.* Boston, MA: Pearson Education, Inc.

East Longmeadow Public Schools District Student Success Plan

East Longmeadow Public Schools met with parents, staff, and administrators to design a multi-faceted support system for all students regarding MCAS testing. The product of the joint meetings includes a plan in which six major components are addressed. The Individual Student Success Plan (ISSP) is required for all students in the East Longmeadow Public School System who have scored in the bottom quartile of the MCAS test in English Language Arts and Math. Additionally, East Longmeadow Public Schools has recently adopted grade-level testing with a nationally normed test to help with early student identification prior to grades 4, 8, and 10 of the MCAS testing schedule. The ISSP is articulated within all of the five school buildings in the district. Success of the East Longmeadow ISSP Program is contingent upon a triad model of participation and accountability that includes the student, the parent, and the school. Each school in the East Longmeadow Public Schools District will address the six components that comprise the ISSP for students.

Student identification is the first component of the East Longmeadow ISSP Program. Students may be identified through demonstrated empirical test scores, including the following: ITBS Math scores, MCAS English Language Arts scores, MCAS Math scores, ITBS English Language Arts scores, and ITBS Reading scores. Additionally, student identification may be made through the affective domain to include staff referrals, parent referrals, and other referrals of various entities. By looking at both the empirical test data and the affective referrals and communications, a holistic picture of student academic life will be analyzed.

The second component of the East Longmeadow ISSP Program addresses assessment data. In this component, scores from the above MCAS tests and ITBS grade-level normed tests are disaggregated to show strengths, weaknesses, and deficiency patterns as it relates to the individual student. Also, the holistic approach to supplying an academic safety net for all students will be reviewed by soliciting staff and parental suggestions.

The third component of the East Longmeadow ISSP Program stipulates the academic patterns that detail the responsibility for addressing each student's ISSP plan. These responsibilities at the school building level are shared via a multi-faceted approach. Success teams may include guidance counselors, academic team meetings of teachers, administrators and parents, IEP team meetings, needs assessment conferences, and other cooperative partnerships. Parents and students will be involved in the formulation of the ISSP. The responsibility to design each student's ISSP is authorized through site-based management and resides at the individual school where the student attends.

Instructional support is the fourth component of the East Longmeadow ISSP Program. These supports may include five types of instructional support for identified students. The first type of instructional support is adapted school day programming. Adaptations may include reconfigurations, adjustments, academic changes, and new curricula programs for the individual student. The second type of support is expanded school day programming. Expanded programming includes new and additional courses that are designed to meet individual needs and new and additional staffing to deliver services for individual needs. The third type of instructional support is extended school day programming. Extended programming includes before school, after school, noontime, evening, and weekend programs designed to meet individual student needs to remedy academic deficiencies in students. The fourth type of instructional support includes summer school programming. Summer programming includes the months of June, July, and August and may include remedial courses, summer camps, and summer tutorial programs for identified students. Finally, the fifth type of instructional support includes unique and other individualized programming that cannot be served through the previous four instructional supports. This programming serves those students whose unique and individual needs cannot be met through adaptations, expansions, extensions, and summer school programming.

The fifth component of the East Longmeadow ISSP Program is evaluation. All ISSP plans are evaluated and re-evaluated twice a year, once during the fall and spring. Additionally, those programs that are offered throughout the summer will conclude with an evaluation component. The East Longmeadow evaluation for ISSP plans include beginning and ending data for individual students, articulated lesson plans, stratified use of curriculum guides, sequenced to Massachusetts curriculum frameworks, and a compendium of teaching strategies. These data elements will be identified, collected, and analyzed to determine the success of the ISSP plans and Program. Additionally, parent and student surveys will be administered to measure the phenomenological aspects of success as indicated by respondents.

The sixth and final component of the East Longmeadow ISSP plan includes communications. This component is based on the triad model in that the parent, teacher, and school must stay in constant communication regarding the identified student as instructional supports are identified, delivered, and measured for each student. Within this triad model all participants (parents, students, and schools) must agree on instructional supports and authorize by individual signatures that the triad model bears equal responsibility for the success of each plan. Schools must design, implement, and deliver instructional supports. Students must attend school ready and willing to try their best and must complete all assignments in school and at home to the best of their abilities. And, parents must monitor their child's work at home, spend time helping their child with directions for homework and communicate with schools frequently. Clearly, when all 3 entities of the accountability triad work – success is achieved by all.

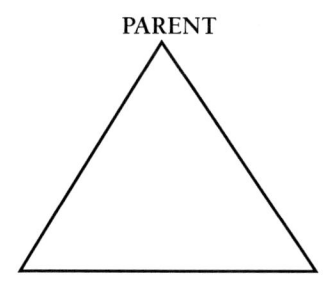

EAST LONGMEADOW SCHOOLS' INDIVIDUAL STUDENT SUCCESS PLAN

STUDENT NAME:_____SCHOOL:_____GRADE:_____

I. STUDENT IDENTIFICATION (✓):

☐ MCAS ELA   ☐ MCAS MATH   ☐ MCAS READING   ☐ MCAS SCIENCE
                                                              TECH/ENG

☐ STAFF REFERRAL_____ ☐ PARENT REFERRAL_____
☐ OTHER_____

II. STUDENT SUCCESS PLAN ASSESSMENT DATA (scores):

☐ MCAS ELA SCORE____   ☐ MCAS MATH SCORE____
☐ MCAS READING____   ☐ MCAS SCIENCE /TECH/ENG____

POWERFUL PARTNERS IN STUDENT SUCCESS: SCHOOLS, FAMILIES AND COMMUNITIES

☐ STAFF REFERRAL_____ ☐ PARENT REFERRAL_____
☐ OTHER_____

Additional Info:_____
_____

III. STUDENT SUCCESS PLAN FORMULATION COMPONENTS (✓):

☐ Guidance Counselor Meeting ☐ Academic Team Meeting
☐ Administration Meeting   ☐ IEP Team   ☐ Needs Assessment   ☐ Other

Additional Info:_____

IV. STUDENT SUCCESS PLAN INSTRUCTIONAL SUPPORTS (specify in detail):

☐ Adapted School-Day Programming: _____
_____

☐ Expanded School-Day Programming: _____
_____

☐ Extended School-Day Programming: _____
_____

☐ Summer School Programming: _____
_____

☐ Other Academic Programming: _____
_____

V. STUDENT SUCCESS PLAN EVALUATION (✓): All plans must be re-evaluated once per semester each year.

☐ Fall Date_____   ☐ Spring Date_____   ☐ Summer School Date_____

VI. STUDENT SUCCESS PLAN COMMUNICATIONS:

☐ Parent / Teacher / Student Conference   Dates: _____

_____   _____   _____
Parent Signature   Student Signature   School Staff Signature

NOTES

NOTES